WHISKEY, WOMEN, AND WAR

WHISKEY, WOMEN, AND WAR

How the Great War Shaped Jim Crow New Orleans

Brian Altobello

University Press of Mississippi / Jackson

The University Press of Mississippi is the scholarly publishing agency of
the Mississippi Institutions of Higher Learning: Alcorn State University,
Delta State University, Jackson State University, Mississippi State University,
Mississippi University for Women, Mississippi Valley State University,
University of Mississippi, and University of Southern Mississippi.

Designed by Peter D. Halverson

www.upress.state.ms.us

The University Press of Mississippi is a member
of the Association of University Presses.

First printing 2021
978-1-4968-4650-1 (trade paperback)
∞

Library of Congress Cataloging-in-Publication Data

Names: Altobello, Brian, author.
Title: Whiskey, women, and war: how the Great War shaped Jim Crow New
Orleans / Brian Altobello.
Description: Jackson: University Press of Mississippi, 2021. | Includes
bibliographical references and index.
Identifiers: LCCN 2021008781 (print) | LCCN 2021008782 (ebook) | ISBN
978-1-4968-3509-3 (hardback) | ISBN 978-1-4968-3510-9 (epub) | ISBN
978-1-4968-3511-6 (epub) | ISBN 978-1-4968-3508-6 (pdf) | ISBN 978-1-4968-3512-3
(pdf)
Subjects: LCSH: African Americans—Legal status, laws, etc.—Louisiana—New
Orleans. | New Orleans (La.)—History.
Classification: LCC F379.N557 A95 2021 (print) | LCC F379.N557 (ebook) |
DDC 976.3/35—dc23
LC record available at https://lccn.loc.gov/2021008781
LC ebook record available at https://lccn.loc.gov/2021008782

British Library Cataloging-in-Publication Data available

For Denise

CONTENTS

PREFACE

In commemoration of the centennial of World War I, the Historic New Orleans Collection created an exhibit on the role of New Orleans in the war. It included a few artifacts and displayed interesting photos and documents related to the war effort. One such document attracted my interest. It was a report about suspected disloyal behavior submitted by a member of an organization that I had never heard of called the American Protective League, an agency with volunteers pledged to hunt spies, report seditious behavior, identify slackers, and help to suppress vice. The subject of this particular report did nothing more than criticize US participation in the war, yet his innocuous remark was enough to trigger a written report to the APL's desk in New Orleans. Had the First Amendment been overlooked? How could such an organization, sanctioned by the Justice Department, exist in America?

My curiosity led me to an investigation of the APL in New Orleans. This, in turn, inspired in me, a New Orleans native, the desire to help fill a gap in the three-hundred-year history of the city—an account of the war years of 1917–18. The passion displayed by these unpaid agents, I found, was only one example of the willingness of New Orleans civilians, in addition to the thousands who served in uniform, to sacrifice their time and money to help defeat the Kaiser and his forces.

Much of this effort was prompted by the popularity of President Woodrow Wilson, the first southerner elected since the Civil War. But Mayor Martin Behrman, ironically a German Jew, was at least as important a driving force in energizing his city to recognize its wartime responsibilities. Meanwhile, he managed the city through the contentious fight over both the Prohibition and Women's Suffrage Amendments, the closing of Storyville—its infamous red-light district, the assault on the city's German population, and what could have been an explosive racial environment as African Americans registered for the draft with Jim Crow hovering low over them. Sadly, the official records of his administrations before and during the war years are scant and insufficient.

Equally disappointing was the discovery that no public records exist of the Progressives Kate and Jean Gordon, major players in the suffrage struggle and in the war on vice. The city's three daily newspapers, however, provided an indispensable resource in telling the story. Archival holdings added substance to the narrative. The previously mentioned Historic New Orleans Collection, Williams Research Center, houses the records of the most important of German civic associations in New Orleans, *Die Deutsche Gesellschaft*, the German Society. While these records are in German, the annual reports of the presidents were crucial in revealing the difficult position they were placed in during the war and were essential in developing the chapter "We Were Among Wolves."

Tulane University's Louisiana Collection maintains a few records of the local APL, although those of Charles Weinberger, its chief in New Orleans, are nonexistent. (Emory University is in possession, however, of his postwar report on the chapter's activities. Otherwise, Ancestry.com now houses National Archives investigative APL agent reports.) Tulane's files on a few of the city's suffragists are available and provide insight into the deep factionalism to win the vote for women. In the collection is also a valuable file on the Louisiana Council of Defense and the minutes of the university's board, which debated the issue of faculty who were required to take a loyalty oath. Tulane's Hogan Jazz archives is an unparalleled resource of the city's musicians and their music.

Tulane's Amistad Research Center has a wonderful collection of materials essential to any serious study of the African American experience. The University of New Orleans Louisiana Collection also offers a good account of the lives of African Americans during the war years, and its Orleans Parish School Board minutes shed light on the steps taken to rid the curriculum of so-called pro-German references. Other archives consulted are those housed at Jackson Barracks, the home of the Washington Artillery. There a publication called "Louisiana in the War" can be found, the most comprehensive overview of the goings-on in the city during the war years. Diaries of soldiers and other primary documents, however, are few in number. (I am indebted to the Amoss family of New Orleans for sharing a relative's letter with me that included a superb eyewitness account of the front at the moment of the Armistice.) The New Orleans Public Library, Special Collections, maintains the records of city ordinances and court cases along with a useful collection of interviews with citizens who recalled the war years. Transcribed copies of interviews with Italian residents of the city are kept at the Jefferson Parish Library's American-Italian archives.

A word about a most under-appreciated profession—the archivists who were so cooperative in assisting me. In each of the dozen different archive collections visited, I received a generous amount of their time and guidance. A special salute goes to Lisa Moore of the Amistad Center, Anna Smallwood of the National Archives, Rebecca Smith of the Historic New Orleans Collection, and Ann Case of Tulane University.

Finally, my wife, Denise, was not only a constant supporter during the entire course of this endeavor, but she also was gracious in finding time from her own demanding work to make enlightened suggestions to the manuscript whenever I asked. I could not have completed this work without her.

WHISKEY, WOMEN, AND WAR

INTRODUCTION

New Orleans, wrote Tennessee Williams in his play "A Streetcar Named Desire," was "a little piece of eternity dropping into your hands." As a resident of the city, he recognized that it was suspicious of post-Victorian America and, like Blanche DuBois, felt ill-suited for it. Like the conflicted protagonist in his play, the city viewed itself as a bit too genteel, too charming for an American society unabsorbed by its history. New Orleans, still proud of its French culture, was disconnected from the hum of progress embracing other cities and remained tenaciously provincial in its outlook. Much of this was a function of its geographic predicament, founded on an inhospitable marsh trapped between Lake Pontchartrain and the Mississippi River. But it was also a cultural island in the South with a profoundly Roman Catholic population surrounded by a vast sea of Protestant disdain and imprinted with a colonial legacy unknown to most others. This isolation allowed it to develop an original culture. Jazz, celebratory funerals, and a permissiveness toward alcohol were all byproducts, as was its easy blissfulness about life, almost an apathy—all of which collided with the nation's Puritan ethic. New Orleans would welcome progress, but it would do so without deserting its soul. "The past doesn't pass away so quickly here," wrote Bob Dylan. "You could be dead for a long time."

Historian Gary Krist understood. New Orleans, he reflected, was the first to build an opera house but also the last to create a sewage system. Fifteen years into the twentieth century, automobiles, airplanes, electricity, telephones, movies, and other inventions taught New Orleanians to acknowledge the modern age, but many remained ambivalent about these transformative achievements. There was uncertainty as well about how Jim Crow laws would be enforced, the races continuing to mingle in parks, saloons, and, most notoriously, in the city's healthy sex industry. The nation's Progressive reform movement would be embraced by its municipal leaders, but only if the reforms did not dilute the sanctity of white supremacy or machine politics. Even the tumult of the First World War failed to leave its signature.

Governing New Orleans during the war was Mayor Martin Behrman, the man who helped to steer his city's narrative into the new century. Behrman boasted an impressive dossier of urban improvements, placing him among the leading Progressives of the South. Under his regime, port facilities were modernized, marshlands were drained, construction began on the Industrial Canal connecting the Mississippi River with Lake Pontchartrain, dozens of city services were updated or replaced, and infrastructure was revamped to accommodate a rude newcomer to New Orleans—automobiles. In the years prior to the war, New Orleans was becoming a much more livable place. But this does not tell the entire story, for the mayor was also a living tutorial for machine politics. As the franchise quarterback of the New Orleans Old Regulars—a cartel of elected officials and appointees who did his bidding—Behrman excelled at the sport, using strong-arm threats and election manipulation as well as anyone.

One wonders how Jean and Kate Gordon, the sisters who devoted their years to improving conditions for the citizens of their native town, go so unnoticed today. Educated, elitist, and privileged, they nevertheless despised the arrogance often associated with that privilege. There were plenty of moving parts in their lives. Sedentary they were not. Coy? Never. They were both hardwired to the Progressives' Social Gospel—applying Christian morality to society's miseries. Acting as an army of two, they were successful in struggles to bring attention to animal-cruelty issues, to ensure that child-labor laws were enforced, to open the doors of Tulane Medical School to women, and to advance public health. In between these battles, the Gordons became the leading evangelists for women's suffrage in the state. Like other Progressive reformers, they too were fluent in their attack on machine government and the numbing regularity of graft associated with the city's substantial vice industry, and it is in this arena where they clashed publicly with their boss-mayor again and again. It was the big stage that Kate in particular relished. No behind-the-curtain work for her. No boilerplate clichés. And she did not care who liked her and who did not.

It is difficult to identify three people in the long history of New Orleans who are more deserving of acclaim, yet each of them had their dark sides. Behrman's years in office were framed by classic boss-rule techniques— patronage and widespread graft. But he played the political game deftly, with humor and without the brashness of a demagogue, entirely visible and untiring in his efforts to coax New Orleans deeper into the new century. The Gordons, in spite of their years of personal self-sacrifice and unflinching altruism, were unapologetic racists, believers in the science of eugenics as the salve for many of society's ills. Contradictions abounded.

While the reach of these three extraordinary people was quite long and enduring, the war was paramount, prevailing over every facet of life in the two-hundred-year-old city between 1917 and 1918. And its Gallic heritage connected *La Nouvelle-Orléans* to its cousins overseas from the war's beginning in 1914.[1] But the stimulus of war could change only so much. Racial segregation had been institutionalized since the late 1800s with the enactment of Jim Crow laws. When war came, African American participation in the military, their leaders hoped, would spike the "racial uplift" movement and mitigate the demons of Jim Crow. That did not happen. The war brought no relief to the toxic climate of racial bigotry. The sturdy edifice of white superiority remained embedded in the New Orleans panorama.

African Americans were not alone in their despair. When war first broke out, people of German extraction were much more readily received than were the town's Sicilians, Chinese, or Irish. But as graphic news reports of atrocities committed by the Kaiser's forces in Belgium filtered into the press, sentiments shifted rapidly. Already characterized as a militaristic *Kultur*, German citizens began to be unfairly associated with these crimes. In New Orleans and across the nation, a fever pitch of fear of often ridiculous proportions mushroomed—Germanophobia. Germans who were not US citizens were officially labeled by the government as enemy aliens. It was hardly an endearing term, inviting harassment and worse. People with German surnames, even those that had been citizens of the US for decades, would be taunted, spurned, or at least carefully monitored.

Fear morphed into hysteria, and when mysterious bombs exploded at manufacturing plants and shipyards in parts of the US, tens of thousands of willing citizens ineligible for what was to shortly become a draft volunteered for an organization meant to assist the Justice Department in identifying German spies and subversives. The local office in New Orleans was swamped by people eager to contribute to the war effort. It was called the American Protective League, an ad hoc organization of well-intentioned individuals who would often violate the most basic of one's civil rights. It did not take much for an APL report to be typed up and sent to Bureau of Intelligence agents. Someone may have been overheard criticizing the president. Another might simply be seen "acting suspiciously" and be brought in for questioning. Patriotic fervor disguised a litany of injustices. Questioning the practices of the APL cast doubt onto the accuser. Three decades later, a new word would be coined for this phenomenon—McCarthyism. The emotional sweep was identical. Only the targets changed.

When it became apparent that the League was engaging in overkill, it turned its attention to far less interesting work like identifying violations of the government's food- and fuel-conservation regulations. When a "Work or Fight" order was issued, meant to cleanse the streets and pool halls of "slackers," the League was asked to assist in this campaign. The mission broadened still further—suppression of all forms of vice near military installations. Working in dialogue with local law enforcement, the federal government's Committee on Training Camp Activities, and the New Orleans Civic League, the APL became a hyperactive arm of the moral police. Agents assisted in the identification of sporting houses, where prostitution flourished and saloon owners sold intoxicating beverages to anyone in uniform. An inebriated or diseased soldier or sailor directly affected military readiness. Decontamination of the city's vices became not only a Progressive goal, but also a patriotic endeavor as well.

The groundwork had already been laid for the Prohibition Amendment, beginning decades before with the Women's Christian Temperance Movement and especially the more recent Anti-Saloon League. During the war years, momentum had swung heavily in the direction of the "dries." Many breweries throughout the nation were German-owned, and the "Kaiser's brew" that they produced, along with the people who drank it, were guilty by association with the vilified Hun leader. Moreover, the nation's allies were already on board with various bans on alcohol, creating a reflex in America that emboldened the forces against Demon Rum.

Local-option laws allowed states to choose to be "dry." Louisiana, however, was not one of them, and liquor distributors there were able to profit from this by supplying neighboring dry states with all the booze they could consume. But when the Supreme Court ruled early in 1917 that crossing state lines with the liquid contraband was illegal, prohibition forces rejoiced. Now supporters of the Anti-Saloon League possessed a precedent for national action. In spite of strong opposition from Louisiana, dry states, already numbering more than a third of the total, would become "bone dry."

The judgement was also a blow against "states' rights." For many, prohibition was an intrusion into the bailiwick of a state's authority, one in which the federal government should not trespass. Others simply viewed it as a violation of a basic recreational male ritual. Nevertheless, it surprised no one when the Eighteenth Amendment was ratified, especially since the War Department had previously set the table with a wartime prohibition edict, never mind that it was intended as a food-conservation measure. Supporting the amendment, like purging the city of its immorality, became synonymous with supporting the war.

Venereal disease was an odious companion to the sex trade, and the city's infamous, twenty-year-old red-light district, called Storyville, was in the government's bombsight. Not only did gonorrhea and syphilis take a toll on a military unit's readiness, it also was an indication of the degradation of a young man's character. Washington welcomed the responsibility to build solid citizens in its ranks. It was not enough to teach good soldiering skills. After their release from service, soldiers must be ready to become solid husbands and fathers as well. Such was the magic of the Progressives, showering even the military with its high-minded ideals. What bolted the doors of the infamous district in 1917 was the War Department, not the Anti-Saloon League.

When Congress declared war in the spring of 1917, New Orleans was eager to answer Behrman's appeal for unanimity with the president. The mayor addressed an anxious audience as "fellow Americans, fellow patriots," challenging them with a question: "What will you people of New Orleans do?" The answer would not be long in coming. The city assembled its resources promptly and spectacularly.

The immediate urgency was the mobilization of men. Almost four hundred thousand registered for military service in Louisiana, and 46 percent of those were classified as Class I, fit for service. Only Wyoming had a higher percentage. New Orleans contributed 84,905 to the total, including hundreds of professionals who relinquished their incomes to volunteer.[2] The Allies also depended on the city's port for shipment of military supplies overseas, its workers able to turn around a fully stocked ship in nineteen hours. And its four shipbuilding and repair plants did much to bolster the nation's ability to provide material support for the troops in France.

The common New Orleanian, however, was an active participant as well, and there is no better example of the willingness of the citizenry to contribute to the enemy's defeat than the five Liberty Loan drives and the twelve other fund drives conducted to raise money for the war. Over $114 million was collected in a span of just nineteen months, $23 million over the city's quotas. That is roughly $68 for every man, woman, and child in the city, or about $1,200 adjusted for inflation. Extraordinary. The people responded to their mayor's appeal. They could indeed claim a share of the victory. Much of the credit for this success goes to the dozens of civic, social, religious, and benevolent societies, including the Red Cross and the Elks, who committed themselves fully to Behrman's call. So too did the commercial community, which helped to publicize the drives by cleverly transforming their stores, hotels, and businesses into repositories for donations and providing lavish publicity for them with no thought of reimbursement for the expenses.

So what did this two-hundred-year-old city inherit from the war? Because of their service in the ranks of the military, African American leaders hoped that the Great War would hasten racial uplift and help to derail Jim Crow. It did not. In fact, seeing Blacks in the uniform of their white friends and relatives merely served to heighten fears among many whites that their own place in society was vulnerable. Segregation's bondage remained uninterrupted.

The Old Regular machine maintained its stranglehold on the city's political landscape in spite of Progressive opposition, and Behrman and his cronies would be reelected in 1924. The city's German citizens were slowly able to shed their tainted reputation, but wartime vigilantism against the Hun would transmute during the decade of the Red Scare into an equally vicious pursuit of similar "threats" to America's values.

The war did indeed arouse support for the Eighteenth Amendment, yet the reformers' romance with prohibition turned out to be little more than a troubled thirteen-year affair, ill-considered and untenable. Progressives claimed that the order to liquidate the city's notorious rectangle of sin, Storyville, was a significant consequence of the war. But it was clear that its closing did not exterminate prostitution in New Orleans. It merely repositioned the working girls to other places in town.

For women, the war begat job opportunities—and not just as nurses overseas or as Red Cross volunteers. They sought and eagerly filled available positions as store managers, automobile drivers, and even mechanics. Dozens joined the Navy to become yeomen or to work as telephone operators, stenographers, or messengers. And the leadership women displayed during the massive Liberty Loan and food- and fuel-conservation campaigns did not go unnoticed. They attended to dependents while wage-earning women were away from home. Others volunteered their time packing supplies for shipment to camps, provided recreational opportunities for soldiers and sailors stationed in the city's military facilities, nursed them when they were ill, and chauffeured officers and dignitaries around town in their personal automobiles. These high-profile activities helped to smuggle in new attitudes, delivering the necessary accelerant in the long struggle for women's suffrage. The Nineteenth Amendment left a permanent mark, albeit an incomplete one, as Black women in New Orleans were still deprived of the vote, and local white women did not register in proportional numbers until the 1930s. Much like the Armistice itself, which brought about only a specious peace, the Great War left New Orleans still toiling with unfinished issues, which would be left to settle in later decades.

Chapter 1

THE SCENT OF WAR

Whirring lazily in the almost-pleasant April afternoon, a ceiling fan provided some relief for the intimate party as they finished their salads. Heavy limbs of tired, ancient oak nearly obscured the wrap-around veranda where family and friends gathered for their last lunch together. The humidity being what it was in New Orleans during the spring, the gentle breeze coaxed from the fan was a welcome respite. No one could really complain, however, given the setting at the Demarest home, a magnificent three-story Queen Ann Victorian whose "front yard" on Exposition Boulevard was the stately Audubon Park itself. Originally a plantation and, in 1884, the site of the World Cotton Exposition (thus the street name), the park once served as a staging area for Confederate and later Union troops during the Civil War. No such activity disturbed the tranquil park grounds now, unless one counted the occasional squirrel scampering up and down the sturdy tree trunks.

Rosina T. P. Leverich, 60, along with her daughter of the same name, was concluding a six-month visit to their beloved city, the first since she had left for London with her young daughter and infant son twenty-three years before. After her husband William's death, the need to be with her mother and sister in the UK was compelling despite having to leave other family members in New Orleans behind. Now, almost a quarter century later, she was back with her adult daughter to reacquaint with them. Laughter and conversation swirled about school events, family picnics, and childhood pranks with Rosina's two sisters-in-law, an aunt, and George, her nephew. Evelyn Demarest, a childhood friend and classmate, hosted the lunch. Glasses were charged and raised for a final toast to the two Leverich women before they departed for New York to board the 760-foot British Cunard liner *Lusitania*. George volunteered with a grin, "Here's hoping for a safe voyage—and no submarines." Everyone chuckled. Three weeks later, the elder Leverich's body was discovered floating to shore near Old Head Kinsale, Ireland. Her son could only identify her body by a gold charm that she had hidden inside her whalebone corset. It was for good luck. The younger Rosina's body was never found. A notation in the Leverich family bible under their names reads, "Died 7 May, 1915. Murdered by Germans."

Oscar Grab, an Austrian-born twenty-three-year-old, had just returned from his one-month Bermuda honeymoon with his new bride when he boarded the *Lusitania*. This trip to Liverpool, he hoped, would advance his fledgling women's fashion business. Leaving her behind in New York was difficult for the young couple, but Claire would keep in close touch with her parents in New Orleans. They were Herman and Victoria Runkel, one of the city's most recognized couples, he being the founder of the famous Runkel chocolate works and Victoria the daughter of another high-profile candy manufacturer.

Grab had read the odd notice in the New York papers from the German government warning passengers about sailing into the war zone in British waters. So once on board, he marched to the ship's purser, James McCubbin, and asked him if there was any reason to be concerned. Echoing most other experts, McCubbin replied that the *Lusitania* was much too fast for any German U-boat. He need not worry.

It was after lunch on the fifth day of the sail, a Friday. Grab emerged from his cabin to do a bit of reading on the Book Deck, anticipating his last night on the liner. The ship was only nine miles from the Irish coast and running roughly parallel to it. At 2:08 p.m., the newlywed put down his book to speak to two other passengers, when he spotted something odd sticking up from the grayish expanse off the starboard bow. It looked, he said, "like a stick in the water." What Grab saw was the periscope of the German U-boat, *U-20*. Riveted, he stared at the foaming wake of a torpedo "very plainly" plowing directly toward him three meters deep. Steadying himself, he instinctively bent over the deck railing, watching in horror as it made impact just below the wheelhouse. The *Lusitania* seemed to shrug off the explosion until a second and much more violent explosion followed soon after. This time, the liner and its ten decks shook and began to rapidly take on water, listing prominently to starboard.

A frantic scene ensued as lifeboats dropped prematurely or were rushed by screaming passengers, many with children in tow. Other lifeboats, in their haste, spilled terrified passengers into the icy ocean as they were being lowered. People, he reported, were "drowning like rats." Rather than risk waiting for a lifeboat (only six of forty-eight were launched successfully), he pulled off his shoes, jumped into the frigid water below, and swam until he was pulled out of the water by survivors in a nearby boat. Eighteen short minutes later, he watched the *Lusitania*'s bow slip under the waves with a hiss, plunging three hundred feet and settling on the floor of the Irish Sea.

England's most important coal magnate, Daniel Thomas, a major investor in the New Orleans–based Mississippi Navigation Company, was accompanied by New Orleanian John Bernhard to New York for his voyage back to London on the *Lusitania*. Thomas had just concluded a major barge deal with Bernhard, the company president, which would send a line of these vessels between New Orleans and St. Louis. It was a huge contract, and Bernhard was happy to escort Thomas to the luxury liner and afford him the courtesy of being with him until it shoved off.

British composure was evident when a white-jacketed steward strode briskly up to Thomas with a telegram just before farewells were exchanged between the two men. Unsigned, it bluntly warned that the *Lusitania* would be torpedoed and that the addressee should not take passage on the voyage. Thomas simply chuckled and handed the message to Bernhard to read. They both laughed, considering it a trick of some kind. (Many other passengers received similar telegrams.) Bernhard joked with Thomas that perhaps he should use his own quite credible influence with the German government to have the ship spared this time around. Thomas then tore up the message and left in search of his cabin. Before debarking, Bernhard passed through the main saloon and noticed the captain speaking to several passengers about the curious telegrams they had all just received. Some of their faces appeared quite worried, but the captain assured them that the ship's great speed would protect them from any attack. All passengers remained on board. Several of those receiving these messages would likely lose their lives in the attack, but Thomas would be saved and make it back safely to his home in Wales.[1]

The Atlantic had always been a reliable sentinel, a buffer zone that separated the US from the ambitions of hard-to-pronounce sultanates and empires that stubbornly refused to recognize the twentieth century. Most New Orleanians had neither heard of Sarajevo, Bosnia. Neither did they read with any great alarm about the assassination that killed an archduke there, the murder that would trigger the Great War. Business would go on as usual. But after the *Lusitania* tragedy, public opinion began to shift decidedly against the Central Powers, Germany and her ally Austria-Hungary. For most citizens, this was unquestionably a heinous act, the mark of a barbaric "Teutonic" nation. Included in the death toll of almost 1,200 were 94 children, 31 of whom were infants in the arms of their mothers. Just 764 passengers survived. The American death toll was 128. The war had finally reached the US coast.

Few Americans had paid much attention to the war's events until the death toll was confirmed, and no one seemed to have noticed the torpedoing of two British steamers, the *Centurion* and the *Candidate*, one day before the *Lusitania* attack in the very same waters off Ireland. (There is no explanation about why confirmation of these sinkings was never telegraphed to the *Lusitania* to forewarn her.) Now the report of their loss amplified the reaction in New Orleans. Both of these tankers had been frequent visitors to its port.

Crowds gathered at the sidewalk bulletin boards posted by the city's main dailies to read news dispatches from England. The early reports were that all passengers were safe, but by that evening, details of the calamity became clearer. The next day, the *Times-Picayune*'s lead editorial took a hard position, as it would for the next two years until US entry into the war: "The sinking, without warning, or without so much as the offer of rescue . . . is a new and sinister thing in civilized warfare." It concluded with a call to Washington to take effective and prompt action so as not to let this horrific act go unpunished.[2]

President Woodrow Wilson's response was more restrained—and tardy. It was six days before he sent a diplomatic note of protest to Berlin. But he did strongly affirm the right of neutral countries during wartime. Moreover, the US would not omit "any act necessary to the performance of its sacred duty to maintain the rights of the US." Further, Washington would "hold the [German] government to strict accountability for any infringement of those rights."

The German reply was swift, calling the attack "regrettable but necessary" as the liner, they claimed, was carrying munitions. In several more notes, Wilson denied that the *Lusitania* was hiding contraband and insisted that the Imperial government disavow the "wanton act" of its naval commander. (Commemorative medals were later minted to remind everyone of German savagery. On one side was an engraving of the sinking ship along with the phrase "no contraband." On the other was a skeleton selling tickets to passengers along with "*Geschaeft uber alles*"—business over all.) The president continued to emphasize the established rights of neutral vessels on the high seas. Two years later, in a joint session of Congress, Wilson again would invoke this principle to justify his request for a war declaration.

The White House's reaction to Berlin was too firm for Wilson's secretary of state, William Jennings Bryan, who resigned because he believed that the president was leading the country to war. Wilson was not a militarist, making clear his moral qualms about war in his famous speech in Philadelphia on May 10th. "There is such a thing as a nation being so right," he explained, "that it does not have to convince others by force that it is right." The following year, he continued to stand unmoved against those who demanded that Americans troops be sent to the trenches of France. Most prominent among them was the vocal Teddy Roosevelt. Despite the ex-president's vast popularity, it was Wilson who had "kept us out of war," as the Democratic Party's slogan proclaimed proudly in that reelection year. The president won with 49.2 percent of the popular vote over the Republican Charles Evans Hughes and three weak third-party candidates. Louisiana sent him 86 percent of its popular vote, a 9 percent jump over his 1912 totals there.[3] Despite the clamor for standing up to German tyranny, Wilson seemed to be the safe choice in that most difficult time.

War in Europe had been roaring on for a year, but it had been not much more than a distant curiosity, albeit something to be wary of nevertheless. This was not America's affair, most believed, despite daily front-page news coverage of military moves on both fronts. Much of the reporting was, however, clearly biased. That bias was evident in New Orleans as well, although there was little need for such propaganda in a city with such deep historical connections to France.

Still, the *Lusitania* story was a game changer. And throughout the years prior to US entry into the war, editorials and letters in New Orleans newspapers were entirely anti-German, with most calling for war or, at least, for a buildup of the nation's military. The image of the German "Hun" was fast developing, and most Americans continued to respect the nation's long-standing relationships with its traditional allies. Continued news reports of German atrocities in Belgium and elsewhere simply validated the favoritism.

Residents of New Orleans had cause to be wary of German intrigue beginning at the arrest in December 1914 of Hans Halle, an unemployed thirty-five-year-old native of Hamburg, who rented a cheap room at the Faust Hotel downtown. Pinkerton agents along with nine detectives from the city's police force picked him up at the corner of Girod and Baronne Streets after almost two weeks of surveillance. An informant supplied information that Halle intended to plant a bomb on a French cargo vessel that carried supplies and munitions from New Orleans to enemies of his native country. Halle, under intense questioning, confessed completely to building a clock bomb designed to explode in six days when the ship was far away in the Atlantic. The device, with a hundred pounds of explosives, was discovered hidden in his hotel. Halle also fingered an accomplice named George Sommers, the owner of the Faust Hotel. Sommers was well known as a former manager of the Rheingold saloon on Common Street, a popular hangout for Germans. He too was later arrested.

While it is impossible to measure the impact of these arrests, it is probably safe to assume that suspicions were beginning to be cast on any German living in New Orleans, alien or not, as early as 1914. Sommers, for example, had even served as a cavalry sergeant in the US Army before moving to New Orleans.[4] Yet many first-generation Germans like Sommers remained culturally dislocated from their country of residence, clinging to their own kind with their language and customs.

Anti-German sentiment often translated into action. Impatient with Washington's vacillation, a few joined the French Foreign Legion to fight even before the US war declaration. Some of the more adventuresome became part of the legendary *Escadrille Américaine* or, as it came to be called, the *Lafayette Escadrille*. The elite unit was composed largely of American volunteers, many of whom were educated and privileged. One such young man was an impulsive and untamed New Orleans native named Edgar Bouligny.

EDGAR BOULIGNY

As both a French and Spanish Creole, Edgar grew up hearing stories about his intrepid ancestor, Dominique de Bouligny, who founded the town of New Iberia, Louisiana, and later served as military governor while Spain ruled the colony in the late 1700s. (Creoles are defined as native-born people of various races who are descended from French or Spanish settlers of colonial Louisiana.) Edgar's grandfather, John, represented Louisiana in Congress in the years immediately prior to the Civil War. Independent, stubborn, and virulently unionist, he received national attention for bravely refusing to vacate his seat when Louisiana voted to secede.

Edgar was stamped with many of the traits of these men in his bloodline, among them being the violent inclinations of Edgar Sr. As a young teen, his father was once arrested for firing his pistol into the belly of another teen who first punched him on the steps of the French Quarter's elegant Opera House at the conclusion of a performance. After firing the gun, he fled into the building through the scattering deluge of people, ran up the staircase, and somehow avoided three shots fired at him by his accoster, who chased after him. Both boys were arraigned in court the following day, where a high-pitched argument erupted between them in front of the judge's bench. After being subdued, they were both sentenced to twenty-four hours in jail and fined $25.[5] Three years later Edgar Sr. was arrested twice, once for causing a disturbance at a voting poll and again for assault with a deadly weapon.[6] Even more serious charges were to follow: the murder of a man in Los Angeles (acquitted) and manslaughter in El Paso for shooting his bookkeeper (guilty—four years in prison).[7]

Only three years old when this last incident occurred, Edgar Jr. was too young to know about his father's criminal misdeeds and fondness for gunplay. Yet the younger Edgar would continue his father's irascible behavior.

At thirteen, presumably for disciplinary reasons, he found himself in a New Orleans boarding school for boys where military science was taught, the College of the Infant Jesus. Even within this closed environment, however, he managed to burglarize over twenty homes and businesses. His parents took their lawyer's advice and had him plead insanity. The strategy worked. He was sent to the Louisiana state mental hospital in Jackson, avoiding detention, at least, in a penal facility. Not long thereafter he escaped, fled to St. Louis at seventeen, and took a job as a bellhop at a hotel in that city. A short time later his wanderlust brought him to San Francisco, where he was shanghaied and forced to work as a deckhand on a steamer to China, then back to San Francisco.

Disillusioned and aimless, he joined the US Army and, in his first assignment, helped to guard that city from looters in the aftermath of the 1906 earthquake. Bouligny left the Army in 1912, but when war broke out in 1914, he felt drawn to the adventure. His affinity for France and sympathy for their struggle against the Germans were compelling. Besides, he was fluent in French, thanks to his mother's insistence on a proper Creole education for her six-foot-six-inch son. He was not alone in his outrage over events in Europe. Cultural ties with the French people remained solid in *La Nouvelle Orleans*, so there was little doubt which side enjoyed its favor. Bouligny joined roughly 120 other Americans in the French Foreign Legion. "I thought France was worth fighting for," he stated simply, "so I went. That's all."

Enlisting in August of 1914 in the Legion, he became one of the first Americans to do so and remained there until May of 1917, when he became a fighter pilot for the notorious *Lafayette Escadrille*. During his stint on active duty, the young airman was wounded four times at the Battle of the Somme, becoming the first American casualty of the Great War. More danger befell him when an enemy bomb exploded under his trench near Rheims. Bouligny was entombed in the debris for twenty-seven hours before he was accidentally discovered and dug up, stunned but still alive.[8] After recovering he was back in the cockpit again, crash landing his disabled biplane after it took fire from the famed German "Flying Circus" in the skies over Albania. Arrogant as ever, he often boasted that the Germans didn't have a bullet with his name on it. Bouligny was awarded the *Croix de Guerre* with three palms by the French military for his heroism in combat.

Before returning to the US, he met a pretty French girl named Odile Hubeau while having photos developed at the shop in Paris where she worked. They immediately began seeing each other several times a week. Deeply in love, they were married nine months later. But what appeared to be an endearing story of a wartime romance in the City of Lights abruptly turned sour when, a day after their marriage, Edgar confessed to her that he was already married to an American! To the lovesick young French woman, that seemed not to be an impediment as long as her hero divorced her, which he did once they arrived in the US to begin their lives together. There they would drive around the country as partners in a photography business. But what followed was only occasional success selling their work to travel publications.

By the late 1920s they were broke, so the couple decided reluctantly to return to New Orleans, perhaps to lean on Edgar's family for financial help. There they rented a cheap French Quarter apartment at 409 Bourbon Street and opened a photography studio a few blocks away on St. Peter Street. It never panned out. Penniless and without direction, the decorated soldier was no longer held in the esteem he had achieved while in uniform. His wartime exploits overseas never translated into a solid post-war career in America, and the discontent stirred his inner demons. Clinging to the memories of his salad days as a pilot in France, Edgar found solace sharing the aerial photos he had taken from his cockpit while flying over the ruins of shelled cities and broken battlefields to American Legion posts and civic associations.[9] During these presentations, Edgar could at least temporarily relive those moments that connected him spiritually to his great-great-grandfather Dominique, whose burial in St. Louis Cathedral among Louisiana governors and bishops attested to the significance of his life. But these talks were never sufficient to tame his tortured spirit.

Adrift, he began rummaging the neighborhood alone at night through any number of clubs in the "Tango Belt," a niche in the French Quarter where the lascivious dance and other sensual diversions continued well into the early morning. Women with unenviable reputations were known to make the cabaret circuit from places like the Oasis or the Black Orchid, where there was always a market for their wares. Wallets were commonly lifted, and overly perfumed waitresses, called "table girls," coaxed watered-down and overpriced cocktails from unsuspecting and innocent customers. Working on commission, the best hustlers could make between $15 and $20 a night.[10] Crime darkened every dance hall, so much so that the police chief required all "daughters of joy" employed at these establishments in the dubious district to register with them.[11]

Edgar would sometimes disappear for days without explanation. He returned home from the sordid dance halls way too late, way too often. Not surprisingly, this led to loud arguments with Odile followed by curses and beatings. By 1931 the marriage was irreconcilable. The forty-three-year-old Bouligny was exhibiting the classic symptoms of what was then called "shell shock" or, in modern terminology, PTSD. The former lieutenant had become only a residue of his old self, an ugly predator—and his still-adoring wife was his convenient and easy prey.

One day he seemed particularly agitated and punched her, knocking the petite thirty-seven-year-old to the floor of their tiny kitchen. When her towering husband came at her again with clenched fists, she shot him with his own .22 caliber pistol, which she had hidden in the kitchen sideboard. As he lay dying, Odile picked up the head of her bleeding husband and rested it on her lap crying over him, sobbing again and again that she loved him, keeping an all-night vigil.

She was taken to the police station, where she detailed in both French and fractured English the recent years of physical abuse. The coroner identified eight bruises on her that he concluded were likely caused by kicks or punches, validating her claim of self-defense. Several of the couple's relatives hurried to the police station to speak on her behalf, including Edgar's inconsolable seventy-seven-year-old mother, who prayed the rosary incessantly throughout the ordeal. "Poor boy. He was never the same after the war," she cried. "He was sick. None of my family feel hard against her." Indeed, Bouligny's family members had been urging her to leave him for some time, but she had always refused.

Odile was swiftly released from lockup without charges. A few days later she was sitting side by side with her mother-in-law at a North Rampart Street funeral home and even lived with her until she sailed for her native France shortly thereafter. So distraught was Bouligny's mother that she could not make herself attend his funeral mass at St. Louis Cathedral. Odile did attend the services but stayed in the background, muttering, "I love him still. I will always love him."[12]

Newspapers from Modesto to St. Louis to Brownsville gave the story front-page status. In a few, the report occupied an entire page accompanied by broad artist renditions of the murder scene and photos of the couple—Edgar square-jawed and looking resolute in his impeccable uniform and Odile prim in the stylish dress of the 1920s. "Shot Her Husband Because She Loved Him," shouted the bold headline of the July 5, 1931, *Ogden Standard Examiner*. "First American Wounded in War Slain by Menaced War Bride," exclaimed the *Brooklyn Daily Eagle*. The former pilot had longed for the attention he had once received as an acclaimed fighter ace over a decade before, yet as Odile made her way back to her native country, that attention was now fraught with disdain for him.[13] Once a national hero, the New Orleanian had become merely a character in a tragic opera. After the funeral, he was buried in the Chalmette National Battlefield cemetery.

Chapter 2

LA NOUVELLE-ORLÉANS

New Orleans on the brink of the First World War was a city of about 340,000 (249,000 white, 90,000 Black), the fifteenth largest city in America. Over 27,000 of them were foreign-born.[1] In 1900 it had been the twelfth largest, gradually falling to seventeenth in 1920 despite gaining roughly 30,000 people since the previous census. Many of its new arrivals were from rural areas of the state, whose share of Louisiana's total population was rapidly losing ground to the state's cities. The demographic was difficult to characterize. Its Gallic, mostly Roman Catholic mixed-race Creole population, still unique and proud of its heritage, had been forced to become part of the general African American community—at least through the eyes of the law and the city's privileged whites. Under the inescapable grip of Jim Crow legislation, people of mixed race were no longer distinct. New Orleans had become, by law, a biracial city. A Black person's level of education, religion, or economic position was now trumped by his or her racial makeup.

Neighborhoods and clubs identifying with those neighborhoods still managed, however, to cling to the fading distinctions. Creoles of Color[2] mainly lived in Tremé or "downtown" below Canal Street, the city's vertebrae. The remainder of its Black citizens lived "uptown" or in a smaller area known by residents as "back o' town" on South Rampart. There was even a one-block-long stretch called Chinatown on the lower end of Tulane Avenue and South Basin Street. There one could find inexpensive cafes, meeting halls, family-run laundries, and tiny groceries. Debutantes made the beautiful mandarin silk coats sold at Chinatown's curio shops a hot item to wear to the opera.[3] Many of the city's whites, on the other hand, lived parallel to the Mississippi River along Magazine Street in what was once called the Irish Channel, in the wealthier Garden District along Prytania Street and St. Charles Avenue, or in the vicinity of Esplanade Avenue and City Park.

New Orleans's best known and oldest neighborhood, the French Quarter, was in transition. Once the preferred home of the city's elite, Frenchtown, as it was more popularly called in the early 1910s, had been losing its shine for white Creoles since the middle of the previous century. Its structures, many dating back to the period following the destructive fire of 1788, still exuded a waning charm with their exquisite Spanish ironwork, red-tiled roofs, graceful arched carriage ways, corkscrew staircases, and vine-draped patios framed by banana trees. But by 1917 it had become a tormented slum—an embarrassing eyesore.

By late morning, the lacy balcony railings that symbolized it were now concealed by the day's wash murmuring in the breeze, reminiscent of the less fashionable neighborhoods of Naples or Havana. Window and door shutters longed for new paint. Murky streets were sprinkled with rotting garbage. The odd perfume of sweet, overripe bananas, stale beer, and mule manure remained idle most days. One could taste the smell. Fortunately, the city's frequent downpours provided some relief from the unpleasant odors. Plumbing and sewerage, however, were reliably unreliable, so complete escape from the miasma was unlikely.

At night the demimonde crawled up to the surface. Gritty saloons invited petty crime and worse. Cheap prostitutes were abundant. Posturing flamingo-like with a leg up on the wall in robes readily open to expose little or nothing underneath, they claimed the street near their tiny wooden "cribs"—very tiny. Each was no more than ten feet across with a single door and maybe a window. Often one building housed a half dozen of them, one after another. Inside there was space only for a sagging bed and a sink—a "get in and get out" kind of place. For the price of a beer or two, the hooker and her well used mattress were yours for 15 minutes. Crib girls paid about $2.50 a night for their sex nest, more in the winter. The exchange of cash for the keys was usually handled by a saloonkeeper on the block. Kids sold bundles of wood or buckets of coal to keep the cribs warm during winters. The women, however, were not allowed to live in the cribs, renting them between 9 p.m. and 11 a.m. daily.[4] To stay out of jail, the girls and their pimps paid a lawyer named Payton $7 a month as a kind of insurance premium. "He could get you right out. You just called him. You hardly ever went before a judge."[5]

"Ratty" music from a half dozen lusty honkytonk juke joints mingled in the night air. Pool tables were cleared for dice games. Narcotics were commonplace. A popular high was a nickel pinch of cocaine, or "nose candy," dropped into a glass of beer or, for an additional nickel, with a wine-and-water mix. Service-industry workers were stimulated by the drug to survive early morning shifts. Selling it was illegal, but the law was unenforced and little effort was made to discourage its use since it was a recreation mostly within the domain of poor Blacks and prostitutes.[6]

Unsavory, dangerous sorts, "good time people," hung out on street corners in the shadows, looking for action. Author Oliver LaFarge, who lived in the neighborhood, explained that "there are never people lacking to advise you in any undertaking or to yell at a cop who was arresting a drunk. Start something that needs help or get into a fight, you'll soon have company."[7] It was simply not a place for a leisurely stroll, and certainly no place to raise a proper Creole family any longer. The ritual of shopping at the French Market after Sunday mass at the cathedral remained, but the socializing ended there. The wife of writer Sherwood Anderson confirmed this while the pair were living in the Pontalba Apartments. Perched on her balcony overlooking Jackson Square, Elizabeth witnessed the flurry of activity around the French Market on one such Sunday afternoon, noticing the unease the gentility was feeling with the neighborhood's residents. These ladies, she wrote, seemed "almost afraid" of them.[8]

Everywhere buildings begged for care, including the Cabildo and Presbytere. The burnished Pontalba Apartments appeared to lean toward Jackson Square as if they were reaching out to Old Hickory for assistance. Even St. Louis Cathedral, the spiritual crown for the city's *crème de la crème*, was in need of serious attention. It was here that the privileged were baptized, confirmed, and married. But the structure was in such grave need of repair that masses had not been conducted there since the 1915 hurricane. And when Archbishop James Blenk died in 1917, his body was interred in the vaults under the cathedral's sanctuary, as was the practice, but officials decided that it would be too dangerous for the public to attend his funeral there.

Cloistered, brick courtyards that were once focal points of family civility, pleasant gardens, brandy, and after-dinner talk became improvised stables that housed all species of animals, who shared space with their indifferent owners. Mules, chickens, and goats drank from once-graceful, disabled fountains and fouled the unkempt patios with their droppings. One migrant family living in the Pontalba even kept a cow in its second-floor apartment.[9] Weeds grew with impunity from cracks in the brick walls and floor tile, a sure sign of gross delinquency by tenants and landlords alike. Writer Walker Percy described the scene: "The ironwork on the balconies sags like rotten lace. . . . Through deep, sweating carriageways, one catches glimpses of courtyards gone to jungle."[10]

The *Vieux Carré's* slow decay had been forcing well-to-do Creoles to retreat to the fresher, more desirable neighborhood along Esplanade Avenue, with its inviting, garden-like median or "neutral ground." This exodus had been going on for some time now. Grand mansions that Creoles had built along this oak-canopied street rivaled those in the Garden District. They would never return to live in the relic their ancestors had built two hundred years before. The grandeur of the *Vieux Carré* was being anesthetized by neglect. Resuscitation of the neighborhood's historic significance would have to wait until the next decade, when preservationists arose to slow its decline.

Meanwhile, with its affordable rents, the *Vieux Carré*, particularly in the downriver sector, had become a sanctuary for a burgeoning immigrant population from Sicily who could afford little else. "Little Palermo," it came to be called—a pejorative term for what was once the city's most exclusive neighborhood. The immigrants were hardly embraced by the city's residents. Many first came to Louisiana to work as agricultural laborers alongside African Americans in sugar or strawberry farms outside of New Orleans. This association with field hands and their eagerness to accept low wages stirred racial animosity toward these "black dagoes." Even their Black coworkers called them scornfully by their first names.[11] New Orleans jazz musician Danny Barker remembered his grandmother's scorn: "Them Sillians [sic] with them black shirts, black suits, black pants, black hats, black shoes, and black mustaches—all that black is death!"[12]

Bohemians of various backgrounds were also attracted to the neighborhood's affordability, and a small art community was beginning to root there. These mostly non-native writers and artists were drawn to the funky drumbeat, the vibe of the place. Its soft, mystical hum allured them. Its palpable connection to the Old World charmed them. It may have been the wagon merchants who crept through its streets selling watermelons, calas, kerosene, and ice. Something drew in these urban adventurers. They just couldn't exactly explain what. They allowed themselves to melt into this anachronism—the creaky-floored coffee houses, the operatic anthem of the peddlers who beckoned with "ba-na-na lay-dee" or "I gotta peaches," the incense of roasted coffee beans and boiled shrimp, and the offbeat, laissez-faire decadence. Whether it was debauchery or self-purification they were seeking, they couldn't be sure. They just knew they liked the place the way it was and were willing to give it the benefit of the doubt. Their presence along with the other groups, ethnic or otherwise, had transformed the *Vieux Carré*. No longer would the French Quarter be truly French.

Except, that is, for the French Opera House. This cherished white monument at the corner of Bourbon and Toulouse Streets was the high church of New Orleans Creole French culture—its nucleus and its anthem. It did not represent the soul of that culture. It *was* its soul. The city's Opera House defined old New Orleans, underscored its distinction from the rest of America's cities, and stood as the primary proof that New Orleans remained unsevered from its European roots. A *Times-Picayune* journalist described the elegant edifice as "an anchor of the old world character of our municipality ... without [which] will be the greatest danger of our drifting into Middle Eastern commonplacity." Here was where the city's old aristocracy, its *grande familles*, sauntered into the building, which glimmered "like a monster ghost in the night."[13] Here is where farewell parties for uniformed husbands and sons being sent off to war, fashionable wedding receptions for the wealthy, and, of course, opera performances all took place. Screened box seats were even available—*loges grillées*, for those who did not want to be seen. The hors d'oeuvres, the wine, the operas, and even the conversations there were all French. *Quelle surprise!*

The elite, including Creoles of Color (tiered and segregated in the fourth gallery), continued to attend these functions, but once out on the neighborhood's streets, the patois was just as likely to be Italian as it was English. Census reports reveal that there were 8,066 native Italians living in Orleans Parish in 1910, composing 28.5 percent of the city's foreign-born (22.9 percent in 1920).[14] The *New Orleans States* even began printing a daily column in Italian called "*Notizario Italiano*" to provide world news for the newcomers.

Black-skirted women with baskets carrying groceries dodged stray dogs on Royal or Conti Streets on their way to their apartments to prepare the family's evening meal. They strode past barber shops, cobblers, mule-driven milk carts, and electric streetcars. Fruit vendors, singing out the day's best bets, competed with scratchy, twelve-inch Victor red-labeled recordings of Caruso wafting through open shutters. Here and there a crudely built toy wagon pulled by a goat entertained a rabble of laughing kids. On balconies facing each other across the *Vieux Carré's* narrow streets, matrons carried on broad, animated conversations as they waited for pasta to boil, bending over the twisting cast iron railings. Oliver LaFarge, while teaching at Tulane, wrote that the lives of his Sicilian neighbors were "conducted at open windows, on the balconies, and on doorsteps, and thence flow[ing] into the street."[15] Scenes such as these bewitched the thousands of soldiers and sailors who would be stationed in New Orleans during the war. Most had never before traveled more than a few miles from their homes in Akron or Austin. Now they would be able to venture into Little Palermo and to write home sharing stories of their glimpse of the old country.

On the upriver edge of this storied geography was Canal Street—the most fashionable retail thoroughfare in the South and the incubator that fueled the city's commercial engine. One hundred and seventy-one feet in width, the impressive urban canyon accommodated four streetcar lines, which slowly plowed up and down its center with a string of ornamental light poles hunching overhead. The cars carried hundreds of businessmen and shoppers daily along the corridor until it finally dead-ended at the river. Since the eighteenth century the street also served, by accident or design, as a kind of boundary or neutral ground insulating the French Quarter from the upriver, mostly commercial "American Sector" of town. Even the city's geography exposed Creole parochialism.

Every morning and afternoon, indigent boys as young as ten, Black and white, hawked the day's newspapers (or marijuana cigarettes) to passengers as they climbed off the streetcars squealing to a halt. These "newsies," as they were called, would be known to sleep in pool rooms or even in the street to get the jump on early editions coming from "newspaper row" on Camp Street. Poor schoolboys, earning about a nickel, would begin crawling around town after dismissal on Friday, hustling whomever they could—shining shoes, hauling trash, or washing porches. Others sometimes sold powdered red brick to housewives who sprinkled it around the perimeter of their property for color. If they were superstitious, it was mixed with the purchaser's urine and an oil used in voodoo rituals to ward off bad luck.[16]

Canal Street, the city's marquee strip, stirred its entertainment offerings. Here one could see the newest movies or vaudeville acts at its five theaters. Even new recruits could afford the dime it cost to see their first movie at the Tudor or next door at the Globe. The luxurious five-hundred-seat Trianon at 816 Canal was packed for weeks in 1918 with its showing of "Lest We Forget," the story of the *Lusitania* starring Rita Jolivet, an actual survivor of the sinking. Squeezed in between were noisy penny arcades, soft drink stands, soda fountains, and cigar shops—lots of cigar shops— bulging with small bands of young uniformed men participating in the city's full-throated nightlife. Every Friday was payday—in cash. The wide boulevard pulsed with soldiers and sailors by mid-1917, once the military buildup commenced. This was especially evident on pass weekends, when it seemed as though the entire city had become a military installation. More than a few found local girls as escorts, their uniforms bestowing on the young men a magical allure.

Military officers located more refined socializing in elegant hotel bars near Canal, like that in the twelve-story Monteleone Hotel, the Cosmopolitan, or, across Canal, the De Soto. The magnificent four-hundred-room, fifteen-story Grunewald was a go-to destination for locals and visitors as well. It was in this sophisticated establishment, the city's tallest, where one of the first night-clubs was born. The Cave was created to resemble a kind of grotto or cavern. Located appropriately in the hotel's basement, tables for their fashionable tipplers were tucked into niches adorned with such curiosities as stalactites and life-sized statues of naked nymphs staring into pools fed by working waterfalls. The tuxedo-clad orchestra was exceptional, the chorus girls were leggy, the dancing was spirited, and the liquor was expensive.

To celebrate the war's only New Year's Eve on the last day of 1917, the Cave, at the stroke of the clock, dimmed the lights as five thousand balloons were released from the ceiling and descended on the well-lubricated guests. They pelted each other till exhaustion. When the lights came back on, the mood suddenly shifted as the orchestra began playing "The Marseillaise" and the national anthem. All then froze to attention. Then came more dancing deep into the early morning.

Things were rocking at the city's other fine hotels and restaurants too. The *States* estimated that $100,000 was spent on champagne and wine alone.[17] Four hundred partygoers slammed the new banquet room at the St. Charles Hotel for dining and dancing. The Monteleone, Cosmopolitan, and De Soto hotels each reported overflow crowds amplified by large numbers of men in khaki and sailor whites. Few celebrants thought about austerity that night, although the Grunewald at least offered a special "Herbert Hoover menu" of fruit and nuts in deference to the nation's Food Administration chief.[18]

Whether it be after an evening of civilized drinking or cheap beer and billiards, troops and tourists alike might still hear French being spoken while strolling on their way home. Most important to the fading Creole institutions, along with the venerated Opera House, was sustaining the language. To this end, several private French-immersion academies conducted by old-guard Creoles continued their mission, hoping to retard the slow death of *la langue française.*[19] According to a 1902 article in *Leslie's Illustrated News,* one-fourth of New Orleanians still spoke the language of their ancestors in daily discourse. Even more of them could understand it.[20] While these numbers were slowly diminishing as 1917 approached, a weekly newspaper printed in French could still be purchased at newsstands. The *L'Abeille de la Nouvelle-Orléans* (the *New Orleans Bee*) had been in business since 1827. Little wonder that the German invasion of France was a particular outrage to the city's folk.

"It was apparent [when I, Martin Behrman, took office as mayor in 1904] that the average American regarded the Crescent City as a city of mosquito-infested swamps, . . . a city of filthy streets and open gutters, . . . a city in which lived a people . . . whose only object was pleasure and easy living." This was no longer the case.[21] Thus Mayor Behrman went off script, jumpstarting his personal crusade near the end of the war to promote his city in periodicals, billboards, and streetcars in twenty-five major US urban areas. It had become, he preached, a commercial heavyweight, a temple for investment ripe for even more. Five different double-page newspaper spreads were purchased for the targeted metropolises, including such eye-catching headings as "America's War

Work Shop," "New Orleans—World Mart," and "When It's Over, We Want You." Complementing this was a sixty-four-page booklet broadcasting business opportunities in New Orleans and the advantages it brought to those who might consider moving there. Entitled "The Book of New Orleans and the Industrial South," it was indeed an ambitious sales pitch, and there were no precedents. The publication was unquestionably meant to boost Behrman's upcoming campaign for reelection in 1920, but it also documented the sincere, robust confidence the mayor had in his city's commercial future.[22]

There was good reason for him to be so upbeat and so ready to blur or even revise the conception that New Orleans was indolent, suffocated by merriment, with its race tracks, all-night saloons, incessant music, and the year-round, spirited sheen of Mardi Gras. When the conversation turned to business in the past, the city was like a misbehaving child who was put out of the room when company arrived. But because of the war, that had now changed.

Railroads were overburdened, so the government began to shift cargo ticketed for Europe to river barges before overseas shipment. That was a first big step. The war energized traffic on the Mississippi and other waterways as huge quantities of war matériel of all types came through the port of New Orleans. Already it was the largest coffee market in the country, with over two million bags handled annually; other commodities began to challenge those numbers. The product diversification was dizzying. Demand was high worldwide for cotton, grain, lumber, oil, rice, and all foodstuffs—quite a reversal from the economic panic of 1914, when prices plunged for most agricultural goods. Sugar, for example, doubled in price through 1916, the port profiting handsomely from the nation's neutrality. Merchants who had once abandoned their stores in sugar-producing parishes were returning. Cotton prices bested those of sugar, tripling in price during those same three years. The city's Cotton Exchange continued to shatter records into the war years. Two weeks after the US war declaration, the exchange moved almost nineteen thousand bales in just one day, the government being the principal customer.[23] Trade also flourished with Cuba, Puerto Rico, and Central and South America. By the end of the fiscal year in June of 1917, total exports had jumped $100 million in value and imports rose $16 million. It was the most prosperous year in the port's history.

Behrman, whose business acumen was well established, boasted that New Orleans was the largest manufacturing city in the South, larger than the five most populous cities in Texas, with factories employing fifty thousand workers and a payroll of $30 million.[24] Most of these plants were modest in size, producing food-related items, suitcases, furniture, clothing, cigars, drugs, and chemicals. Oil refineries just outside the city were on the threshold of a boom. With the coming of the war, government contracts invigorated an already healthy economic landscape eager to take on more—a humming engine begging for a higher octane.

Near where the still-unfinished Industrial Canal met Lake Pontchartrain, the Doullut-Williams plant, the largest homegrown manufacturing plant in the city, received a contract from Uncle Sam to build eight 9,600-ton steel ships for $14 million. That contract alone provided employment for 2,500 draft-exempt men. Ideally situated with easy access to the Gulf and served by both the new Public Belt Railroad and Southern Railway, the sixty-acre giant was nearly an autonomous city in itself with its own electrical, sewage, and contamination systems. Another shipyard, the Johnson Iron Works, opened a second location during the war on Bayou St. John. Also blessed with rail connections and Lake Pontchartrain access, it yielded dozens of tank barges and tugs.

Across Lake Pontchartrain on its north shore, two more plants, Jahncke and Southern Shipbuilding in Madisonville and Slidell, manufactured cargo vessels and submarine chasers. Two thousand more men took well-paid jobs at the Jahncke yard alone. Milneburg, their neighbor on the south shore, saw the construction of its own new shipyard with a contract for $2.5 million in hand. Further down the lakeshore, the Richardson Aeroplane Corporation, another local concern, began building a tandem biplane for coast patrols and mail service. And in Chalmette, below New Orleans, a new shipyard opened that would employ over ten thousand. Smaller supporting businesses sprouted up near these larger enterprises. The commercial snowball began rolling. Wages drifted up. People were spending. Tax revenue rose. Even the postal service reported increases in profits.[25]

Other construction projects boosted this soaring growth. Buildings sprouted up to shelter the large numbers of servicemen who were now training in Louisiana. Soldiers at Camp Nicholls in City Park pulled in an estimated payroll of $125,000 a month, much of it spent locally. Feeding the hungry men cost another $55,000, padding the pockets of the city's food wholesalers. Camp Beauregard, resurrected from fifteen square miles of forest, became a small city of over thirteen hundred buildings of varying size. Though it was located several hours north of the city, hundreds of New Orleans contractors and service providers were tapped to build these structures. New mess halls, horse stables, health facilities, quarters, and other buildings were also erected at Jackson Barracks, home to the city's own Washington Artillery. The Army purchased land on the east bank next to a site where the Industrial Canal was being dug and began the construction of three large structures to be used for its Quartermaster Corps. More buildings went up at West End's naval cantonment, and the Algiers naval facility was expanded to become a major logistical support center with a new hospital and a dry dock for ship repairs. Along with the manufacturing contracts, the New Orleans economy, already strong, was fortified with about $70 million as it drank from the war's fountain.[26]

Yet it was not simply the tonic of government contracts that catalyzed the city's development. The American Contractors' Association provided an unmistakable index of economic growth even before Wilson's war message. In 1916, it announced that building permits in New Orleans had jumped 115 percent over the previous year. No other large city even approached that number. (Philadelphia was second with an increase of 67 percent.)[27]

Banks provided more irrefutable evidence of this spike in prosperity. Eleven of the city's institutions reporting at the end of 1917 claimed double the deposits of three years before—$172 million. The president of Whitney, the city's most prominent bank, was buoyant: "Our deposits have never been so large nor our business so good." Twenty years ago he had come to New Orleans, he continued, and the largest bank had deposits amounting to about $6 million. "Today," he proclaimed, "there are 33 million."[28] Bank clearances shot up. The *Item* reported that credits doubled and then tripled. The twelve state banks within the city's boundary boasted resources amounting to $134 million in October of 1918, $14 million more than it enjoyed the year before.[29]

Office space in downtown New Orleans was impossible to find as new businesses were attracted to town. Higher paying jobs were abundant, and locals were spending their money. So too were the city's visitors. The Association of Commerce, the predecessor of the Chamber, exploited the closure of Europe's great cities to tourism by marketing New Orleans as "America's Most Interesting City," a new branding that would replace the older "The City That Care Forgot." Stickers emblazoned with the new moniker were pasted on overseas packaging and tattooed on public billboards at train stations. It seemed to be working. Hotels weeks after Mardi Gras 1917 reported high occupancy rates from both national and international travelers. "Up until this year," a hotel clerk revealed to a reporter in a *Picayune* story, the hotels' prosperous season once "ended with Mardi Gras." No longer. These tourists, along with the thousands of Uncle Sam's young men in town, must have been spending their money at the city's big retailers. Maison Blanche, Krause's, D. H. Holmes, and Marks-Isaacs were all reporting the best sales in their history.[30]

Another muscular economic incubator for New Orleans, although less legitimate, was its notorious red-light district. While it was in a state of gradual decline in the years preceding the war, servicemen stationed in the city in 1917 improved its customer base significantly. Musicians, bartenders, working girls, and madams were happy to entertain their young clients eager to empty their pockets—away from the watchful eyes of parents. The saga of Storyville, the city's "restricted district," would be one of the most memorable of the war years.

Chapter 3

"ABANDONED TO LEWDNESS"

If the Mississippi River was the front gallery of the French Quarter—the main entrée into the old city—Storyville was its notorious backyard. Here was the old city's *faubourg* of sin, a suburb on the northwest edge of the French Quarter. Bordellos offering an assortment of fantasies had flourished there since 1897 despite its location—just a short ten-minute stroll from Canal Street's chic shopping, hotels, and most serious business operations. City councilman Sidney Story had in that year proposed a municipal ordinance meant to shrink and confine the city's burgeoning sex trade and its "lewd and abandoned women" to a defined area of twenty square blocks. The ordinance was following the Progressive Era's errand—segregating the immorality of prostitution and all of its accompanying social ills in order to recreate a purer and more righteous America. Neither shrinking nor segregating the trade worked. Moreover, the ordinance technically did not legalize the trade; it simply made prostitution illegal outside its boundaries with a mind to protect it from lawsuits.

Storyville seduced hundreds of thousands of visitors from all over the US to its bawdy houses, including sports legends like Babe Ruth, Jim Corbett, Ty Cobb, John L. Sullivan, and composer George M. Cohan.[1] During its twenty-year existence, the district was established as one of the city's most important industries and economic engines, not only attracting clients but also directly employing roughly twelve thousand locals. In 1914 these included three hundred pimps, two hundred musicians, five hundred or so domestics, hundreds of saloon workers, and other attending contractors. Historian Al Rose estimated that in 1917 and 1918, $10–15 million was spent in the tenderloin district, stoking the already robust commercial posture of wartime New Orleans.[2] "You can make it illegal," deadpanned Mayor Martin Behrman, "but you can't make it unpopular."

He was right, of course. Behrman usually was. In addition to his city's vigorous horse racing—i.e., gambling—industry, Storyville's sweeping notoriety tempted more visitors of the "sporting set" to come to New Orleans than any of the city's more virtuous charms. Bourbon Street early in the new century, save for the Opera House, was not much more than a residential street sprinkled with a few small retail outlets.

A man could choose without guilt from a prix fixe menu of appetizers, entrées, and desserts—willing women of all ages, services, prices, ethnicities, and colors. In the Deep South where Jim Crow racial segregation was universal and uncontested, Storyville's girls were as racially diverse as the services they sold. But there was a limit to their immorality—the soiled doves in a few of the more exclusive sporting houses were often not allowed to smoke, curse, or drink with the patrons. And music was usually not offered on Good Friday and other holy days, although the primary enterprise was uninterrupted.[3] It depended on the madams, who were the autocrats within the wicked walls of their domains. Drunken patrons were politely escorted out. Opium, or "hop," on the other hand, was permissible. There was no need to leave their establishments to get high. They would simply send a pianist or a youngster, a "bellhop," to buy it from an unscrupulous pharmacy over the counter or from a grocery in Chinatown.[4] Champagne and expensive booze were for sale, but beer was generally not.

Prices charged for female services in the most opulent establishments ranged from $5 to $50 depending, of course, on the level of companionship desired. Jelly Roll Morton, who as a fifteen-year-old began playing jobs in Storyville, remembered that many of Mahogany Hall's girls wore lace stockings and garters high up their thighs stuffed with bills that designated the girl's price.[5] A tantalizing lift of a dress and a quick wink—what better way to advertise?

Before selecting a partner for fleshly pursuits during the next hour or evening, well-heeled clients in a few of North Basin Street's fourteen pleasure palaces sipped cognac and relaxed amid lavish Victorian furniture and statuary, polished grand pianos, antique clocks, swirling staircases, and oil portraits of aristocrats under imported cut-crystal chandeliers. The ambience framed an obvious paradox—human degradation amid gilded luxury. Fantasies were in easy reach. Food was not. Santiago the pie man, however, blowing his bugle to attract customers, was a reliable presence on the street. According to Louis Armstrong, who as a young boy sold coal to the crib ladies for a nickel a bucket, Santiago "could swing it too." The waffle man and his mule wagon made an appearance most nights—the gamblers "all but chained his wheels to keep him from leaving."[6] Good music was in abundance as well—from the nimble fingers of skilled pianists flaunting their latest jazz improvisation. It was quite an environment.

The quality of the sporting houses, the girls, and the prices declined, more or less, as one penetrated deeper into the district, further from the river and Storyville's Champs-Elysees, North Basin Street. It was on these less embellished streets that one was more likely to spy neighborhood pimps and river roughs hanging out, rolling dice, and talking trash. The toughest corner, the tenderloin's back door, was the intersection of Iberville and Franklin (now Crozat) Streets, where three saloons attracted a criminal element. The music escaping from these dives, like the women for sale, was gritty and unpolished, just the way they liked it. Regular customers were aware of the district's bottom shelf. But how was a newcomer to know this?

Novices were assisted in their hunt for a taste of licentious pleasure by a unique publication. Photos with sexually suggestive descriptions of available women from the best "sporting houses" were printed in the "Blue Book" for the convenience of the curious. This forty-to-fifty-page annual directory of bacchanal was published by the so-called "mayor" of Storyville, restaurant and brothel owner (and state representative) Tom Anderson. The pamphlet was available in hotels, saloons, or peddled just as one stepped off the Southern Railroad terminal, located on North Basin Street's neutral ground. This proved to be quite a bonus for the dozens of madams and women who worked there.

The trains unloaded a healthy customer base to the doorstep of the "restricted district," or simply "the district" as it was called in the press and in the respectable parlance of the day. This was especially true during the prime horseracing months of October through April. After a seven-year hiatus when antigambling forces managed to convince the state legislature to outlaw racing, the law was repealed in 1916. The starting gate was again opened, and a reliable current of gamblers from around the country eagerly returned to place bets during the day at one of the area's two tracks.

If they hit a race or two, or even if they didn't, they just might decide to watch a wicked sex circus or other indecent acts on the curtained stage of Madam Emma Johnson's establishment, the House of All Nations. According to an early history of the district, sometimes audiences demanded something even more salacious and passed around a hat. If enough money was collected, "specialists" were called in for certain exhibitions. These acts were so sexually vile that Johnson had drapery hung between her young pianist Jelly Roll Morton and the warped performances on stage. This only sparked more curiosity in him, so the budding artist admitted cutting a slit in it on one occasion to sneak a peek at the action before him.[7] Others might opt to spend an hour or more with a young octoroon or mixed-race girl in the evening, hell-bent on Sazeracs and sex. For a quarter, the Blue Book allowed patrons to flip through its pages and select from the ladies of the Little Annex, where they "know how to do things as you like 'em." A visit to 338 North Franklin Street, one ad beckoned, "will teach you more than a pen can describe." In between the provocative text, lawyers advertised in its pages next to ads for cigars, whiskey, cafes, piano tuners, and even a medicine that claimed to cure gonorrhea.[8]

It was wide open, explicit sexual commerce, a feast of erotica that men from prudish midwestern America or the rural Bible Belt could hardly ignore. How could they? The place was an alternate universe of glitz and permissiveness. Partially dressed, smiling tarts in bubble-gum-pink stockings waved at them, showing a bit of bosom and leg from the windows of their cathouses as the trains came to a long, slow halt. From second story perches at the Arlington or Tom Anderson's place, reputed to be the first saloon in America wired for electricity, strumpets clad in lingerie would welcome wide-eyed visitors by using their thumbs to pantomime oral sex. Philip Werlein, president of the respectable Progressive Union, a predecessor of the Chamber of Commerce, once demanded that the railroad erect a screen to block the passenger's view of the local talent.[9] With the support of the Travelers Aid Society and church groups, he had also petitioned the city to move Storyville to a more remote spot. The mayor dismissed these overtures as "unnecessary" and the appeals went nowhere.[10]

Morality aside, even the more pragmatic argument that Storyville was detrimental to the city's commercial prestige came to naught. The district would remain where it was as long as Behrman was mayor—without any camouflage and within a stone's throw of Canal Street, polite society's conventional thoroughfare. Sunday afternoons, in particular, were awkward on Canal. That was when Storyville's working girls slipped out of their brothels and relaxed a bit by taking in a movie or doing a bit of shopping alongside the city's more demure and modest class. The invisible boundary was breached. This situation was unacceptable to the administration of Newcomb College, Tulane University's elite sister school for women. It would address the matter aggressively. Between 1911 and 1917, hoping to protect its students from the sexually indiscreet women, the school's leaders prohibited them from walking down Canal Street on Sundays, with or without chaperones.[11]

Prefaced by the French maxim "*Honi soit qui mal y pense*" or "evil to those who think evil of it," the Blue Books hoped to add a bit of Gallic exoticism by portraying the district's feminine offerings as classy society girls, indexed either alphabetically or by address. They were also conveniently categorized by the historic New Orleans racial pyramid: "W" for white, "N" identifying a Negro, and "Q" for Quadroons. (In the 1906 publication, "WJ" was added indicating that the woman was white and Jewish.)

Sister teams and one pair of twins were available for sex—for a pretty price. There were even mother-daughter duos for sale to complete the depravity. Special services or a bed with the most coveted girls were expensive. One madam claimed that a "good house girl" could pull in $150 to $250 a week, but prices were not listed in the Blue Book. Descriptions of ladies of pleasure in gilded, suggestive poses were designed to entice even the most timid. Miss Grace Simpson, for example, called her cathouse on Customhouse Street (later Iberville St.) "a temple of joy where every man of sporting proclivities should visit." Her ladies were "noted for their clever ways in making everyone feel happy and contented." Gypsy Schaffer's girls "will let nothing pass toward making life a pleasure." And at an Iberville St. address, one could find Miss Isabelle, "a fervent priestess of Venus ... capable of offering twenty sacrifices in one night on the altar of love."[12] The last Blue Book, printed sometime between 1913 and 1915, advertised brothels offering 706 available women in Storyville, a number that accounted for neither the hundreds who worked the unlisted cribs and assignation houses or those who worked in brothels that did not purchase ads.[13] One scholar speculated that there were at least two thousand at any given time working within the district.[14]

If a Blue Book was not enough to satisfy an inquisitive browser, he could turn to a column called "Society" in the weekly five-cent tabloid, *The Mascot*, which exposed personal news and gossip about a few working girls who had yet to achieve the level of sophistication and charm that qualified them for the pages of the Blue Book. "It is safe to say," concluded one piece, "that Mrs. Madeleine Theurer can brag of more innocent young girls having been ruined in her house than there were in any other six houses in the city." Still another was the unabashedly bold rumor rag, the *Sunday Sun*, sold at newsstands and saloons. In this weekly one could read a column called simply "Scarlet World," which reported more prurient and often humorous news from the district. "Boys, if you are looking for a good time and wish to save a doctor's bill, we severely advise you to give [Carlisle's] all the room possible. When it comes down to the real thing in the way of low down tarts, then this is the place you are looking for." The tabloid even identified a drugstore on Customhouse and Marais Streets where "it is not lawful to sell cocaine but it is sold here just the same." The drug was sold as a medicine with such brand names as "Crown" and "Dr. Gray's Powders."[15] Boasting dozens of cabarets, cafés, saloons, approximately thirty bordellos, and dozens of cribs from the most raucous and bawdy to the most tasteful and luxurious, Storyville became a destination in itself for many who looked to indulge in the city's unholy diversions.[16] "No other city of the country," claimed *Collier's Weekly*, "runs vice of every kind so wide open."[17]

STORYVILLE'S SISTER

Just uptown from its more infamous neighbor, the so-called Black Storyville contributed mightily to that vice as well. It beckoned a narrower group of clients—the African American community, although there is evidence that it was probably more racially ambiguous than its name implied.[18] The two stood as the New Orleans version of Sodom and Gomorrah. Under prodding from Public Safety Commissioner Harold Newman, who himself was goaded by a reform-minded pressure group calling itself the Citizen's League, the city council decided "from and after" March 1, 1917, to dismember the downtown tenderloin turf of its nonwhite *nymphs de pavé*, 28 percent of Storyville's occupants in 1910.[19] City Ordinance 4118 crowbarred out from the legally defined district any "woman notoriously abandoned to lewdness" who belonged to "the colored or black race," proving that it had heretofore been an asylum from Jim Crow like no other public space in the South. Moreover, these fallen women could not "occupy, inhabit, live, or sleep in any house, room or closet" outside a specified four-block area uptown from Canal Street—Black Storyville.[20]

Sexual race-mixing, which had been for many the most reprehensible element of the district, had finally reached its limit of civic tolerance. The order was meant for the clients as well: "The appearance of a white man in the Negro district will cause his arrest," the commissioner warned, and "should a Negro woman even stroll in the white district, she will be jailed." (Black males worked in Storyville but were not allowed to be customers there.) Storyville, convulsed by this new order, had yielded to Jim Crow's ball and chain.[21]

It seems quite a paradox today—"reformers" fortifying the barriers of racial segregation. But the concept of white supremacy was, at the century's turn, curiously aligned with activists who pressed for this ordinance. Many reformers believed, both Black and white, that separating the races was a necessary invigorator for social change and a safeguard against racial disharmony. The Black elites in the Society for the Uplift of the Negro Race, for example, strongly endorsed Newman's ordinance.[22]

The ordinance was seen as especially disruptive to a unique and historic piece of New Orleans culture—its uncommon rubber stamping of sexual play between the city's whites and its rich population of cinnamon-skinned quadroon and octoroon women—"fancy girls." During the French and Spanish colonial periods, plaçage was a socially acceptable custom whereby a wealthy, ethnically European man would contract with the mother of a mixed-race woman and enter into a physical, common-law relationship with her in return for property and a higher standard of living. Storyville was a kind of twentieth-century version of plaçage, perhaps the most enticing element of the district for visitors searching for an exotic sexual partner. Here they found the erotic comfort of an octoroon's tawny skin. It was exactly this racially heterogeneous tableau of the available women in the top-drawer establishments that enticed adventuresome men from as far away as Europe to travel to New Orleans and harvest this forbidden fruit.

Many New Orleanians, however, had not warmed to mixed-race concubinage despite the city's long history of indifference to sexual permissiveness. Twenty years of living under the mantle of Jim Crow had changed attitudes and mores. The segregation ordinance, one *Picayune* reader offered, was supported by every Black in the city "who believe, as do the whites, in keeping the races pure. It was never intended by our Creator," he pontificated, "that the races should so mix or mingle, or all would have been the same color."[23]

A few of the more enterprising of the district's octoroon women were able to elevate themselves to become very prosperous brothel owners. Alabama-born Lulu White was one. Owner of the famous Mahogany Hall, she advertised a "stable of octoroon beauties" residing in her four-story urban palace, which offered five luxurious parlors, lush boudoirs—each with its own bath, and even an elegant elevator to speed the rendezvous.[24] Her guests paid a tidy price for these plush furnishings, helping to pay for the eye-popping diamonds she displayed on every finger. If Lulu had to move, her trade would never be the same even if she opened for business elsewhere in town.

Another baroness of the evening was Willie Piazza, Storyville's octoroon "Countess." The daughter of an Italian-born Mississippian and a woman of unknown racial heritage, she favored Russian cigarettes smoked from a two-foot-long holder made of gold and ivory and socialized with her patrons wearing expensive gowns and a diamond-studded choker.[25] Yes, the enterprise they conducted was a high-profit racket with a reliable customer flow. All this and more would be lost once the law went into effect. Madams White, Piazza, and all the other women of their pedigree, it seemed, would have to relocate.

Willie Piazza, who had once shot at a customer for assaulting one of her girls, was especially furious. Not about to vacate her resident mansion and operation without a fight, she refused police orders to vacate, hired a good attorney, and sued the city along with a few other of the tight-knit roster of cathouse matrons. The Countess's most powerful argument was economic—as the legal owner of her Basin Street residence, the ordinance violated her rights. The city was guilty, she claimed, of attempting to illegally seize a citizen's property without due process of law.

In the first round, Piazza was found guilty of violating the contested ordinance. She managed, however, to win her case on appeal to the Louisiana Supreme Court. The city's position was that it had provided a "separate but equal" space for "colored" prostitutes—Black Storyville—but the justices were not persuaded by this argument in spite of the reference to the famous quote and jurisprudence from the *Plessy v. Ferguson* case.[26] Less than two weeks after the Supreme Court victory, however, the city, now enlightened, passed a replacement ordinance that legalized the language of its predecessor. This time the law read that it was only unlawful for African Americans to work in Storyville. They were not forced to leave if they lived there.[27] Injunctions were filed against this revised ordinance as well, but by that time Storyville was declared closed by order of the War Department.

Many of the banished women reluctantly moved a few blocks west to Black Storyville, knowing that their income was sure to plunge. The new venue of vice was not unfamiliar terrain. A substantial commerce in African American sex was unofficially established there well before the troublesome decree was passed. Historian Alecia Long confirms that the two districts, despite the law, were never strictly segregated and were divided almost equally between Blacks and whites.[28]

In Black Storyville, "back o' town," rent was cheap and gambling dens thrived alongside a labyrinth of wilting saloons selling cheap whiskey, murky jazz tonks, and dimly lit dives. Dance halls often provided separate rooms enclosing hustlers playing cotch, a card game similar to poker. Ashtrays and bar stools didn't match, and the incense of stale yeast spilled from the glasses of Jax lager lingered along with the lingerers. As the post-midnight hours crept on, the pageant turned primitive. The music, in a tight dialogue with the dancers, became lustier. "Women danced on bars with green money in their stockings," alleged one of the neighborhood's abundant lost sisters in a 1945 interview, "and sometimes they danced naked. They used to lie down on the floor and shake their bellies while the mens fed them candies."[29]

Unsurprisingly, it was high-poverty territory. Children as young as eight squirted down the brick and cobblestone streets barefooted looking for anything to do to make a few nickels so they could buy a "poor boy" sandwich or gamble it away on the curb playing "cooncan," a form of gin rummy, or craps. Others were persuaded to attend class at the Fisk Colored School at Franklin and Perdido Streets, where Buddy Bolden and later Louis Armstrong learned to read and write from decaying textbooks. (The school was finally closed in 1917 when the school board caved in to pressure from a Black civic group, who argued that it was unconscionable to have children walk to school in that environment.)

Lyle Saxon, the director of the Federal Writers' Project in Louisiana during the Depression, portrayed the scene as he explored the dark streets back o' town: "Music boxes blasted from every lighted doorway. Black men swaggered or staggered past, hats and caps pulled low over their eyes . . . or set rakishly over one ear." The smells were equally enduring, a strange brew of "stale wine and beer, whiskey, urine, perfume, and sweating armpits." Inside one hangout there were drug addicts, street people without a dime, and laborers who were depleting their Friday paychecks, all having quite a time. Dancing alone, an obese woman snapped her fingers to the beat. Young, perfumed Jezebels, sweating along with the others, approached a few who "sagged over the bars, their eyelids heavy from liquor and reefers," searching for "slow drag" dance partners and more. One of the girls screamed over the music, "I'll do it for 20 cents, Hot Papa. I can't dance with no dry throat. I wants 20 cents to buy me some wine." Then she raised her dress and "showed some linen."[30]

Squeezed in between were small cafés, several barber shops, the husks of abandoned residences, and a few multipurpose halls owned by fraternal organizations like the Odd Fellows and Masons. There was even a place of worship, the Mount Zion Baptist Church, where Armstrong and his mother attended services. The presence of Sicilian corner grocery stores and the nearby Jewish businesses on South Rampart Street touted the neighborhood's diversity.

There were no Blue Books for Black Storyville. None were really needed. Anyone could find a scarlet lady just by asking around. Even a precocious young teenager like Armstrong, who had certainly seen more than he should have growing up in this, his own neighborhood, could help provide directions. And during his later gigs at Matranga's dance hall, one of the toughest fleshpots, the budding cornetist likely became acquainted with several of the local female solicitors. (His mother was in the trade for a while, and he himself would later marry one.)

No guidebook was necessary. But keeping people's wits about them was. Music and song trespassed into every building, though their refrains were often the robberies, drunken debaucheries, and stabbings that threaded through its streets. That was Black Storyville's other soundtrack—sin and struggle. An hour or so before sundown on Saturday nights, bands booked to play until 4 a.m. would set up just outside the Funky Butt to draw customers.

One Baptist pastor converted his church into a dance hall because it generated more money. It was notoriously dangerous. Jazz master Kid Ory recalled that "if you didn't have a razor or a gun, you couldn't get in there." Armstrong concurred: "It was a real rough place. You'd have to take your razor with you, 'cause you might have to scratch somebody before you leave." In the streets outside, even youngsters had to be vigilant. "You had to fight and do a lot of ungodly things to keep from being trampled on."[31] Residents called their neighborhood "The Battlefield" for good reason. Despite the area's crime, white community indifference led the police to generally assume a low profile there. Much like the other needs of the New Orleans African American community, particularly in areas such as health and education, these residents were usually left to fend for themselves.

Just before the war years, other sounds arising from the gut of the African American community were beginning to be heard throughout the city as well. Before long, the new musical genre of jazz would become one of America's most important contributions to the creative arts.

Chapter 4

"THAT BARBARIC THROB"

Attempting to manage all of this from his office in City Hall was a New York-born German Jew. Martin Behrman was an infant when his parents, Henry and Fredericka, moved to New Orleans. His father died soon after arriving, forcing Fredericka to open a humble bazaar in the French Market to bring in a few dollars for herself and her only son. They lived together in a cheap corner apartment on Bourbon and St. Philip, attending public schools until his mother died when he was only 12. It was a hardscrabble existence but a life not unlike that of many of his neighbors. Without a family-support network, Martin was forced to forego high school. He did manage to learn to speak both German and French while in elementary school, a skill he would put to good use as a politician. In his teens he landed a cashier's job at Samuel's Dollar Store on Canal Street for $15 a month with no thought that he would one day command a position of honor on that same thoroughfare oversee-ing dozens of parades, welcoming international dignitaries, and delivering patriotic speeches during the war years. After a time he moved to a modest home on Pelican Street in Algiers, on the west bank of the river, having accepted an offer to clerk in a grocery there. He later became a salesperson for a wholesale grocery operation, making friends, remembering names, and harnessing his relentless self-will and energy. Algiers would remain his home for most of his life.

Money did not appear to motivate him. Political power did. It was the accelerant that gave him his undented drive. One wonders if Behrman's conversion to Catholicism in heavily Catholic New Orleans was less about his spiritual beliefs than it was his need to further his political aspirations. Married at 22 to Julia Collins of Cincinnati, he skipped from one appointed political job to another, paddling his way upstream to the headwaters of the city machine while forging opportunistic alliances with the right people along the way. Patience, hard work, fierce ambition, and the support of local ward leaders and precinct captains finally won for him the mayor's office in 1904 at 39 years old. He would later comment that campaigning for votes was little different from selling produce.[1] The portly Behrman, who resembled a young Grover Cleveland with his husky, scrub-brush mustache, would be elected to that office an extraordinary five times, four of those terms consecutively and two without opposition. No other mayor in the city's history could match either these political accomplishments or his work in freeing New Orleans from the creaky clench of the nineteenth century.

During those seventeen years as the city's chief administrator, he strengthened his political grip by deftly deploying his most persuasive weapon—patronage. The Sewerage and Water Board alone, for example, controlled over four thousand jobs. There existed, however, hundreds of less than legitimate jobs dispensed by Behrman in order to either maintain or nourish loyalty. Perhaps most infamous of those was that of "sidewalk inspector," responsible for reporting cracks in the concrete to the public works department.[2] As he doled out favors to businessmen with illegal no-bid contracts and strongarmed the election machinery by installing the city's seventeen powerful ward leaders, Behrman made political maneuvers like a Russian grandmaster playing chess pieces. Votes also came his way from Storyville's dens of desire—even though women could not yet vote—from hotel rooms, and even from the dead. Election results often were suspect. In some precincts where ward leaders were in firm control, the number of votes tallied exceeded the number of registered voters.[3]

With assistance such as this, Behrman became the unrivaled boss of the Old Regulars, the political machine that had once anointed him as its candidate back in 1904. Well-oiled and reliable, its operatives were made up of an assortment of business, ethnic, and political leaders who worked with the mayor to form a kind of benevolent dictatorship over the city. This model skirted many of the precepts of democracy—particularly the integrity of state and local elections and its inclination to favor political supporters with contracts and jobs. But it was at the same time quick to respond to pressures from vocal civic and religious groups for reforms and infrastructure improvements. The Old Regulars' report card was muddled with contradictions. The same is true of its leader. Like a few other urban-machine overlords, Behrman is remembered for his positive leadership and effectiveness.

The mayor chaperoned New Orleans through the turmoil of World War I and two transformational amendments to the US Constitution. New schools were built, and long-delayed sewerage and drainage upgrades were executed. Much of this success was due to Behrman's comfortable relationships with power brokers, showcasing an approach that always seemed more intuitive than scripted. Yet he retained some scar tissue—the ugly wart of a big city kingpin. He was indeed the Crescent City's Machiavelli. Democracy's mechanisms often got in the way and were discarded. The ends, he might have said, justified the means.

Throughout the war Behrman was imperishable, appearing in an abundance of the war's fundraisers, promotional functions, and public forums. Hardly a citizen could say with honesty that they had not seen the mayor in person or heard him speak. Never laying claim to masterful oratory—he preferred handing off a required speech to one of his staff members—he was clearly invigorated by the war, creating another persona for this son of penniless immigrants. The mayor slowly understood the importance of being visible during the war years, lifting the city's citizenry, displaying a cool demeanor and resolve, always reminding them that they must sacrifice for the cause.

It was not unusual for him to deliver a half dozen speeches in a single day, zigzagging across the city in a whirl. A sign on his desk faced all visitors to his office: "Don't Park Here." Translation: let's make it short—I don't have time. A typical itinerary on a single day in July of 1917 took him to an event at the French and British consulates at 11:00 in the morning, then scrambling to a gathering of the Louisiana Exhibitors League, a festival at City Park, a Woodmen of the World convention, a meeting of the Annunciation Playground board, and finally a 5:00 p.m. patriotic affair at the Strand Theater.[4] Somewhere in between he must have had something to eat. His popularity soared, polling more votes than President Wilson in the election of 1916. Clearly, his German ethnicity was no liability even as the nation conducted a war with the country of his ancestors.[5]

PLAY

New Orleans culture was experiencing a renaissance during the Behrman years, one that would arise deep from the belly of the city and eventually become its identifier. From the antebellum days of Congo Square's weekly festivals for the enslaved and Free People of Color on the very edge of the French Quarter, music and dance have been inseparable from everyday life in New Orleans. It was there that the *bamboula* thrived. Drums and banjos playing raw and uninhibited music accompanied dancers, male and female, who swayed, shook, and trembled into a crescendo of improvised movement. To the enslaved who participated, the dance made them feel free, at least for a few hours. In more refined neighborhoods, music was no less important. But by the 1880s, the more disciplined repertoire of string and brass marching bands was rapidly being supplanted by the more youthful sound of ragtime.

Sometime near the turn of the century, another change took place. Perhaps it began with Jelly Roll Morton, who claimed that he was first to invent what would become known as jazz. The New Orleanian took his cue from the syncopated rhythm of traditional ragtime, but he flirted with what would later become a jazz piece by first simply accelerating the tempo of contemporary dance numbers and marrying ragtime with the blues. Doctrine be damned. The fresh sound's appeal to younger Black and white audiences, soldier and civilian, was overwhelming. Both the songs and the dances, like the respectable *quadrille*, became more "ratty" with slow drags and sexually suggestive lyrics. Some tunes, like "Stick It Where You Stuck It Last Night," had no "suggestions" at all. At some joints, said Bolden, "them whores would perform something terrible 'til they'd get out of hand, shaking down to the floor and dropping their drawers and teddies . . . a beautiful sight to see."[6]

While it is impossible to truly credit who invented this genre, it is easier to explain why New Orleans was its incubator. Cultural diffusion was more evident in the port of New Orleans than in any other American city by the early 1900s. There were white Creoles and mixed-race, French-speaking Creoles of Color, the latter having occupied its own social class of relative privilege until Jim Crow. Along with the city's Anglos, their European classical music connections could have influenced jazz musicians to maintain a loose melodic structure throughout the number. Added to the mix were thousands of newly arriving Sicilians, who heard similarities between the music of street bands in their new home and those in Sicily itself. And there were the descendants of the enslaved whose musical inclinations were embedded into their Congo Square traditions.

Equally important to this cauldron was a distinctly laissez-faire, liberal attitude about life that pervaded New Orleans. Calvinist it was not, nor had it ever had been. *Le bon temps rouler* was the city's mantra, its lyric, so it is not difficult to understand that its musicians were not always willing to follow the established architecture of printed measures and notes. This mingling of ethnicities and cultures, each continuing to maintain its distinct identity while interconnecting, is a tempting metaphor for the musical mélange called jazz. If New Orleans with its joie de vivre had not been the place of its birth, then it probably should have been.

Most adults seemed at the very least to be intrigued by jazz as long as it did not replace the comfort music of their youth. A 1917 story ran in the *Picayune* entitled "Savage Dance Music of Africa Drives Away Gloom of the World." The writer attempted to hail the new music, doing so with a clumsy syntax that mirrored the untidy tempo of jazz itself: Ever since slaves were brought from Africa, he wrote, "that barbaric throb and crash of jazz, that nerve tingling rhythm, has put numberless thousands on their toes and sent their bodies swaying and whirling in a mad effort to interpret in motion the appeal that leaps from the unfaltering regularity of beat that underlies the droning smoothness of the tumultuous din."[7] Not everyone was as delighted. Jazz was not unlike other new trends that defied convention and evoked ridicule. An editorial in the same conservative *Picayune* excoriated the new musical species, blasting it as "a manifestation of a low streak in man's tastes that has not come out in civilization's wash." In this house, it continued, jass [sic] is "down in the basement, a servant's hall of rhythm." The author could not understand how its "cult" of acolytes "love to fairly wallow in noise."[8] The *New Orleans Item* was no kinder. "Every musician must play out of tune." They are "seized by epileptic fits" and perform like they are "contortionists."[9] Dancing to its random sound was the most troubling of all. Many older folks, Black and white, looked on it as a menace, a symbol of unwanted change—a perversion of familiar, beloved tunes, which jazz musicians derisively labeled "sweet" music for "dicty" folks with money. They especially feared the enchantment this dancing had for their children and its ability to overreach racial boundaries.

Jazz was insolent. That was a large part of its appeal. Its revolutionary message crossed Jim Crow perimeters, fascinating young and urbane whites to a musical species that evolved from the bowels of the African American experience. And it was a participatory, not a passive allure. That was just unacceptable to some. Historian Jennifer Atkins defined the new dances that evolved from jazz even more broadly. Women were "testing the limits of social acceptability through their bodies" as it brought couples together in "sexually explicit arrangements" and helped mark the advent of sexual liberation for women. "Getting sweaty" and "dancing with partners of the opposite sex became morally tricky, especially for women."[10] Even more alarming, the critics believed that these new, primitive sounds encouraged racial mixing—a kind of "musical miscegenation," wrote Charles Hersch, staggering Jim Crow just a bit.[11] Forty years later in Tupelo, Mississippi, a young Elvis Presley would hear a similar torrent of criticism from the very same narrow corner of older, self-righteous music dilettantes. In both cases these disapprovals would eventually be reduced to mockery.

Apprehension about the slow, poisonous leak of jazz music into the aristocratic Creole culture of New Orleans continued through the war years. A week after the Armistice was declared, the French Opera House hosted what was considered to be one of the finest orchestras in the world, *La Societe des Concerts du Conservatoire de Paris*. Every dignitary, it seemed, was present along with nearly every black tie and long gown in New Orleans. Given the cozy relationship between the Americans and French, forged by the war and the lingering high spirits of the Armistice, anticipation was high for a fine musical performance. Governor Ruffin Pleasant, seated in the first row, was ready to present a wreath to the conductor before the performance. As he stood to do so, he was interrupted by the sound of a jazz band strutting down Bourbon Street announcing an upcoming boxing match. Pleasant sat down to wait its passing so he could be heard, then rose once more to complete his task once the band passed on. A reporter from the *Item* wrote that faces in the fashionable audience "expressed polite horror" at the crude jazz interlopers, but their feet "kept polite time" with the beat of the snare drum. "God preserve us," mumbled one disgusted guest.[12]

Whatever one's tastes, the streets were swollen with music—heard often, even from the decks of ships docked on the river or on streetcars where trios played for tips. There was such a demand for it and gigs were so abundant that bands in the city grew smaller to address the shortage of musicians.[13] Parades, funerals, and fish fries were all expected to have live music. Lawn parties set up bands on front porches, playing well into the night. Fueled by beer and whiskey and illuminated by *flambeaux* planted into the lawn between dancing couples, these parties often morphed into neighborhood gatherings. Hired "ballyhoo bands" played on busy street corners or on decorated flatbed wagons to advertise a new product or store opening. Dairy stables all over the city were cleaned and hired out for dances that lasted late into the next morning. Bands serenaded outside the home of a friend or relative who was celebrating a birthday. Anonymous soloists playing guitars, mandolins, or sometimes classical violins harbored at busy corners wishing for a coin flip from an approving pedestrian.

Children even participated in this street music culture using homemade instruments like tin cans and pots, playing in "spasm" bands for tips. "Kid" Ory, the jazz trombonist, began learning about the beat of the city by singing in a "humming" band for cookies or treats as a child.[14] Some got their start participating in "cutting contests," where two or more bands would meet coincidentally in the street and take turns trying to outplay each other. These became so popular that groups of Black jazz musicians would be booked in advance for "band battles" and featured at expensive society picnics. Joe "King" Oliver, Ory, and fellow jazz impresarios King and Sidney Bechet were in demand at fancy uptown and Esplanade Avenue house parties too. As his mentor, Oliver likely invited the young Louis Armstrong to sit in for these jobs or at subscription dances at the old Tulane gym, a regular spot for the college set during the war years.

Storyville provided steadier work for a few noted musicians like Jelly Roll Morton, but they were found mainly in the plushest establishments where twenty cents got you a shot of I. W. Parker or Murray Hill whiskey, twice the price for the same in a "tonk." Even then the "professor," as the lone pianist in the parlor was called, provided about the only music brothels had for customers. Granted, patrons were often there for more than music anyway, but the pianists served to further lubricate the scene. Coin-fed mechanical pianos were common in lesser establishments. Seven-piece orchestras were more likely to be found in the cabarets and dance halls, which were scattered downtown outside the district and into the French Quarter. None of them had singers. For a mere $1.50 a night they played, tips not included. Sleeping late the next day, they gulped pitch-black French Market coffee until these night crawlers returned to play again at 8:00 that evening.[15] Better than punching a clock.

More respectable venues for the bands provided additional opportunities to make a living, and many played for more than one group a day if their lips held out. The *Belle of the Bend* and the SS *Sidney*, river excursion boats, which sailed up and down the Mississippi, were popular spots for nightly dances. Benevolent societies, community and business associations, and religious groups like the Knights of Columbus booked boats regularly. Fate Marable's New Orleans Band had a nightly gig—a dicty job on the *Sidney* playing more traditional waltzes, sometimes distilling a bit of ragtime into them too. Its star cornetist was the seventeen-year-old from "back 'o town," Louis Armstrong, who undoubtedly imported a bit of the pulse from the music joints he had reaped as a player. He was accompanied by "Pops" Foster, Johnny St. Cyr, and others, each of whom won fame later as jazz icons.

Patrons sat on long benches facing each other, the dance floor dividing them with the band at one end. Young, unattached military men, admitted free each Monday and Friday, were particularly fond of this seating arrangement. It allowed them to search for and lock onto a cute girl before risking the long walk to the other side of the floor in search of a willing dance partner. It was also a proper way for local girls to meet an attractive soldier, marine, or sailor. Pairs were quick to discover the dark and romantic decks, with the Mississippi below, outside the enclosed dance floor—perfect for even more familiarity.

More music, lots more, could be found at the city's three amusement areas along the brackish, gray water of Lake Pontchartrain. Twenty cents would get you a round trip ticket on the eighty-six-year-old Smokey Mary, the first railroad built west of the Appalachians, packed with locals, soldiers awaiting orders, and musicians hoping to make a few bucks. It left on its six-mile ride from the river to the resort of Milneburg on the shore of the lake, chugging down the Elysian Fields neutral ground north across a scowling marsh, unpopulated woodlands, and farms where hunters still stalked game. Here was a modest but very popular area with a mile-long elevated boardwalk that gave access to restaurants, a hotel, cotton candy and ice cream vendors, watermelon stands, and picnic areas. A white lighthouse built in 1838 stood sentry in the midst of it all, avowing that the area once accommodated a port.

Sunday patrons, their numbers swelling with men in uniform, strolled on a wide wooden pier to Quarella's, a café and dance joint set on high pilings extending several hundred yards out into the lake. It was a world away from the city, and lovers easily found solitude in the long hike to the tip of the pier. There was even a bath house available for changing into "bathing costumes" for swimmers, and the hint of saltwater spiked everyone's appetite for fresh shrimp, blue lake crabs, and especially dancing. Bands, both Black and white, set up on performance platforms or played at Quarella's late into the evening seven days a week. Up and down the shore a colony of over a hundred rather raffish, sometimes crumbling fishing camps rested tenuously on pilings, reminders of the city's intimate relationship with seafood—and hurricanes. There was no indoor plumbing. One could peer down open toilet lids to the lake below. Yet blissful, bronzed fishermen sucking away at their Old Golds continued to tend their nearby crab nets hoping for a nice catch to boil for dinner.

Kid Ory, Armstrong's idol, had his boat ricochet from camp to camp with his combo aboard busking for tips from vacationers. Bands like his would compete in cutting contests to grab spots near the most generous camps. One popular white band might be across the water just a few yards away from a band made up of African Americans, each scrambling for position in a kind of water-bug symphony. Both were playing the new sound. Jazz was beginning to find its way to the waters of Lake Pontchartrain.[16] Another music idol, Sharkey Bonano, decided to live in Milneburg to save him the trouble (and the twenty cents) of commuting there from town. On weekends it was not unusual to find dozens of ad hoc jazz bands setting up outdoors between the piers. Jelly Roll Morton captured one moment with his *Milneburg Joys*: "Rock my soul with the Milneburg Joys. Play 'em mama, don't refuse. Separate me from these weary blues."

That last line from Morton's number would be prophetic for African American artists after Louisiana's most pervasive segregation laws were passed in 1898. This tragic legislation marked an alteration to the easy, unique synergy that existed between the races in New Orleans, within both the bands and the audiences that huddled near the stages to see and hear them. Virtually all public facilities, including restaurants, hotels, theaters, saloons, night clubs, parks, playgrounds, schools, libraries, and cemeteries, became racially segregated. These restrictions, however, were very slow to be enforced. With the war came more rigid enforcement of Jim Crow laws. Once the sweeping restrictions were policed, they jolted the New Orleans music scene. One by one, some of the city's most respected jazz entertainers "separated from these weary blues" and fled to more racially tolerant cities like Chicago and New York. Among them were King Oliver, Louis Armstrong, Jelly Roll Morton, and Sidney Bechet.

Meanwhile, the Milneburg scene was becoming seedy, especially given the number of young military men coming into town who were looking for a few hours of fun while training for a job designed to wring out of them precisely the opposite. Many of the fishing camps, it was said, were being rented out by the hour. Not a good sign. There were certainly other opportunities for sexual liaisons elsewhere in New Orleans, but these outposts were places a poor Navy recruit could afford before leaving for the war zone. The *Picayune* chose its words carefully: "Boys and girls were said not to be making the best use of [the camps]."[17] Beds were found in the women's bathhouses, and "pajama parades" became a favorite pastime on the boardwalk and on the camps' porches.[18] A good many "shop girls," female factory workers who were considered loose and yielding, made their way to the outpost. They were nicknamed "Hernshine Canaries" because a good number of them were employed at the local cigar factory by the same name. Their signature apparel was a pair of "baby doll" shoes that sported straps across the instep and white stockings, both of which were turn-ons for the guys. "If they didn't want to go along with us, we pushed them into the lake," grunted one of the camp regulars.[19]

Two other amusement areas on the lake east of Milneburg competed for the servicemen's dollars. Spanish Fort near the mouth of Bayou St. John was much tamer and family friendly.[20] It boasted a concert brass band led by a Professor Tosso and mostly Sicilian musicians reluctant just yet to venture into jazz. The big draw was the bandstand and pavilion built for dancing. After a terrible fire there in 1906, the new owner, the N.O. Railway and Light Company, built a connecting streetcar line, making it easy to access it from the city center. Owners accessorized it with a spectacular roller coaster, an alligator pond, an interesting shrubbery maze, a scary Ferris wheel, and several concession stands completing what residents liked to call "the Coney Island of the South." The 1917 spring season opened with a patriotic ceremony capped off by a flag raising on the new seventy-foot flagpole, the national anthem, and a speech by the mayor.

West End Park, where the New Basin Canal met Lake Pontchartrain, offered another option for recreation and relaxation. Everyone called it a park, but it was actually a large deck extending out over the lake's waters. An expansive garden greeted visitors at the entrance, its rose vines twisting through a trellised arch leading to a dancing fountain that fired spikes of water high into the sky, spraying giggling kids standing nearby. Intruding far into the lake at the end of a wide, curling pier stood the glistening two story Southern Yacht Club with its broad, sweeping verandas. Steps led up to its ornate rooftop gazebo, which governed the shoreline park from high above the lake's waters. Members only, please.

A big attraction for families was a vitascope used for movies projected onto a huge outdoor twenty-by-forty-foot screen that covered the bandstand. Music, of course, was frequent and fun. Then there were seafood restaurants, a challenging roller coaster, and oak trees everywhere providing shade from the summer sun. A clam shell road along the linear New Basin Canal linked it with downtown. Once a streetcar line was laid parallel to the road, it became an easy twenty-minute ride. Service was twenty-four hours during the summer. One could even elect to continue on that same line to Spanish Fort, for those who were still capable of braving another park the same day. During busy times, fun lovers did not have long to wait, as the clacking streetcars appeared at West End about every five minutes. Free admission to all three of these spots made them especially attractive to the city's military population.

Blacks, of course, military or not, were not welcomed. Not anymore, that is. Spanish Fort's owners, faced with declining attendance, had just twenty years before ignored the swelling momentum to legalize segregation. In fact, in 1896 they had specifically invited the city's African Americans, along with its white patrons, to enjoy the resort.[21] That announcement reflected the complexity of racial attitudes as the city slowly transitioned to the adoption of Jim Crow legislation. Admittedly, opening the gates to Black citizens was a strictly economic decision, and no more. Yet, there is no evidence that this liberal policy created any discord at the time. Spanish Fort's delicate patience with racial mixing, however, would shortly end, surrendering to Jim Crow's clutches. By 1917, its Black jazzmen would be playing to all-white audiences, audiences that were becoming more and more aware of the terrible war that was being waged closer than ever to their homeland.

Chapter 5

REX, COMUS, AND THE WAR'S APPROACH

The sinking of the *Lusitania* made clear to Americans their vulnerability. Future collisions with Germany's submarine force, yet unchallenged, would be impossible to avoid without a complete embargo of transatlantic trade. Recognizing this grave potentiality, Wilson launched the Council of Defense in 1916 to inventory and coordinate the nation's manufacturing and commercial resources. Later its mission would broaden to include facilitating such things as bond sales, conservation, and draft registration. It was a kind of clearing house and advertisement arm for most all government war programs. The organization emanated down to the state, parish, and even community levels in order to better personalize its efforts.[1]

That same year Congress passed the National Defense Act, which expanded the standing Army and National Guard, established the Reserve Officers' Training Corps, and allocated funds for hundreds of military aircraft. It was a meek response to the so-called "preparedness movement," whose main sponsor was the popular former president Teddy Roosevelt, who had been hammering Wilson relentlessly since the *Lusitania* sinking for his reluctance to move the country toward war. The Naval Act of 1916 was more substantive, allocating money to build ten battleships, six heavy cruisers, ten light cruisers, fifty destroyers, and thirty submarines. It was becoming evident that the president's tight grip on neutrality was beginning to loosen, one finger at a time.

There were other signs of the deepening crisis. Regulations on Atlantic shipping were tightened, and a merchant marine was established along with a naval auxiliary fleet. Over ninety German and Austrian merchant ships in American waters had been seized and its crews interned since the outbreak of war. Once US entry was imminent, Wilson gave the order for port officials to prepare to take custody of the officers and crew members as they were considered war prisoners. Ships were needed to transport troops and supplies to the war fronts in Europe, and these foreign vessels would be refitted to help fill the shortage.

By early 1917 there was an unmistakable sense of the inevitability of being drawn fully into the terrible conflict. Germany announced a return to a policy of unrestricted submarine warfare against neutrals on January 31st, tightening its naval blockade against the Entente powers of England and France. It was an act of desperation, for the Germans had been unable to break the stalemate in the trenches of the Western Front. The Kaiser was now willing to risk war with the US, believing that strengthening his U-boat blockade would serve to weaken and finally collapse the British and French ground forces. There had been confrontations on the Atlantic during the past years, but the German high command, careful to appease the US, had heretofore backed down. The demands of war, however, often change policy. Berlin had decided to roll the dice.

President Wilson, elected less than three months before with a boost from the slogan "he kept us out of war," would remain fixed to his administration's position. The right of neutral ships to sail the oceans was inviolable Wilson insisted, even though US ships continued to carry thousands of tons of contraband to Washington's putative allies. Neutrality was no more than a thinly veiled diplomatic charade. But in response to the Kaiser's U-boat decision, Wilson broke diplomatic relations with Germany four days later. In a few weeks the president would also issue an executive order arming US merchant ships with the full knowledge that an exchange of gunfire would very likely hurl the nation into the war. The US also purchased the Danish West Indies, later the Virgin Islands, for fear that the Germans would conquer Denmark and establish a U-boat base on the islands. From this time on, cabinet meetings were dominated by the buzzing of updates from each department on war preparations that many believed had been postponed for too long. It was now only a matter of time.

American citizens were in a state of heightened nervousness. In just the one week following Germany's return to unrestricted submarine warfare, dozens of merchant ships, many flying flags of neutral countries, were sunk in the war zone near Britain. One of the victims of these attacks was a US seaman who was aboard a sinking British freighter. The passenger liner *California* was torpedoed not far from where the *Lusitania* was attacked. Several US nationals were among the survivors. In late February another Cunard liner, the *Laconia*, was hit by two torpedoes before capsizing off the Irish coast. Two Americans drowned. (US cruise lines asked the government to mount four- and five-inch guns on its ships' decks for protection, but the request was denied and cruises were thereafter suspended indefinitely.) The *New Orleans Item*, the city's evening daily, was more temperate than the *Times-Picayune*, campaigning for moderation in the face of growing militancy. "The American masses do not want war," it insisted in a February 21 editorial, "not because they are cowardly, but because they are brave . . . , brave enough to exercise restraint."[2]

In New Orleans there was more evidence of the deteriorating situation. A French steamer, the *Honduras*, a well-recognized regular customer at the port, exchanged gunfire with a U-boat on the 16th of February near the French coast. There were no casualties, but the incident brought the war a bit closer to home. A piece of New Orleans commerce was now at war. Live machine-gun firing sessions began on the shore of Lake Pontchartrain's west end to train the local navy militia. The targets were mock periscopes, and every hit was awarded with cheers from the spectators who lined the shore.[3] Five steamers (three German and two Austrian) that had been interned by authorities for several months in the Mississippi were ordered by port officials to relocate five miles downriver, a safer distance away from the city's main port facilities. There was fear that the crews would try to scuttle the ships if and when war was declared. A torpedo boat and revenue cutter escorted the ships to prevent escape. The War Department closed the mouth of the Mississippi to ship traffic between sunset and sunrise, a drastic move for a port city. Not since the Civil War had such an order been given.

MARDI GRAS

For a few short weeks in February 1917, anxiety over a looming war declaration from Congress was tempered by the frivolity of the Mardi Gras season. It would be a grand tonic for the citizenry, a reliable constant in the city's culture. Here was a celebration for every strata of New Orleans society. Creoles and the elite had their royalty, debutantes, lavish balls, and parades. African Americans had their own parading organization too, the eight-year-old Zulu Social Aid and Pleasure Club. Then there were the flamboyant, historic Mardi Gras Indian tribes who, fortified by drink, pranced through their neighborhoods with unrestraint, accompanied by booming drumbeats and exotic call-and-response chants. "Oowa-aa, Tu-way-pak-a-way, Oowa-aa, Tu-way-pak-a-way."

African American prostitutes got in on the fun too. A few years before the war, several formed erotic "Baby Doll" dancing groups from Black Storyville to compete with their sisters across Canal Street by demanding the most attention. This never presented much of a problem. Dressed provocatively in short, lacy bloomers, long stockings, and bonnets, they sucked on milk bottles (filled with adult beverages), smoked cigars, and stuffed cash in their garters

to throw at the men. As they bumped and grinded slowly down neighborhood side streets to the throb of bass drummers, "walking raddy" with faces
painted in pink chalk, they most certainly attracted the male admirers who
slinked through the spectators to gawk at them from the curb. They were
asserting themselves with their sexuality in a society that demeaned both
their race and their gender, although the real intent was much simpler—to
show up their white sisters in Storyville. "Them . . . bitches thought their
behinds were silver," remembered one of the dolls. "We had all the niggers
from everywhere following us. They liked the way we shook our behinds,
and we shook 'em like we wanted to." Modest and refined she wasn't. "We
showed them whores how to put it on. . . . When them Baby Dolls strutted,
they strutted. We showed our linen that day, I'm tellin' you."⁴

On Lundi Gras, the day before Fat Tuesday, Rex, the King of Carnival,
"Monarch of Mirth," and his entourage, arrived at the foot of Canal Street on
the krewe's royal launch chaperoned by a chorus of salvos fired from the ships
anchored nearby. "The guns were let go," wrote a *Picayune* reporter, "and one
could have imaged himself in the war zone in Europe."⁵ Shrill whistles from
plants and commercial boats added to the celebration. Nearby, the krewe of
Zulu's king, escorted in rented limousines from the Geddes and Moss funeral
home, lampooned the arrival of his counterpart Rex, when he and his earthy
officers, dressed as African warriors in black face, were pulled by mules up
the New Basin Canal in a banana barge. This comedic caricature of Rex was
becoming a must-see attraction, drawing hundreds of spectators from the
conventional activities of the carnival season.

The bewigged Rex in his white tights and jewel-encrusted satin cloak conducted a proper parade down the slalom of Canal Street. Below a bank of
lounging clouds, police on horseback preceded the monarch, gently coaxing
back a legion of onlookers. Then came the monarch himself waving a gold
scepter from his chariot high above an estimated twelve to fifteen thousand
bemused enthusiasts. Following him were marching soldiers, sailors, and National Guardsmen for the few short blocks to the magnificent Greek Revival
building, Gallier (City) Hall. Awaiting him there was another throng so dense
that many who had tickets to the raised bleachers erected on its steps could
not find seats. Governor Ruffin Pleasant sat in front next to the mustached
mayor, who in a vested suit and satin top hat, with a gold watch bob dangling
free from his bowling-ball midsection, looked very much the part. Following
the traditional toast to Rex, Behrman presented his majesty with the key to
the city, as was the custom, bowing and using the highest of gilded Victorian
oratory. For the next thirty-six hours, Rex would reign over the city.

Also among the marching units in the parade was the crew of the recommissioned *Maine*, dressed smartly in their dress uniforms and in perfect cadence with their band's drums. "It is doubtful," the reporter continued, "that the machine-like marching of Uncle Sam's men was ever so vividly impressed upon Orleanians. The thoughts of preparedness were probably uppermost in the minds of the people, in view of America's standing on the brink of war." Oddly, once the parade disbanded, the *Maine*'s sailors were ordered to return to their ship immediately. Also unusual was the prohibition against civilians who wished to visit the battleship, a routine practice when a military vessel docked at the port. But these were not routine times.[6] Perhaps the ship's commander determined that his crew had experienced enough of the city's seductions. Beatrice Hill, a back 'o town prostitute, recalled decades later that the sailors were a bonanza for her occupation. All of them "wanted a brownie. High yellows fared poorly . . . unless they got in those freakish shows."[7]

Temperatures in the upper seventies blessed the torrent of fun lovers that appeared on Mardi Gras day, February 20th. Canal Street from Elk's Place to the foot of the Mississippi was clogged by a swaying deluge of elbow-to-elbow flesh, many of whom were already swilling beer well before noon. The city was so jammed with visitors that over fifty Pullman cars parked in rail yards were set aside for those unable to book a hotel room. Special trains pulling three hundred cars brought in both foreign and domestic visitors. Two steam paddle wheelers docked at the Bienville Street wharf accommodated several hundred more revelers. Dozens of others rented cots in boarding homes or train depots for $2.00 a night.[8]

To the delight of many families, the New Orleans-based Washington Artillery and its hundred horses arrived home to enjoy the party after eight months of mostly tedious duty on the Mexican border. Each soldier was required to report promptly to the Fair Grounds race track the next morning, where a temporary camp was erected for them until they could be discharged, but at least for one day they could celebrate with the carnival of humanity in the way that young twenty-year-old males are apt to do after a long stretch out of contact with civilization.

The krewe of Rex paraded as it always had on Fat Tuesday morning for the pleasure of the thick multitude awaiting their sovereign for the day. As was the tradition, the parade of twenty mule-towed floats halted so the monarch could toast his young queen, Miss Emily Douglas, who stood on an elevated viewing platform in front of the Boston Club on Canal Street. The membership of this highly exclusive men's club always produced the next Rex. In 1917 the honor went to Charles H. Hamilton, the prominent coffee broker. Later that evening lights stringing the width of Canal Street formed a glimmering canopy for the parade of the oldest of Mardi Gras krewes, Comus, celebrating its sixtieth anniversary. The pageant's floats were further illuminated with the help of Black flambeaux carriers, dancing for craning fans who tossed coins their way. As with the other all-white krewes, this was the only participation allowed for the city's African Americans in the parade.

There was a newcomer to the 1917 Carnival. In order to emphasize that New Orleans would not simply become bystanders if hostilities commenced, the Association of Commerce mounted a parade of its own with a war preparedness theme. Composed of an impressive 150 floats representing over 90 different local manufacturers, its purpose was to introduce local resources that could be harnessed for war. One float exhibited a National Guard machine-gun crew, who were rewarded with sustained applause as they fired blanks from a Lewis .30 caliber.

Costumes were popular, particularly for younger revelers who loved becoming pirates or cowboys for a day. Contests awarding cash prizes were held throughout the city for the best. One that probably drew the largest swarm of gawkers took place at the corner of Frenchman and Derbigny Streets. For two blocks, the curious stretched their necks to watch as female impersonators climbed a platform to display their risqué wardrobes. "Promiscuous Maskers Attract Much Attention," read a playful headline in the *Picayune* the following day. "They fairly overran the place, lending a feminine influence" to the mob on the street. On St. Charles Avenue the same reporter, clearly enjoying his assignment, spotted an attractive young girl standing "languidly" on the Rex parade route attired in a costume which was in an "exceedingly abbreviated condition," fit, he guessed, "only for a beach." He went on to write that "her white shoulders gleamed in the sunlight and her shapely limbs were liberally displayed." A cop who was eyeing her laughed when another leaned over to whisper to him that the object of his attention was actually a man.[9]

Much more bawdy diversions took place as night fell on Mardi Gras. A few select old-line krewe members from Proteus, Momus, Comus, and Rex, along with other special guests, were invited to the oddly named "Ball of the Two Well Known Gentlemen," a private "French," i.e. erotic, soirée conceived in 1882 to mock the stuffy balls the invited guests had just left. This bacchanal boasted its own court and a resplendent, bejeweled queen chosen for the honor from Storyville's most desirable white girls. Dressed in the most opulent, glittering gowns, they parodied the traditional balls in the most outrageous fashion to the great delight of the district's regular clients, who shelled out as much as $100 for a night with their favorite masked maid.

Like King Zulu's comic prance through the city's streets, the balls were another jab at the priggish krewes whose members came entirely from the city's tuxedoed, white elite. They were easy targets for the working-class satirists. But it was all in the spirit of a good time, and the privileged in attendance, some of them sober, likely enjoyed the pageant more than most. They relished laughing at themselves and their haughty organizations as the prostitute/queen glided by, saluting the appreciative audience with her scepter followed by her dazzling, debauched maids in court. Author James Gill called the offbeat affair the apex of the Carnival season "for assorted johns, prostitutes, politicians, and policemen who grew rich on bribes for turning a blind eye on the whorehouses." Even the wives of the most highly regarded men in New Orleans society sought access to invitations, so deep was their prurient interest in the lives of the demimonde.

French balls were open to curious spectators without invitations—particularly tourists, military officers, and natives—searching for a kind of entertainment available nowhere outside of New Orleans. Once more unsavory elements began crashing the parties, however, a strict invitation system and an admission fee was charged to keep the ball more exclusive. Women who wanted to witness the fun were admitted free if they passed muster with screeners at the door. Presumably, many of these women were the coworkers of those in the court, who were there to celebrate their "debutante" friends as they spoofed the tableaux of Rex or Comus.[10]

Mardi Gras parades would be suspended in 1918 and 1919 because of the war. There would only be a few minor balls held those years, and the mayor outlawed masking in 1918 since it might, in his words, "give an opportunity for enemies to work destruction." Students had to go to school on Mardi Gras for the first time since the Civil War, but one does not cancel a big party without confronting teenage rage. Trouble brewed at Warren Easton High where a student-led strike and boycott had to be subdued. Classes were held as usual, but it is safe to say that not many polynomials were being divided that particular Tuesday.[11]

More signs of the impending war appeared during the early weeks of spring, 1917. Visitors were no longer allowed at the Algiers Naval Station or the National Guard's Jackson Barracks. Boy Scouts with binoculars helped patrol sensitive areas day and night. Servicemen were ordered to the US Mint on the perimeter of the French Quarter to protect the valuable machinery stored there. The water purification plant in the Carrollton neighborhood was placed under strict military surveillance. National Guard soldiers on two-hour shifts were told to keep all strangers away from the port's cotton warehouse and grain elevator. They were fortified with sandwiches made daily by gracious women and girls living nearby. Signs were posted along the river levee near the installations with the warning, "Enemy Aliens Stop! You Must Go No Further!" The soldiers were ordered to shoot if intruders did not comply. On April 1st a crew member on an interned German vessel was arrested for loitering at the foot of Canal Street on the river. Photos of large New Orleans buildings were found in his pocket.[12] Times were tense. Triggers were happy.

The most conspicuous indication that war was at hand was a Red Cross membership drive in February, an immense affair attracting hundreds of women volunteers who canvassed neighborhoods seeking the $1.00 membership fee. Mayor Behrman urged all to be generous as "the U.S. may at any moment find itself in collision" with Germany. One of the most passionate enthusiasts was the pastor of Trinity Chapel, Reverend Gordon Bakewell, a Civil War veteran. "I have seen soldiers . . . preferring death . . . to injury because they could not be given proper treatment in the hospitals," he thundered. No person should refuse the solicitors.[13]

The entire city stood at ramrod attention for the Monday event. Schools were closed. Red Cross ribbons were pinned on policemen, railway workers, store clerks, and hundreds of others. An electric sign flashed in red over Canal Street bearing a reminder of the effort. Cars driving below it trumpeted the occasion with placards fastened to their hoods: "We have done our duty to our country. Will you do yours?" Every streetcar in the city boasted signs with the same message. The school board even loaned classroom blackboards to help broadcast the amounts collected as they came in. One was placed in the huge show window of Maison Blanche. Others were positioned at major intersections in the commercial district on Canal and its feeder streets. Red Cross flags were on display everywhere too, in case one somehow overlooked the other adornments. In the final tally, the membership drive attracted almost five thousand new members in the local chapter, up from three hundred.[14] Several hundred of those new members were employees of Maison Blanche department store, whose store owner, S. J. Schwartz, paid the buck for anyone who could not afford the membership fee.[15]

PREPARATIONS FOR WAR

Roman Catholicism was a major feature of the city's French and Spanish colonial legacy, given a boost by the more recent immigrants from Ireland and Sicily. It nourished the city's pulse, its modus vivendi. The Lenten season after Mardi Gras was a time of reflection and prayer. In 1917, however, even nonbelievers were meditative. People understood that severing diplomatic relations with an adversary presages war. Mardi Gras offered only a brief respite from these sobering events. There was no return. One could now only guess what would nudge Washington closer to the edge.

The president had concluded that war would come "only by the willful acts and aggressions of others." On March 1st such a bombshell dropped. Reports confirmed that Berlin was secretly attempting to entice Mexico and Japan into war against the US. It was the infamous Zimmerman Telegram. In this explosive diplomatic note, announced to the nation in the press, Germany also attempted to seduce Mexico by pledging financial aid to its government if it agreed to a military alliance. To sweeten the deal with Mexico, Germany further promised to restore all territories annexed in 1848 by their un-neighborly neighbor north of the Rio Grande. Texas, New Mexico, and Arizona were specifically mentioned in the dispatch.

Even the remaining Americans who continued supporting the Central Powers were confounded at this Teutonic treachery. It was outrageous to believe that the Kaiser would be so unscrupulous as to prescribe cleaving American territory. But to have the unabashed audacity to admit to the intrigue was bewildering. Plausible deniability was an available option, yet the Imperial government exposed its hand nevertheless. It was yielding to its own extremists. "There seems no reason to doubt any longer Berlin's purpose," lamented an editorial in the *Times-Picayune*.[16]

Militants were now in the ascendency. The local chapter of the United Spanish War Veterans adopted a resolution condemning senate isolationists who "belittled our glorious nation" by filibustering the bill to arm US merchant vessels.[17] Letters swamped the city's newspapers, most all condemning the lawmakers as traitors. "What we need in this country," wrote one who signed his letter "A Red Blooded American," "is a law to provide severe punishment to anyone who embarrasses the nation in a crisis."[18] Or perhaps each of the dozen senators should be awarded the German Iron Cross.[19]

A few did indeed view the senators as real statesmen who understood the gravity of the vote. "Armed neutrality . . . is a misnomer existing only in the imagination of those who want to barter lives and blood for gold," complained a doubter. In the same edition, another concluded that "this is not our fight."[20] The hastily assembled Emergency Peace Federation placed a full page ad in the *New Orleans Item* and other US papers imploring its readers to write their representatives in Congress to slow the "stampede" of the war hawks.[21] But the majority opinion was solidly behind the president's decision to arm the ships and to flex some American muscle.

In mid-March a recruitment campaign was launched (offering a monthly salary of $28.75) in order to buttress the state's paltry National Guard forces—one infantry regiment, the Washington Artillery's one battalion, a single cavalry troop, and a field hospital. In sum there were perhaps fewer than seven hundred mostly part-time men on hand for duty. The US regular armed forces were in the same woeful condition, ranking seventeenth worldwide in size, below Romania, with under 250,000. Governor Ruffin Pleasant contributed a statement of his own. Being careful not to arouse panic, he called the recruitment only "precautionary" given the "fanatical cases of German sympathizers over the country, resorting to . . . blowing up public utilities."[22] Pleasant never suggested that they might be sent to France to fight, although this remained a real possibility. As a former colonel during the Spanish-American War and as commander of the state's National Guard, he was taking cautious, prudent steps.

Fed by gratuitous anti-German propaganda from Britain, jingoistic voices began demanding action. An organization called the National Security League (NSL), a right-wing pressure group founded in 1914, led the push for military preparedness. Business at the New Orleans Cotton Exchange was temporarily suspended on March 24th while members participated in a flag-raising ceremony led by the NSL's state chairman, Frank Hayne. In his brief address, he insisted that the US had already been at war with Germany for some time and denounced as traitors anti-Wilson pacifists and anyone opposed to the draft. Loud cheering assured him that he was speaking to sympathetic faces.[23] Each of the city's newspapers concurred that a draft was indeed necessary, no doubt spurred by the torpedoing and sinking of the steamer *Healdton* off the coast of Holland in a "safe zone" identified by the German command. Seven Americans drowned. One of the survivors was engineer G. W. Embry from New Orleans, whose last letter received by his wife read, "I am going to come home soon. This business is just too dangerous."[24]

The very next night the NSL sponsored another event, a "monster" prowar rally at the Athenaeum auditorium on St. Charles Avenue and Clio Street to urge Congress to authorize compulsory military training (and universal flag displays). An estimated 3,500 crammed into the building, a small US flag placed on each seat for all to wave during rousing sound bites from the speakers. All aisles were jammed with people standing and shouting. Galleries were filled to capacity, and dozens of Boy Scouts weaved through the place distributing programs.

After the national anthem, all heard from the governor, Mayor Behrman, and other dignitaries. They listened to strong-armed demonizing of pacifists, isolationists, and hyphenated Americans, an indication of the growing hysteria associating non-natives with threats to Anglo-American values. And preparedness was pushed: "Do you know," sang out St. Claire Adams of the National Security League, "that the whole army of the U.S. is but twice the size of the police force of New York City?"[25]

By far the loudest and most sustained applause came when Dr. H. Dickson Bruns, a Civil War veteran and a respected local physician, directly rebutted isolationist Senator James Vardaman of Mississippi for his opposition to military conscription. An avowed supporter of lynching, he once stated that education of African Americans would only "spoil a good field hand and make an insolent cook."[26] The segregationist "White Chief," as he was called, would never countenance an army that included African Americans. His voice rising, Bruns excoriated Vardaman and roared that the South would "take care of that issue as she had in the past." It was a full minute before he was able to proceed over the wild cheers of approval from the floor.[27]

In late March recruitment offices for all of the services began extending hours of operation, opening even on Sundays. Boys as young as seventeen were allowed to enlist with parental consent. Four elderly Civil War veterans set up shop on the corner of Canal and Baronne Streets to encourage enlistments. "We served in 1861," read their makeshift sign. "It's your turn now."[28] Businesses promised to pay the difference between an employee's salary and his military pay for one year. Loyola law school waived final exams for those students who enlisted, and students in their final year were automatically graduated. Tulane followed suit.

These measures, however, failed to attract more than a trickle of enlistments until war was declared. For example, the Navy set a quota of eight hundred men for Louisiana by April 20th. On April 2nd, the day of Wilson's war message to Capitol Hill, fifty applied but only fifteen passed the simple physical.[29] The same predicament faced the Marine recruiting station on Camp Street, where 85 percent of their hopefuls were rejected for various reasons.[30] Tulane University sent out a call to form an artillery unit made up of both students and graduates for the local Washington Artillery. One angry reader of the *Picayune* had a solution to the shortage—Behrman and other elected leaders should themselves enlist. Wearing an American-flag lapel pin and singing the national anthem was not patriotism, he complained. Rather, real patriotism means carrying a rifle in a trench in France.[31] (Behrman's son and two of his nephews did enlist in the Army.)

As the vote in Congress loomed, anxiety escalated. Rumors swirled. Was the city safe from attack? Was it true that there were U-boats lurking in the Gulf? Would Forts Jackson and St. Philip, designed to guard the river's mouth, provide protection from enemy ships that might punch through to

New Orleans? Many citizens remembered too well how inadequate these two sister forts were in 1862 when Union gunboats easily swept past them during the Civil War. The city surrendered without a fight soon thereafter. These fears prompted the chief of coast artillery to assure the public that they were indeed safe. Defenses had been significantly upgraded since then. No fleet in the world, he reported, could pass them today.[32]

None would accuse the male staff of the Grunewald Hotel of being war skeptics. Motivated by a growing awareness that the country was ill-prepared for the coming crisis, the young men willingly formed a quasi-military squad under their chief clerk. It was a simple public gesture of support for the president and no more. While the men were never armed, they learned the fundamentals of close-order drill and military courtesy using the rooftop of the hotel to train while off duty. The hotel's general manager, Gaston Saux, soon found that guests at the hotel began addressing him as "Colonel." Erect, white uniformed bellhops at the St. Charles Hotel began a well-orchestrated practice of stomping in cadence through the lobby in single file during a change of duty. The last man in file peeled off smartly at his new post as the others, head and eyes straight ahead, continued their march, mimicking the military's changing of the guard. The performance always drew a host of appreciative hotel guests.

There were other such groups as well. Maison Blanche on Canal Street, which soon would be hosting daily patriotic concerts for customers in its third-floor concert hall, was reportedly the only retail center in America that conceived of its own version of a militia. Made up of forty-seven of its male employees, these "home guards" drilled like the other ad hoc groups. But they were the most public, performing their tight marching routines at places like Heinemann Park to standing ovations before the Pelicans, the city's triple-A baseball club. Businesses under the guidance of the Citizen's Protective League mounted quasi-militia units, like the Insurance Men's Preparedness Squad, purportedly to help protect private property. Neighborhood groups created their own home guards, enlisting draft-exempt men or those over forty-five who were still willing and capable of handling a weapon. They too drilled with fervor each week.

Only slightly more serious was the hasty organization of two more "militia" groups, formed most likely for the purpose of giving its members a sense that they were contributing in some way. A unit of volunteers called the Battalion of Auxiliary Police was assembled in order to augment the local police in the event that emergency circumstances demanded more men to maintain public safety. They drilled once a week at a public space called Eastman Park near the boundary of Orleans Parish and Metairie. National Guard officers were selected to train and equip the men using a military model. Others instructed Warren Easton High School students in the rudiments of drill and ceremonies after dismissal. Veterans of the Spanish-American War and the Philippine Insurrection, too old for the military, joined the Emergency Guards, whose mission was to defend the city against the possibility of a military attack. The curious could watch their weekly drills on Chartres Street near the cathedral.

Not to be ignored, the city's commercial community sought to display its backing for the administration and the coming war by staging an event on April 5th at the Board of Trade's auditorium on Magazine Street. The usual politicians were present, including Governor Pleasant and the mayor, who coordinated the conclave with dozens of other mayors across the country. They were joined by several of the most visible New Orleans commercial leaders and an audience of over a thousand, who formed a procession, marching into the hall following a color guard and a band playing a peppy version of *Dixie*.

After the national anthem, Mayor Behrman was introduced. He respectfully rose from his chair and stepped slowly to the podium gripping a small American flag and steeling himself for what would become one of his most memorable public moments. After reaching the microphone, he stood for a long half minute with an emotion scarcely seen in the mayor, peering at the assembly before addressing them with a controlled monotone. With his head slightly bowed, he began his soliloquy with a whisper: "Fellow Americans, fellow patriots. The crisis has come—a state of war actually exists." It was the voice of a father whose only son had recently joined the Army. Then his head lifted: "Now, what will you people of New Orleans, you people of Louisiana do?" Hundreds in the crush of people brayed in chorus, "Fight, fight!" After pausing Behrman uncoiled in animation, pointing at them and shouting, almost in anger: "If your homes were in danger, if the lives of your brothers and sisters were in danger, I know what you would do." Loud choruses of cheering spliced nearly each sentence. "Now that your country . . . is in danger, we must all respond to the call!"

Once the governor and the other dignitaries spoke, a resolution that was to be telegraphed to Pennsylvania Avenue was read, expressing "loyalty, patriotism, and allegiance" to the president from the members of the Board of Trade, the Cotton Exchange, the Sugar and Rice Exchange, and the Association of Commerce. Finally, the entire auditorium stood to sing *America the Beautiful* and to give three cheers for Wilson before spilling out of the building. The entire affair, it seems, was designed to communicate to the president that they understood how difficult it was dealing with his opponents, ever mindful of his own campaign pledge the past year to keep the US out of the European war. Would the Great War become "Mr. Wilson's War?"[33]

The clock was ticking. Loudly. The lead editorial in the March 31st *Picayune* illustrated the sense of head-hanging resignation that the majority of the citizenry felt. Most unusually, it bold-faced several paragraphs for emphasis. "It is not now within the power of the U.S. to have peace," it claimed, "even on the 'at any price' basis proposed by ultra-pacifists." Berlin was responsible for funding, from "secret sources," the home-grown pacifist agenda. Pro-Prussians are "straining every nerve" to advance "Congressional betrayal." Germany "has already begun the war upon us; non-resistance and submission would only encourage ... more outrageous aggressions. The only argument they recognize is the argument of force." The editorial concluded with a fervent call to all New Orleanians to write their representatives urging them to "stand by America and the President who has worked so hard and so long ... to keep peace with a power that has broken every law of God and man, ... and invoked methods of warfare banned by civilized governments for centuries."[34]

On April 2nd the president, after agonizing over his decision, reluctantly brought his war message to Congress, the first chief executive to address a joint session of Congress in over a hundred years. The War Department added a cavalry troop to Wilson's security force on his way down Pennsylvania Avenue to the Capitol, such was the state of the nation.[35] The Senate voted 82 to 6 in favor of it on the 4th (eight abstained). No one in the chamber applauded. The conclusive House vote came two long days later on Good Friday. Fifty of its members voted against the war resolution—a good reflection of the nation's ambivalence about sending its young men to France.

The votes were more expressions of abdication than enthusiasm. The United States was now officially at war. The *Item*, which had been more irresolute in its views on what the US should do, was preaching harmony and support for the president now that war had come. Its editor even suggested to the Orleans Parish School Board that Wilson's speech be read in every school to all students. It was. Interestingly, the *Picayune*, without need for comment, printed on its front page each of the fifty names of those in the House who voted against the war resolution.[36] America's "ceremony of innocence," to borrow a phrase by William Butler Yeats, had finally drowned in the "blood-dimmed tide."

Within hours, the War Department issued orders to seize all German ships throughout the nation that had been interned since the beginning of the war. The crew members had been allowed to continue to live on their ships. A few actually were paid to work on a farm on the west bank in Algiers during their internment. But now they had all become war prisoners.

In a well-planned coordinated move at 3 a.m., sixty-five agents of the US Marshal's office travelling five miles downriver by tugboat and armed with pistols, simultaneously stormed aboard the *Breslau* and the *Andromeda*, the two German vessels moored near Chalmette, and arrested their sleepy crews. There was no resistance. The captain of one of the ships had his six- and fourteen-year-old children aboard. While their mother was back in Germany, they attended public school in New Orleans. Now they would be placed under the care of the immigration office while their father and his crew were sent to Fort Oglethorpe in Georgia, an internment camp, for the remainder of the war.[37]

The government also ordered all enemy aliens over thirteen, male and female, to register with authorities, be issued identification cards, and surrender weapons, ammunition, explosives, signal devices, and code books of any type. Women married to enemy aliens were given the same classification. If they lived within a half mile of a military installation or manufacturing plant, they had to move their residence. Permission was necessary before any enemy alien could travel, and none were allowed to board vessels of any kind except public ferries.

One week after the war declaration, New Orleanian C. W. Hutson, a Civil War veteran, penned a letter from his modest home on Panola Street. His message to his son, a senior at Annapolis, likely encapsulated the general sentiment of his city on the brink of war: "Already the call to get ready for [war] has done us a lot of good. We need waking up and it has been a gain to have shown the absurd pacifists that in a real crisis the country will have none of this nonsense!"[38]

Chapter 6

ANSWERING BEHRMAN'S CALL

The paucity of early enlistments nationally, even after Congress declared war, was troubling. Public opinion was divided, for there were legitimate dissenters—socialists, isolationists, and others—who were not convinced that it was America's war to fight. The movement's distrust of big business swayed many, especially poor, rural folk, to believe that a conspiracy was afoot to drag the US to war.

Beyond these war skeptics, there was a much simpler reason to explain the nation's polarized response to Wilson and the interventionists. The answer can be found by examining the developments that prefaced the war declaration. Missing in 1917 was a single incident—an episode that would animate America's martial spirit. There was nothing like Lexington and Concord in 1775 when British soldiers, it was believed, fired on undermanned Massachusetts militiamen. There was nothing like the (reputed) violation of the Texas border in 1846 leading Congress to declare war against Mexico. There was nothing like the bombardment of Fort Sumter in 1861 to convince the Union that Lincoln should expand the size of the army and ready it for war. There was nothing like the sinking the USS *Maine* in 1898, the provocation for America's war with Spain. And of course, there was the attack on Pearl Harbor. These tripwires were missing in 1917. The *Lusitania* was torpedoed a full two years before Wilson drew up his war message. While her sinking motivated a shift in public opinion against Germany, it cannot be regarded as an immediate sparkplug. Universal endorsement for the war was tepid in several quarters.

In the three weeks since April 1st, only twenty-six thousand men had enlisted nationally, far below the numbers the War Department claimed were necessary. Each state had its own quota—but only 462 enlisted in Louisiana during those same weeks, one-seventh of its apportionment. Mississippi's numbers were worse—only one-twelfth of its quota of volunteers.[1] Something had to be done. Wilson, who was initially against conscription, was persuaded by War Secretary Newton Baker to move on it, undeterred by loud opposition in various corners of Congress.[2]

Now solidly behind preparedness, the *Item* for ten consecutive days in mid-April printed a mail-in petition to Congress demanding approval of the military conscription law pending on Capitol Hill. The *Picayune* pushed hard too, printing a boxed editorial on both April 23 and 24, urging that telegrams be sent to each member of the Louisiana delegation in Congress to support conscription.[3] Most other newspapers across America were in league.

Some expected southerners to oppose a draft and shadow the racially charged warnings from Senator James Vardaman, who ranted that conscription would mean racial blending. "There is enough of this black virus in the body politic of America today," he preached on the Senate floor, "to mongrelize her entire population."[4] Vardaman feared arming African American inductees, crying out from the steps of Jefferson Davis's home in Biloxi, Mississippi, that he knew of "no greater menace to the South than this."[5] The still-simmering memory of the Civil War, the Reconstruction period, and carpetbagger manipulation, lent substance to his appeal. Resentment against the federal government in Dixie persisted. Government leaders even considered sending lecturers there to explain the advantages of a draft, anticipating a political battle, but the scheme was aborted when it became clearer that most southerners were behind their Virginia-born president, the first elected from the region since before the Civil War. Vardaman did not speak for the entire South. His nineteenth-century rhetoric fell flat in the face of the Kaiser's military might and the plight of Europe. Conflicts that invited use of the military—like the Spanish-American War and the more recent Mexican revolution—had soothed much of the South's bitterness toward Washington.

Even so, an undisputed draft was not assured. The Selective Draft Law slipped through a divided Congress in May, targeting eligible men between the ages of twenty-one and thirty-one (in a subsequent draft, between eighteen and forty-five). Locally appointed neighborhood boards would euphemistically "select" from those registered and decide on eligible deferments. The term "draft" was saddled with a bad connotation from the Civil War and was therefore strategically rebranded. Too, by having local citizens make judgements about who could be deferred, the government believed that it would soften the blow by divorcing itself from this odious task. The "d" word also recalled the highly unpopular provision allowing men of means to hire others to take their places during the Civil War, making for a "rich man's war and the poor man's fight."

Perhaps it was the threat of being conscripted that boosted volunteer recruitment for the famed Washington Artillery, although the dozens of street meetings, parades, and appeals at movie theaters likely contributed to the swell of late recruits too. This National Guard unit, based in New Orleans at Jackson Barracks, had served in every war since its inception in 1838. By the end of April, it mushroomed to a full regiment, roughly eight hundred men—mostly local. Help for the Allies was on the way. Mayor Behrman's challenge, "What will you people of New Orleans do?" was finally being met with growing numbers of enlistments.

Tulane University, like all other institutions and businesses in New Orleans, was a significant contributor in providing men for service. Forty percent of its medical-school faculty and more than a thousand of its alumni and students saw military service, including two colonels and the Washington Artillery's commander. Forty-four of them lost their lives.[6] The university even organized a short-lived alumni chapter in France. Military training was required for all male students during the spring semester of 1918 in the Student Army Training Corps. Many of the university's professors teamed with army officers in facilitating the SATC, a federal program designed to prepare young men for military service. Non-college students received instruction in such areas as auto mechanics and wireless telegraphy. The others received three hours a week of military training to prepare them for commissioning as officers.

Training took place at Camp Martin, a tent city temporarily located at the Fair Grounds racetrack until moving to Tulane's campus once barracks, a hospital, and other buildings, fourteen in all, were completed. These wooden structures occupied much of the quadrangle from Gibson Hall to Freret Street, virtually turning the campus into a military encampment. Over three thousand enrolled in classes—women as well as men, and were paid $30 a month. Pulling kitchen-patrol duty was ignominious for the privileged private college boys. But for junior class historian Douglas Kerlin, being forced to double-time everywhere was his personal hell. "We were quick timed to our meals, quick timed to classes, quick timed to the university at night for study period until it became such a habit to us to be quick timed that we actually ate and slept at quick time."[7]

Right next door, Loyola University, just five years old, formed its own SATC and offered several more military-related classes for the public. Women were invited to take the skill-based classes offered there as well, a first for the institution. Across the street, Audubon Park was transformed into a space for small-unit infantry maneuvers for the officers-to-be from both universities. Soon, those two neighbors on St. Charles Avenue more closely resembled military compounds than institutions of higher learning.

With the recent move of the Newcomb College co-eds to Broadway Avenue next to Tulane and its male students, fraternizing between the two schools was sure to blossom, notwithstanding Newcomb's strict rules on socializing with student-soldiers. Even simple communication between them was restricted. One pair of women, however, believed that they had found a way to circumvent the rules. They devised a method to signal a fraternity house from their dormitory using lights, window shades, and whistles to pass messages to the frat brothers. Unfortunately for the enterprising women, a chaperone discovered the clandestine ploy, resulting in a two-week confinement to the campus for the entire dorm. The male students escaped punishment entirely, perhaps because they were already suffering under the custody of their military overseers.[8]

Hundreds more adults would have eagerly raised their hands to be sworn in to the military had they been able. Meeting for their annual reunion in Alexandria, Louisiana, the United Confederate Veterans resolved, in the soaring literary style of the times, that "the Louisiana Division ... would have representation in the army of the United States on the battlefields of Europe, were it not absolutely precluded—even the youngest of its members—by the physical disabilities incident to the flight of more than three score years and ten, the allotted span of human life." The resolution was approved by a voice vote from the floor accompanied by a version of the rebel yell, its volume—not its enthusiasm—tempered considerably by age.[9]

There was something about that yell. It was their heirloom, a ghoulish eulogy to the Lost Cause. But even more the vets, most now in their seventies, believed in its battlefield magic. So it was that a group of former Confederates from Louisiana were actually invited by the Texas-born commander of the newly organized 82nd Division to travel to Camp Gordon, Georgia. During basic training there, the retired rebels would teach the young recruits how and when to holler the sacred scream. "Our boys will use it when we go 'over the top,'" affirmed General Eben Swift, who clearly believed that this was no pointless waste of time. "The battle cry of their fathers will again ring out in defense of freedom and democratic principles."[10]

Pride in the Confederate army ran throughout the ranks of Southern troops and sailors. Still wary of any Yankee, many replacements were uncomfortable when slotted into units with Northerners. It had not been long enough to forget the terrible war and the stories their grandfathers had told them. A letter to the *Picayune* from one such New Orleans recruit was representative of the dilemma. In his case, it was listening to his regimental band play "Marching Through Georgia" ad nauseam. Wishing for unity in the army, he believed that the song was divisive. The words wounded him, and he admitted cursing it whenever he heard it play.[11]

Almost two months to the day after the war declaration, 35,255 New Orleans men had registered under the Selective Service Act.[12] Hundreds also lined up at the Navy and Marine recruiting stations to volunteer at the last minute rather than submit to the unknowns of a draft. A volunteer, some believed, was preferable to being inducted, even if it meant risking the chance for a low draft number. Many of those standing in line would ultimately be rejected—some by failing the physical exam or because of illiteracy. Marine Corps regulations also could block a prospective recruit for "undesirable" issues. And, in a curious twist in gender roles, a wife's refusal to give her consent to her husband's enlistment also merited a disqualification.[13]

On July 20th, the selection began in Room 226 of the Senate Office Building in Washington at 10 a.m. in front of an audience of newspaper journalists, military brass, elected officials, and cabinet members. An oversized glass bowl sealed at the opening with thick Manila paper bound by five rounds of thick twine sat on a small table near one end of the room. It was from here that fate rested for tens of thousands of young American boys. Ten thousand and five hundred grayish-black gelatin capsules filled four inches of the bowl, sharing space with a wooden stirring spoon decorated with red, white, and blue bunting.

The US Provost Marshal General Enoch Crowder explained the entire selection process. Inside each transparent capsule was a tiny piece of paper, white on one side and black on the other. A red number was printed on the white side that matched the number on a selectee's registration card. This would determine the order of the draft. Baker then rose to select the first number.

The seal was broken, and the capsules were stirred while Secretary Baker removed his glasses so he could be blindfolded. He was then led to the bowl, his hand guided to its opening. He reached down and drew the first pellet, held it high above him, and said in a solemn voice, "I have drawn the first number." Then he handed it to a clerk, who broke it open and announced, "258." Another attendant carefully wrote "258" on the chalkboard behind them. Members of Congress then selected the next few, which were 2,552, 9,613, and 4,532. All 10,500 numbers were finally tallied by 6 a.m. the next morning. General Crowder maintained a vigil in the room throughout the ordeal just to make sure there were no mistakes. "Should anything go wrong it would throw the entire country into turmoil."[14]

If one's enthusiasm for military duty was a bit shaky, conscripted or otherwise, there could be an escape—marriage. Registrants with a dependent spouse or dependent children under sixteen would be placed in a deferment status, as determined by his draft board. Husbands were still eligible for service but safe for the moment until the War Department decided that more recruits were needed. One *Picayune* columnist could not hide his disgust for what he considered gutless Yankee behavior in New York: On the eve of registration day there, hundreds rushed to get marriage licenses at a rate of about 1½ per minute. "Slackers Rush to Wed in Final Forlorn Hope to Hide Behind Skirts," read the derisive title on page one.[15]

The number of marriage licenses issued in New Orleans also spiked. From April through June 1917, there were 248 more marriages than over those same months in the previous year—a 23 percent increase. And during the entire nineteen months of America's involvement in the war, all but four months saw an increase in the number of New Orleans nuptials when compared to 1916.[16] The actual total of New Orleans nuptials was certainly higher than the numbers indicate, for dozens more took place at training camps elsewhere. It was easy for lonely and anxious eighteen-year-olds to fall in love with girls they had only just met at a Salvation Army social.

As the months went on, the marriage deferment became extremely unpopular with both the general public and the local boards who had to infer whether the marriage was entered into with the intent to evade induction. And there were no specific guidelines for board members to make judgements. Inconsistencies were common, even among boards in the same towns. In order to rectify these deviations, Secretary Baker agreed to amend the regulations. No longer would a marriage contracted after January 15, 1918, offer immunity from the draft (with certain exceptions for dependent children).[17]

Many, of course, were not "slacker marriages," as they came to be called. Spousal benefits were available for soldiers killed in action. There were even reports that some women of dubious character were playing a dangerous game with this—traveling from camp to camp, inducing innocent young men to marry them and then moving on to marry again so as to become beneficiaries for multiple husbands. This forced at least one camp commander to disallow his men from marrying without his authorization.[18]

Frustration grew as more and more men were called up. The manpower shortage was magnified as Black agricultural laborers fled their farms, lured by higher paying jobs in northern war industries—without the Jim Crow millstone.[19] Then there was the quivering indignation for those seen playing pool or lingering at a soda shop, for the vast majority of citizens were rock solid behind their mayor's call for self-sacrifice. Exemption boards became particularly wary of African American men who claimed deferments because their parents were dependent on them for support. Many of these men were unskilled, made no more than $30–40 a month and, the boards believed, were more likely dependent on their parents than the reverse.

Growing fury with slackers (and worries about labor shortages) led Washington, in May of 1918, to issue a "work or fight" order targeting those immediately eligible for military service (Class 1) in possession of an uncalled draft number. An awkward spectacle had been unfolding whenever new draftees in route to training camps passed dozens of fit, idle young men. The order was designed as a remedy, also targeting those who were waived by their draft boards because of dependent responsibilities. No man would remain immune from the draft indefinitely. He must find work or he would lose his deferred status.

New Orleans Chief of Police Frank Mooney, seeing an opportunity to contribute to the spirit of the order, gave instructions to his policemen to step up enforcement of the state's companion vagrancy law.[20] But Mooney took it a step further. Utilizing the city's loitering ordinance, even oglers who stood on the street flirting with women would be booked. And if lingerers could prove no means of support, they too would be arrested.[21] Cops set their sights on gamblers and those who lived off the earnings of women. Downtown cigar stores, pool rooms, and saloons were prime gathering spots. "Work, enlist—or go to jail" was their slogan. Mooney was emphatic: "The American Sugar Refinery needs 200 men; the New Orleans Railway and Light Company needs 250, and the general contractors need 500. You will issue to all your officers orders to round up all idle men, both white and black."[22]

The governor later published his own order requiring all men to carry a card with their employer's signature proving they worked for at least a forty-eight-hour week at that job.[23] According to a survey from a government agent, an estimated thirty thousand "idlers" were in New Orleans who could contribute in some way to the national purpose. The report broke down the numbers as such: five thousand colored men, ten thousand colored women, and fifteen thousand white men. White women were not counted, presumably because society, particularly southern society, did not as yet hold them to the same expectations as other groups—like Black women. The same survey tagged the city with 50 percent more idlers than in any other city in Louisiana and four other southern states.[24]

Many of these men were not exactly "idle," holding jobs in the service industry. But they too were stigmatized and considered as jobless by some. The great majority of these men were also legitimately draft exempt. Others failed the physical exam or were deemed undesirable for a variety of other reasons. But this hardly exonerated them in the eyes of a mother whose son was dodging artillery bursts in France. It was a relatively small percentage of the population, but the resentment directed toward them was palpable.

Resident aliens? They too were subject to the draft if they had filed a declaration of intent to become a citizen. Many who had not filed volunteered because it placed them on a fast track to citizenship, waiving the long residency requirement and streamlining the process altogether. The government's immigration service reported that a surprising 18 percent of the US Army was composed of men born outside the US.[25] New Orleans native Mary Connoly, in a 1971 interview, recalled that her mother articulated what was likely the most common attitude running through the Italian community in New Orleans. Connoly remembered well what her mother told her draft-age sons: "This country gave us a home and gave us an opportunity for a better life. . . . No matter what my feelings are to the old country or anyone else's feelings," Connoly remembered her saying, "your obligation is to this country. All of our obligation is to this country—first!"[26] Some, understandably, were not as keen to serve, especially if it interfered with a successful career.

PETE HERMAN

One of the most famous athletes in the history of New Orleans sports was the world champion boxer Pete Herman who battled with his draft board over his classification. Peter Gulotta, his birth name, was the son of itinerant Sicilian parents who settled in the French Quarter at the turn of the century. Work was abundant for someone willing to put in the hard hours for little pay unloading cargo from the riverboats, and Pete's father was happy to land a job there. It was a hardscrabble life and, not unlike many others his age, Pete dropped out of elementary school to work as a shoeshine boy at a barber shop to help support his family. He was a celebrity of sorts, performing for the customers who watched him snap the cloth and swipe the leather in a blur with his amazingly quick arms. According to his grandson, little Pete was eventually making more than his father just on tips. In two years he had become the main provider for his family.[27]

During breaks at the shop he read magazines like the *Police Gazette*, which often featured sports stories—especially boxing. Just five foot two inches and weighing 118 pounds, he learned that his quickness translated well to the boxing ring. Adoring fans called it the "shoeshine punch," the rapid-fire body punching that few opponents could endure. He was only 16 when he began fighting professionally at the New Orleans Athletic Club, and in 1917, the twenty-one-year-old became the world bantamweight champ in front of a boisterous local audience. New Orleanians, always great boxing fans, were in love with their diminutive, rags-to-riches hero.

Pete's draft board, however, was less inclined to favor him. Selected for the draft, he quickly applied for a deferment based on his claim that he had dependent parents, a wife, and a sister with three orphaned children. Pete did, however, have three brothers who the board decided were capable of caring for them. Failing the appeal, he joined the Navy Reserve. Despite his widespread popularity, the boxer's eagerness to seek an exemption irritated many. Herman was an exceptionally fit athlete. He should easily qualify for military service, and his presumed wealth, it was thought, would be more than sufficient to provide for his family.

W. K. Patrick, the talented *Picayune* cartoonist, landed a staggering uppercut on the champ with an inflammatory cartoon entitled "A Streak of Yellow?" In the drawing, Herman held one glove up against an open-armed Uncle Sam, while his other glove pointed to a money bag. The caption read, "Nix on the 'My Country' stuff—that's the only feller I'll fight for."[28] Opinions were mixed. One complained that local newspapers "don't publish cartoons of all the boys who could go to war and whose families would prosper.... No—they pick out a poor Italian boy who ... has reached the highest point in his professional career."[29]

Herman was eventually given the job he wanted, training other sailors for his unit's boxing team. It was not uncommon for pro athletes in both world wars to be assigned a duty that allowed them to perform their special talents for the morale of their fellow servicemen and women, a job no less important than that of a clerk typist or a supply room private. Pete also boxed challengers in exhibition matches, sometimes ten to fifteen a day, and took quite a beating. The slightly built bantamweight was in the beginning stages of blindness, losing his sight during bouts but then recovering it afterwards. Determined not to retire, the pugnacious fighter kept his condition a secret from even his manager and continued to fight after the war. Pete lost his sight completely in his final match but, with unmatched tenacity, muscled through the bout by talking to his opponent and inducing him to stand toe to toe with him so he could attack with his furious body punches. Marty Mulé, a sportswriter, called it "boxing by braille." He won by a decision.[30]

Of the total who registered for the first draft at the 13 neighborhood selection boards scattered throughout the city, 22,165 were white, 10,250 were African American, and 1,662 were aliens. (Numbers from the Provost Marshal were slightly higher.) Administrators warned, however, that the totals for African Americans were not necessarily accurate given that many did not know their exact age.[31] And given the tenor of the times, it is doubtful that these people received much help interpreting the complex law.[32]

This should have been expected given the deplorable state of education for African Americans in New Orleans. From 1900 to 1914, the school board, for example, prohibited education for Black children after the fifth grade. An enrollment increase of over twenty-two thousand students between 1900 and 1920 forced the construction of thirty-nine new schools, yet fewer than one-sixth of them were dedicated to Blacks despite representing a third of that enrollment spike.[33] Unsurprisingly, the 1910 census reported that 18.2 percent of the city's Blacks ten years and over were illiterate.[34] Given that compulsory school attendance was seldom enforced and that New Orleans had only just opened its first public high school, McDonogh #35, exclusively for African Americans in 1917, it is little wonder that many were turned down for service despite the best intentions.[35]

One of the tests used by selective service to measure "intelligence" was the Devens Literacy Test. It was designed to progress from the ridiculously easy—"Does a baby cry?" and "Can a hat speak?" to the more difficult—"Are diamonds mined in the ocean?" to the most challenging—"Are pernicious pedestrians translucent?" Potential recruits were coded on a range from "very superior" to "mentally defective." In between these, a person could be found to be "literate enough to learn a skill," "illiterate," and more. It was simply a matter of adding the number of correct answers to the yes or no questions. The school board directed teachers to assist with scoring and classification. While certainly not a perfect instrument, it did allow for some level of differentiation when it came to assigning recruits to an appropriate assignment or specialty.[36]

More would register in the second draft for those men who had turned twenty-one in the previous twelve months. The fourth and final registration in September of 1918 expanded the age range to include both younger and older men. All who were between 18 and 45 (instead of 21–31) were now forced to submit their names for the lottery as well. One of those was eighteen-year-old Louis Armstrong, who listed his employment at Pete Lala's 25 Club, a café and music venue on Conti Street. With a draft number of 4,177 and less than two months from the Armistice, he was never called.[37]

The registration cards themselves tell a story. Printed diagonally at the bottom left corner of the short, twelve-question card used in the first draft was a directive: "If person is of African descent, cut off this corner." It was an odd method for the government to identify a registrant's race, but it clearly was done so clerks who handled the cards could expedite the segregation process. Race identification was modified on the second registration cards. A person was required to select from among these choices: white, Negro, or Indian. The government added a fourth choice, "Oriental," to the cards in the last registration. "Hispanic" was not among the possibilities, despite a US population of almost eight hundred thousand in 1910.

A reporter writing a routine article in the *Picayune* covering the first registration inserted some levity in his story by referring to an incident that took place at a registration office in Algiers. Because men with dependents were exempted, all registrants were asked simply, "Do you have anyone depending on you for a living?" "Yes boss, a wife and six children," one replied. "Do you know of any reason you should not be taken into the army?" asked the registrar. "No boss," the registrant answered flatly. "You can takes me right off, so long as I gets away from dat wife and children."[38] Neither Chinese nor Sicilians were immune from the mild mockery as all three major dailies sometimes phonetically recreated their accented dialogues as well. This device was more about good-natured ribbing rather than for cruel ridicule as it would seem to contemporary readers. Yet it was also a thinly veiled reminder that these groups, while fellow citizens, each occupied a different— a lower—social class, and one line of demarcation was drawn by diction.

REGISTRATION FOR WOMEN

Harnessing the country's manpower for war was a priority, yet women were not overlooked. In order to take stock of the resources they could provide to bolster the war effort, all women across America were asked to voluntarily register so as to determine their whereabouts and skill levels. In Louisiana, however, registration was compulsory for women over the age of 16. Agricultural, clerical, social service, industrial, or Red Cross relief work were just some of the options. They were asked what they could perform, what they would like to learn, and whether they wanted to volunteer or be paid. Women were assured that they would not be inducted, nor did registering (or not) affect the draft status of their male relatives. Neither would they be punished if they bailed out of a commitment.

Nevertheless, the Women's Committee, Council of Defense, who conducted the registration, knew it would be intimidating. Great effort was made to allay any uneasiness. Trained volunteer speakers, called "four-minute men," gave assuring talks in theaters and sports arenas to propagate this and other government messages. Newspapers ran notices for days. Churches and synagogues were even brought into play to reach their congregants. Mailing a letter to all clergy members, the committee urged them to help tamp down any anxiety by reading it to their congregations. "It is a misunderstanding . . . which has caused alarm," it read. "A record is to be made of women, and they <u>must</u> register; but they will not be <u>made</u> to do anything else. If they <u>wish</u> to offer service, they may; but they will not be <u>made</u> to."[39]

Booths covered by 1,245 volunteers for the registration were open all over the city on October 17, 1917—in schools, polling places, public buildings, and private homes. Maison Blanche, always up front for events such as these, built a booth at its entrance. With unmatched zeal, an avalanche of women lined up to complete the forms. At the closing time of 9:30 p.m., there were still hundreds in line who were unable to register, so a make-up date was scheduled. It was a stunning demonstration of faith in government—and in their mayor, whose plea for sacrifice during the war was not just directed toward men. The turnout also acknowledged that women, even southern women, were emerging from dismissed roles.

By the next day, the tally indicated that roughly 48,500 women had registered. Black women, counted separately, accounted for over 20 percent of that number. Beaming at this public testimony of unselfishness, the *Picayune* squawked that St. Louis, with over twice the population, registered only twenty thousand. With the make-up date, the numbers eventually exceeded seventy thousand.[40] Mrs. William A. Porteous, chair of the local Women's Committee, was exuberant: "It is the greatest thing New Orleans women ever did! Many men did not believe that we would register over 10,000." Typical of the eagerness shown to do their part in the war, several of the registrants professed that they were ready to go anywhere in the world on twenty-four-hour notice for any emergency. Others were not as generous. One wealthy woman from a fashionable section of town claimed curtly that she "had no time to give."[41]

While they were waiting in line for the registration table, women were asked to complete a "Hoover Pledge Card," named after the nation's conservation tsar Herbert Hoover, promising to conserve food at home given the shortages that abounded. The cards were a clever way to instill a moral obligation to assist in the war effort by conserving food and fuel resources. Most seemed happy to sign the pledge. Once registration was complete, each woman was handed a card to display in a window at home indicating that the resident had indeed registered her name. Homes not displaying a card would be visited by volunteers to coax those who were reluctant or who were unable to register on the appointed day. Public disdain could be a powerful motivator. It was pushy, but this was wartime. There was little room to tolerate those who did not demonstrate their patriotism.

OFF TO WAR

On September 18th, three months after the first draft registration, four trains
leaving from all three New Orleans stations were poised to deliver the first
contingent of 1,073 white selectmen to Camp Pike, Arkansas. African Americans would leave for training three weeks later and would make up 40 percent of Louisiana's quota of men. Navy and Marine recruits, all volunteers,
were sent to their training facilities in small groups upon enlistment.

Cluttered around each station were hundreds of teary-eyed women, tight-
lipped men, casual admirers, and crowd-stirring bands repeatedly playing
the South's anthem, "Dixie." No one ever tired of hearing it. It was a mantra
of sorts, and it roused the masses like no other tune could. Mothers clung
to their sons muttering, "Do your duty," and "God keep you," before the final
goodbye. Sisters and girlfriends fainted as the men boarded. The *States* reported seeing no less than a dozen prostrate women lying on the shoulders
of their male relatives.[42] Waiting rooms were choked with people overcome
with emotion. Fathers, husbands, and brothers sobbed. "It would have taken a
person of granite to have kept feelings chained in the midst of such emotion,"
wrote one reporter. Police struggled to maintain control with orders to keep
everyone away from the tracks, but a few finally rushed past the police line.
People "climbed through and beneath cars waiting on the track at the risk
of their lives" in order to locate their loved ones.

As the cars lurched forward, the men scrambled to find space in a window
for one last wave, their loved ones slowly retreating from view. Once they
were under way, they were handed a box lunch of sandwiches and fruit, six
hundred of which were prepared by Fabacher's Restaurant, a popular Royal
Street institution. The Boston and Choctaw Clubs prepared dozens more.
Their stomachs filled, the recruits began to enjoy the seven-hour ride. Many
had never before traveled on a train or left Louisiana, so there was a hint of
excitement inside the clacking cars. Friends managed to find each other. Card
games broke out. Dice rolled on the aisles. A few were already writing letters.
Others read. If there was any fear among them, it was in deep disguise.[43]

Along the way, selectmen from other towns were picked up, and wild
scenes similar to that which occurred in New Orleans were duplicated. In
Thibodaux, a group of Confederate veterans sent off their hometown boys
by singing the *Marseillaise*. A band in Lafayette played the British favorite
"It's a Long Way to Tipperary" as a group of French-speaking Cajuns hopped
aboard. As they spoke little English, an interpreter was required when they
reached the camp in order for them to go through processing.[44]

The advanced guard of the much-anticipated American Expeditionary Force (AEF), under the command of the marble-jawed General John J. Pershing, began arriving in the war zone in the middle of June. Desperate as they were for the fresh American troops, skepticism about their capability and durability was widespread on the continent. The impression made by their commander, however, did much to ease that apprehension. Just two years before, Pershing lost his wife and three daughters in a tragic fire. He seemed to blunt the severe pain of his loss by focusing on his mission. You knew just by looking at him—sturdy, determined, competent. Steel-eyed in his perfectly fitted uniform. He appeared to be perpetually standing at attention. While not bestowed with the Eisenhower grin or the oratorical skills of MacArthur, he was exactly what was needed. At that moment. On that stage.

First it was to London in relative secrecy, where he met the royal family and Prime Minister Lloyd George. After three years of artful press reports and propaganda campaigns designed to wean the US away from neutrality, the British had finally pulled in the big catch. Then it was off to Boulogne and later Paris, where the sight of the general with the French war minster literally dropped many of the Parisians to their knees. Coming just two weeks after the alarming news that almost half of French infantry divisions on the front had refused orders to advance from their trenches because of low morale, Pershing's debut was a fortunate bit of timing. Tens of thousands lined the avenue to the Americans' headquarters, the motorcade squeezing through an ocean of waving American flags and the sound of bands playing the "Star Spangled Banner" and the *Marseillaise*. It was just the beginning of an intense romance between the French Andromeda and her American Perseus.

The next day Pershing was escorted to the most hallowed spot in all of France. The crypt where Napoleon is buried was severely restricted, but the commander was nonetheless ushered there by France's Marshal Joseph Joffre and the governor of the *Invalides*, who provided Pershing this singular tribute. The custodian silently inserted the great key in the brass gates that guarded the chamber where the revered ruler lay. The two Frenchmen then drew aside to allow the general an extraordinary honor. Pershing removed his hat, took a deep breath, slowly turned the key himself, and stepped into the emperor's final domain. There, he was presented with Napoleon's sword. Kings had been allowed the distinction of entering this sacred sepulcher, but they were only allowed to view the precious relic in its glass case. Nor had any Frenchman been given this privilege. But no Frenchman had been able to defeat the Kaiser's army. Perhaps this American, on this very spot, would somehow be canonized by Bonaparte's spirit and become his agent in this time of peril. It was Marshal Joffre's unspoken prayer. Here now, in Pershing's hands, was the thunderbolt of Zeus. He held the blade still for a moment, and then slowly and reverently raised it to his lips, kissing the hilt. The marriage of these two nations' armies was finally consummated.

On the fourth of July, the general laid a simple wreath of red roses atop the resting place of the Marquis de Lafayette. As an ally during the American Revolution, the nineteen-year-old and his French forces were deciding factors in the victory. His only son, George Washington Lafayette, had sprinkled soil from the battlefield of Bunker Hill on his father's grave, such was the bond that was forged between both nations. Here now at Picpus Cemetery in Paris, that communion would be forged once more. Staff member Lieutenant Colonel Charles Stanton, in perfect French, spoke for his commander at the tomb. (Pershing's French was limited, and he hated public speaking.) The colonel addressed the reverential crowd gathered to witness the scene and then, at the close of his brief remarks, dramatically turned to face the beloved Frenchman's grave. With a raised arm in salute, he sang out, "*Lafayette, nous voici!*" "We are here!" Just magnificent.[45]

At almost exactly the same time that Pershing arrived in Paris, an Italian delegation trained to New Orleans for one of its stops around the US, demonstrating Italy's gratitude for America's entry into the war. Among the dignitaries was Guglielmo Marconi, inventor of long-distance radio transmission, now a commander in the Italian navy. It was he whom everyone wanted to see. A menagerie of Italians, Anglos, and Creoles began to gather at the Southern Terminal as early as 4 a.m. waiting his arrival. By mid-morning, thousands gathered to hail him as he and the rest of the commission stepped off the train and into a motorcade. Fifteen vehicles rushed down Canal Street to City Hall where a speaker's platform was erected for the occasion. There, over a dozen Italian organizations, including the societies of Christofer Columbo, Cepalutana, San Guiseppe, and Santa Lucia, assembled under their colorful banners and flags resembling a military formation.

Mayor Behrman greeted the visitors warmly and proclaimed with a dose of hyperbole that New Orleans was "the Rome of the West." Italy and Louisiana, he went on, have much in common. Both are known for their gaiety, laughter, song, and, with a grin, mostly for their beautiful women. The delegates followed. Speaking mostly in Italian, they were constantly interrupted by a harmony of howls from the approving Sicilian citizens of the city swelling beneath the platform.[46]

But the largest crowd response was left for the famed inventor. They called out for the trim, uniformed Marconi to speak, and he rewarded them with a few words, also in Italian. Later the party inspected the port facilities where dozens of Sicilian oystermen lined the river to welcome the mission, blowing on the conch shells they typically used to signal their arrival at the wharves after a harvest. It was off to St. Louis the next day, but not before Tulane University awarded each of them honorary diplomas at its graduation exercise in Gibson Hall.

Two million Americans would eventually be deployed to Europe over the next sixteen months until the war's end. They would be anointed in what would be called "the war to end all wars." The main front, just eighty miles northeast of Paris, was in paralysis—stalemated and uniquely bloody because of modern automatic weapons, accurate artillery fire, poison gas, and barbed wire. The interminable miles of defended trenches, like a tangle of frozen serpents, made offensive tactics almost suicidal. But the lines were beginning to weaken. Now that the AEF had arrived, there was great hope that Paris would be saved and the enemy's lines would wilt given the weight of all those fresh and enthusiastic young Yanks primed to deliver France from the iron fist of *des Allemands.*

Huge celebrations everywhere welcomed the "Sammies" in Paris, and a special commemoration was orchestrated on July 4th before they were even a week on French soil. The parades were less for the American troops than for the Parisians, whose spirits were in desperate need of a boost. It worked. Just glancing at the marching columns of stolid, eager faces unstained by combat buoyed their collective will. The balance of the war was still very much in doubt, but simply the knowledge that American troops were arriving created an immeasurable morale lift. "*Vive l'Amerique!*"

The Washington Artillery readied for deployment. It first went into temporary quarters in April at Camp Nicholls in City Park, occupying a space that would later become Tad Gormley Stadium. There it often trained in front of a thicket of curious onlookers, although on occasion the soldiers spilled into the new neighborhood of Gentilly for war games, startling a few residents. The other large Louisiana unit participating in the war was the 1st Louisiana Infantry, formed at the start of the Civil War and now under the command of Colonel Frank Stubbs of Monroe, Louisiana. The men were from cities and towns throughout the rest of the state, although a few New Orleanians appeared on the 1916 roster of the unit's medical corps and machine gun company.[47] The reconstituted regiment was also ordered to the Camp Nicholls staging area, where the Washington Artillery made room for them.

The four thousand men of the two units barely endured City Park's evening assault of hungry mosquitoes and the summer's suffocating humidity while their officers tried to prepare their men for combat. That was not easy. Given their tiny location within an urban environment, weapons qualification on rifle ranges, for example, a fixture in garrison training, was of course forbidden. Long marches were arranged, but only the most meager tactical exercises could be conducted given the geographic limits of their compound. Instead, training consisted mostly of the staples of a military garrison—close order drilling and inspections. It was worse than tedious after a few weeks of the same. The drilling especially seemed more suitable for Boy Scouts. There was dummy hand grenade training and choreographed bayonet exercises as well, the latter designed more to maintain physical fitness and to develop the élan of an infantryman than for skill development.

To keep morale from plunging too low, about the only thing that could be done was to stage athletic competitions between units and schedule concerts and dances. Sundays were "home dinner days," when volunteer families, through their churches or synagogues, took in a serviceman or two of the same faith for the afternoon. Passes for the entire weekend were distributed by unit officers, but this had to be done most judiciously given the considerable temptations that lurked a short streetcar ride from the camp. A recruit from Salt Lake City wrote home in a letter that New Orleans was "a hard town for a soldier. We can't save anything here."[48]

And it wasn't just the aroma of hot beignets or the unique cries of the tamale hawkers on the streets that beckoned. Wayne Pettijohn, a volunteer from a small farming town in north Louisiana who guarded the river levee, was likely exposed for the first time to some of the city's more wicked goings-on, his maiden voyage into the hinterland of vice. The remark this innocent made in his diary was representative of many of the young men stationed in the city, who were at least temporarily untethered from the prim conventions of the rural South. One week before Mardi Gras he wrote simply that New Orleans "is getting pretty wild."[49] One can only guess which details he left out of his journal entry that day. New Orleans brothel owner Nell Kimball was not evasive: "Every man and boy wanted to have one last fling of screwing before the real war got him. Every farm boy wanted to have one big f___ in a real house before he went off and maybe got killed."[50]

In October, the Washington Artillery was ordered to Camp Beauregard near Alexandria, Louisiana, small elements at a time, where it became federalized as the 141st Field Artillery Regiment of the 39th Infantry Division under the command of New Orleans architect Colonel Allison Owen. Once called Camp Stafford, the post had been used as a training site for the National Guard until 1903, later becoming the assembly area for the New Orleans based regiment during the 1916 Mexican border crisis. Hundreds of permanent structures were built in 1917 to accommodate the forty-four thousand men who would eventually train at the fifteen-square-mile facility.

From the ranks of Owens's regiment, seventy-five men who were fluent in French were ordered to France in the spring of 1918 to perform military-police duty. While on board, a general officer conducting an inspection asked one naive Cajun at attention how long he had been with his unit. He replied innocently, "Three months, and you?" Nonplussed, the general was advised by a staff officer that it was common in French Louisiana to answer a question with another question.[51]

The unit's columns were further depleted in the summer, when four hundred more of Owens's soldiers were sent as replacement troops for various units in France. The remainder of the 141st left for France on August 14th, 1918, where they were stationed near the village of Guipry and later Coetquedan. Under French military supervision, their training continued until November 8th, three days before the Armistice. But there was little in the way of celebration with these doughboys. After months and months of monotonous training, firing their big howitzers at dummy targets and cleaning rifles until their barrels glistened, the war was abruptly called off while they were positioned on the very edge of the battlefields. It was like making the Olympic team and then suddenly being told that the games were canceled. One officer captured the general attitude of the unit. The war's end, he lamented, "ruined a perfectly good war before we got to the front."[52]

Once the men first stepped on French soil, they were surprised at the warm reception given them. Cornelius Puneky, who grew up on Magazine Street, wrote about the "special welcome" he received when the locals learned that he was from New Orleans. "They all seemed to know the early history of the state and how closely it has always been linked to France."[53] Then too there was the unexpected availability of French women. Prostitution was legal and relationships were fast and easy.

Lieutenant James McConnell, from uptown New Orleans, was incredulous. In letters to his mother, the newlywed wrote repeatedly about contemporary Gallic sexual mores. "I am thoroughly disgusted with the French women, as they have absolutely no modesty and are not immoral but simply un-moral as they have no morals at all." He related an instance when he brought his unit of over two hundred men for a swim in the ocean. Standing on a mound of sand nearby were fifteen to twenty unblushing women and girls watching the naked men, laughing and enjoying the attention they received from the Americans. "If they like a man, it is alright to sleep with him whether he is married or not. I thank the Lord that I married before coming over to this country." They could not understand why sex with them would be a problem since the soldiers' wives were so far away. "I spent most of my time last night telling Parisian beauties that I was married and did not care to sleep with them." In another letter he told how an innocent stroll down a Paris boule-vard with another officer was interrupted at least fifteen times "by young girls who wanted to take us to their rooms." And they were "pretty and vivacious!" McConnell explained flatly that they simply like American officers. But he overlooked one item—Americans had money to spend.

African American Yanks were in an even more enviable position in France. In a total social reversal, their complexion suddenly became an advantage. White troops were quick to notice. McConnell commented, "The Negro soldiers are making a tremendous hit with the lower class of French women, and they won't have anything more to do with white men after having gone with the Negroes." He remembered watching over one hundred women "cry-ing and wailing" as a ship loaded with a transferred Black regiment pulled away from its dock. The lieutenant never revealed even a hint of racism or jealously in his letters, but he did envision the potential for racial unrest when these troops returned home. "This very same thing is going to cause a number of lynchings . . . , and then look out for trouble."[54]

Soldiers had much more leisure time on their hands after the Armistice. Passes were distributed much more liberally. This, of course, created more opportunities for fraternizing and socializing with a young *belle femme.* Military intelligence officers feared that miscegenation might inflame white soldiers. One officer in particular, an African American himself, expressed his disapproval of racial mixing. "No American white man . . . wants to see colored men mingling with white women in sporting houses." Neither did Blacks want to see whites with women of their own race—"a practice which is in vogue at this late date in the South." He warned that "an American race war" would erupt in France if Black troops were not returned to US soil quickly. "International marriages," he warned, "would not be looked upon favorably by either race at home."[55]

The French flirtation with race-blending was short-lived. Most Black Americans would not return to France once they were discharged. Their brief presence on the continent, however, helped to implant a seed that would blossom and endure—American jazz.

Aside from Claude Debussy's new sonatas dedicated to French soldiers, what really wowed the French was the new sound magnetizing young lis-teners in America at the time—the deconstructed, unscripted rhythms of jazz. In addition to the formal regimental bands, which played at parades or military ceremonies, improvised brass or jazz combos appeared, most notably in Black units. These groups, typically with seven to eight pieces, played with donated instruments for their own entertainment at YMCA huts, hospitals, and officer parties. They also were invited to play off post at public concerts, introducing to the French civilians their unique, liberating sound.

An estimated one thousand uniformed African American bandsmen played in military units from 1917 to 1919.[56] A handful of them were from New Orleans. Jim Robinson, for example, was drafted and assigned to the 525th Engineers, where he helped to build supply roads to the men on the front. Robinson was persuaded to take up the trombone by his unit's bugler, another New Orleanian, who promised to teach him how to play. He learned well enough to become part of the Saint Nazaire Stevedore Band, one of the most well-received "jump up" jazz bands in France. After the war he continued playing with various bands of renown, including Bunk Johnson's and the Preservation Hall Jazz Band. Ninth Ward trumpeter Maurice Durand played in several brass bands in New Orleans, helping to supplement his meager wage working in a broom factory before he too was drafted. As a member of the 816th Pioneer Infantry Regiment, he remained with his unit in France until September of 1919, when it finally received orders to return home. During those months after the Armistice, he played with the unit's headquarters band, touring France and entertaining its war-weary citizens, hungry for a bit of joy and curious to view a piece of America through its unconventional music.[57] Cultural diffusion had run full circle. France's imprint on its longtime colony remained palpable into the twentieth century. Now New Orleans was finally able to reciprocate with a gift from its home-grown culture.

Back at Camp Nicholls, the men of the 1st Louisiana were anxious to be assigned a combat mission, more than ready to hand Camp Nicholls back to the thoroughbred racehorses where it belonged. But it suffered the same fate as its sister regiment when it too was ordered to Camp Beauregard, only to be forced to dispatch six of its companies to France in late 1917 to augment newly forming infantry divisions. The regiment was being cannibalized. Its losses were somewhat filled by draftees from Fort Pike, Arkansas, to the dismay of the men who looked upon these "selected" men, somewhat unfairly, as inferior in both skills and *esprit de corps*. They were the bullpen staff, not seasoned enough to win a job in the starting rotation. This additional complement brought the regiment to roughly three thousand men. Before long, however, more than half of its men received orders to France as replacements, further diluting its unit integrity.

Plunging morale, always a fear for a command, began to strike some of the soldiers at Beauregard as they waited for orders. This was especially true for those who received letters from loved ones who implored them to come back home because of a need or simply because they were missed. It was most difficult for young recruits to resist these overtures, most of whom had never before been away from their hometowns and families. The letters caused anguish and uncovered torn loyalties between family and country.

General Campbell Hodges, 39th Division commander, recognizing the problem as the numbers of AWOLs increased, was forced to write a letter in May of 1918 to Governor Pleasant asking him to engage Louisiana's Council of Defense in addressing this problem. According to Beauregard's courts-martial records, six of every seven men arrested for going AWOL admitted that it was the "pitiful appeals" from home that prompted them to "go over the hill." Eight simple words were all it took: "I want to see you. Please come home." Were it not for these letters, the men could well be "happy soldiers going diligently about their work." The general's communication set in motion a publicity effort throughout the state directed at families with relatives in the service asking their cooperation when writing their sons and brothers.[58]

What remained of the 1st Louisiana did reach France in September of 1918, but the regiment was almost entirely shredded when practically all of its remaining men were ordered to report as replacements for other units already engaged in the fighting. It was the worst fate that could have happened to it, for maintaining unit integrity not only created healthy competition between the various Guard regiments, but it also served to heighten the camaraderie and esprit de corps that was fundamental to the success of any fighting unit.

National Guard units not only went through training together, creating an unshakable bond in itself, but they also knew each other as neighbors. Often their officers were their family's doctor or banker. Many played ball together, had the same biology teacher, and went to the same barber. This relationship welded them to each other like nothing else could, forming the tightest of friendships and devotedness. During combat, the trust and love that developed built warriors who would die for each other. It would take months for replacements, on the other hand, to develop such relationships with members of their new units.

The Louisiana Naval Battalion, four hundred strong with headquarters at an armory on Camp Street downtown, was called to arms near the war's start. Most of its sailors were quickly assigned to sea duty out of Charleston, South Carolina, while a skeletal organization remained in New Orleans. The 2nd Louisiana Cavalry set up a headquarters on Common Street, but with neither equipment nor money, its first appeals to the War Department for authorization went unheeded. Louisiana-born General Hodges, however, eventually organized the regiment as a headquarters company at Camp Beauregard for the 39th Division. The men made it to France, but, like the others, most became replacements with units already deployed to the front.

A few New Orleans units did remain intact. Tulane University recruited staffing for a base hospital composed almost entirely of its alumni and medical school faculty, the first base hospital ordered overseas from the South. The so-called Loyola Base Hospital was assembled by the dean of that university's postgraduate medical school, Dr. Joseph Danna, a Tulane Medical School graduate. The one-hundred-bed hospital was composed of thirty-five doctors, two hundred enlisted men, and a hundred nurses supervised by ten Daughters of Charity nuns, four of whom staffed Charity and Hotel Dieu Hospitals in New Orleans. About a third of the staff spoke Italian, including the Sicilian native Dr. Danna.

The hospital was stationed just fifteen miles from the Italian front and was often overwhelmed with bloodied Italian soldiers. Several American Red Cross volunteer ambulance drivers—who brought in more than sixty-six thousand wounded for treatment—were decorated for bravery by the Italian government. One of them became a casualty after sustaining over two hundred shrapnel wounds from an Austrian trench mortar on the Piave River near Venice. Two men standing near him were killed. Despite the Illinois native's grave condition, he somehow managed to drag another wounded comrade to safety under heavy machine-gun fire. The eighteen-year-old hero was taken to Dr. Danna's hospital, and after surgery and five days of treatment under the care of the nuns, he was transferred to a fully equipped hospital in Milan for additional procedures. But before he left, he slipped a piece of shrapnel taken from his hip into a small pouch as a souvenir of his experience. That tiny metal shard would remind the young man of his close brush with death that July day in Italy. It was an experience that Ernest Hemingway would often harken back to in the future.[59]

The story of the contribution made by New Orleans citizens in the war effort will never shine as brightly as it did during the Civil War simply because few of the roughly twelve thousand uniformed men from the city reached the front lines. Yet there were certainly individuals who deserve recognition. Thirteen Louisiana natives received the Distinguished Service Cross for valor in combat, and five were from New Orleans. Henry J. Adams single-handedly captured roughly three hundred German troops, including seven officers, by boldly attacking a dugout where they hid near Bouillonville, France. Paul E. Blust risked his life by low crawling to rescue a wounded comrade under intense automatic weapons fire, dragging him to safety. Displaying unusual courage, James P. Behan dodged artillery bombardments while repairing critical telephones lines near Cherry-Chartreuse, France. Violent enemy fire did not deter Charles Butler from rescuing a wounded officer by snaking two hundred yards in advance of his front line. For over five hours, Dan Sullivan carried vital messages between his commanding officer and a platoon leader under constant machine gun fire from a nearby enemy position. Dr. Stan Bayne-Jones, who grew up a block from Lee Circle, was probably the first American medical officer overseas, winning the British Military Cross and the *Croix de Guerre* while serving with the British in Flanders and on the Italian front. Later, he was cited by General Pershing for his heroic work during the second battle of the Marne.[60] There were undoubtedly scores of others who displayed such courage, but whose eulogies have never been written.

New Orleans would produce more than its share of historically important general officers as well. Born in Algiers on the west bank of the river, two boys from the Collins family would reach that rank. James served on Pershing's staff and retired as a general in 1946. Joe, his younger brother, reached the rank of major in WWI. "Lightening Joe's" fame would come in the Second World War, where he became the Army's youngest corps commander at forty-seven and emerged as one of the most highly regarded generals of the war. Perhaps the most well-known Louisiana veteran of the Great War was John Lejeune from Point Coupee Parish, a hundred miles from New Orleans, who would become the Commandant of the Marine Corps after serving as the commander of the Marine 2nd Division. Thought by many to be "the greatest of all Leathernecks," he is the namesake of Camp Lejeune, North Carolina. Among other decorations, Lejeune received the Distinguished Service Medal from President Wilson himself on January 8th, 1919, the anniversary of the Battle of New Orleans.

There were also those who would never return from France. Katherine Dent, a nurse assigned to a base hospital in France, died there from pneumonia a month after the war ended. She is the only known female casualty from New Orleans, joining 128 others who were killed in action in the Great War.[61]

These combat deaths, of course, rise above all other contributions made to the war effort. But there exists another story of sacrifice that must be told. The civilian population of the US mobilized against the enemy as well, sacrificing its time and money to buttress the war aims of its country. Few other times in its history had the nation—men, women, and children—answered the bell so enthusiastically. This was certainly true in New Orleans where Mayor Behrman's solicitations were answered with the tenacity expected of a dutiful city at war.

Chapter 7

"BUY BONDS OR BYE BYE LIBERTY"

Meeting the mayor's challenge to join ranks with the government meant, above all, raising money. Already in debt in 1917, Washington would require a massive infusion of money to conduct the war. William McAdoo's Treasury Department therefore issued "Liberty Loan" bonds, paying 3½–4¼ percent, beginning just eighteen days after the war declaration.[1] Newspaper ads printed the suggested amount of purchases based on a family's income. Percentages were incremental and aggressive—$609 or 20.28 percent for a $3,000 a year income, for example.[2]

There were four nationally directed campaigns throughout the country during the war years and one in 1919, the first ending on June 15th, 1917, to encourage citizens to buy these bonds. Sales drives would be conducted for the next twenty-three months at intervals of about six months. Each dollar spent, the message went, would buy resources for the nation's fighting men. One $50 bond, it was said, would pay for a hundred hand grenades or two rifles. Locally, the New Orleans chapter of the Council of Defense was in charge, centering their appeal on native patriotism.

Residents of the city pledged over $9 million for the first drive, easily surmounting its quota by $1.2 million. It didn't hurt that on the deadline in June, papers were reporting that General Pershing was being greeted by massive, cheering hordes in London and Paris. The story had to have generated a renewed fidelity to the nation. Images of the trim general standing erect in the midst of a swarm of waving hats and American flags reminded people that it was America who would help deliver the French from the Hun's clutches. Businesses contributed generously, including the railroads, commodity concerns, and law offices. But the majority of the purchases came from average citizens—the clerks at Marks Isaacs department store, workers at the river's warehouses, and even the poorly paid, like the women cigar rollers at the Hernsheim factory who coughed up $1600 for bonds.[3] Race hardly mattered. One humble Chinese resident shuffled into a bank hauling a large sack over his shoulder stuffed with small bills totaling $4,000. He was ready to use it all for the bonds. Hoarding the currency for years, he found this to be the right time to do his part.

An October cool front in 1917 swept through the city for its second bond rally. Excited citizens, ready for an excuse to go outdoors to luxuriate in the low humidity, left their homes and businesses at noon to watch a half dozen "machines" perform a low flyover, releasing paper "bombs" that hyped the campaign. A few lucky folks caught certificates that entitled holders to free bonds. Kids and adults both scrambled for them in stiff competition, the children expecting and receiving no mercy from the adults. Most had never before seen a plane in the sky, and the pilots did not disappoint, circling and swooping over neighborhoods throughout town.[4] Even individual celebrities took on their own special projects. Sophie Tucker and her band, for example, in town for an engagement at the Orpheum Theater, set up in a truck to perform on the curb in front of the Cotton Exchange at noon on a busy weekday to generate money. Her cause?—the "smoke fund" for the purchase of tobacco products for the Yanks.[5]

Three nights later an armada of the Loyal Order of Moose, Elks, Boy Scouts, Spanish American war veterans, and seventeen different Italian societies paraded down Canal Street, slicing through a wave of admirers. White-caped Red Cross nurses, four abreast, advanced as well. A *Picayune* reporter observed that the ovation given the white nurses was "not a bit more enthusiastic than was accorded the Negro women who followed." Then came a small horde of Shriners. Inserted in the midst of their mounted "Arab Patrol" members was a woman on horseback dressed as the armored Maid of Orleans, Joan of Arc, who waved at the cheering masses high in her saddle. Near the parade's end, a motor truck carrying a tall mock-up of the Statue of Liberty generated "prolonged applause."

After the parade disbanded at nightfall, citizens remained gathered at the foot of Canal Street to witness a much more spirited than usual Governor Pleasant light a bonfire on the downriver side of Canal. Once the flames reached higher, he turned and crossed the neutral ground carrying a torch through a drove of citizens to light another directly across the street. The popular leader, once the captain of the LSU football team, then returned to the platform now illuminated by the two blazes flanking the stage, adding Wagnerian mystery and unleashing excitement throughout the assembly. On the neutral ground between the two burning fires stood the imposing Liberty Monument, a white granite obelisk that commemorated the battle between a few thousand men from a paramilitary group, many of them former Confederate soldiers, against platoons of mostly police and state militiamen in

1874. At least thirteen were killed. It was a relic of the Reconstruction era when white citizens demanded restoration of home rule, i.e. white rule, and the removal of their current governor.

Mayor Behrman mounted the wooden platform, one of four erected earlier in the day for the rally's speakers. A cluster of clouds convened about the moon, the crescent's glow struggling to brighten the face of the fifty-three-year-old leader. He faced his huddled audience, the monument towering behind them and directly in the mayor's view. He could hardly neglect a reference to it. All thirty-five feet of it stared at him in the shimmering reflections from the fires, begging him to recall the battle that erupted forty-three years before at that very spot when the mayor was a youngster. Several of those before him now had likely taken part in that struggle, each of them ordained with a distinction in New Orleans that nearly equaled that of a veteran Confederate soldier.

Standing high above them, he looked down the long corridor of Canal Street, the vicar on the altar of his grand cathedral, and began his homily. "It is proper," Behrman began, "that while patriotic bonfires are being lit all over America in the cause of freedom, we in New Orleans should hold ours within a stone's throw of yonder statue [monument] . . . in honor of the men who fell . . . in the interest of better government." He matched those defenders of home rule in Louisiana with the soldiers of the AEF in France. Like the protagonist at the climax of a stage drama, his soliloquy decried autocracy and asserted the willingness of Americans to die in order to restore democratic government for Europe. After urging all to buy more bonds, he yielded to the governor for a few remarks—very few—in deference to the awakening wind and diving temperature assaulting them. Pleasant knew the lyrics, but he couldn't carry the tune. His speech fell flat, taking his seat to meek applause.

Last in the tableaux of speakers was Miss Florence Huberwald, a professional singer and a leader in the local suffrage movement who possessed enough wattage to energize a malingerer. Her face quivering in the fading flames of the bonfires, she delivered the most enduring body blows in her talk—the weather be damned. Her address had nothing in common with the mayor's aria. It was smashmouth and terse with a strong whiff of blood-boiling fury. "If there are any German reservists left in the U.S.," she boomed, looking left and right and then pausing, "they had better move to towns where there are no lamp posts handy." To a rousing applause, she ended with a challenge. Decide now to buy a bond and "strike a blow for your altars, your fathers, yourselves, and your native land."[6]

Appeals for these purchases were never timid. A diverse gathering of the city's major religious leaders and their congregations met at the Athenaeum to demonstrate solidarity in the war effort and to promote bond sales. Six hundred listened as seven different priests, rabbis, and pastors sang out for the cause. The last was the rector of Trinity Episcopal Church, Rev. R. S. Coupland. He admonished the audience bluntly and succinctly, closing the ninety-minute event: "If you do not purchase a liberty bond [by the deadline], you are the same as a pacifist or a slacker." Newspapers could be abrupt as well. "Is it possible," the *Picayune* asked in an ad, "that you think more of your money than the life of your boy?"[7]

The loud shrill of boat whistles and the clanging of church bells kicked off the city's third drive on April 6, 1918, at exactly 11:45 a.m. in commemoration of the president's signing of the war declaration a year before. French actress Sarah Bernhardt added star power to the opening parade down Canal Street. She led the monstrous procession seated in a white carriage festooned with roses and pulled by six white stallions handled by Boy Scouts at each animal's head. Balconies sagged with folks savoring the panorama. Despite a heavy rain, a multitude of people clotted the street to see a conveyor belt of fifteen thousand marchers slithering from St. Charles and Calliope to the city center.

First came a mounted brigade of the city's finest followed by a long line of various units in uniform. Lots of them—canteen workers in olive drab, grandmothers in Red Cross whites, and bands from a dozen organizations, each playing Cohan's enormous hit "Over There" in varying degrees of skill. It didn't matter to the swell of people, who cheered loudly upon hearing it. Besides, it was perfect for a march. Those who did not sing along with the music clapped in time. Most eloquent was an estimated one thousand nurses from both the military and the Salvation Army, heads and shoulders back. School children massed behind them, both Black and white. Some carried placards. "Buy Bonds or Bye Bye Liberty" one warned. The rest waved flags. And, of course, there were military units from each of the branches. Children struggled to see it all, many on the shoulders of their fathers, especially when several "mock" British tanks rolled by. In the midst of this train of people was a single float mounting a huge bass drum beaten by enthusiastic Boy Scouts. On the nose of the float was fixed a large sign: "Stop the reign of hell with a rain of shells. We, little fellows, can beat the drum—you help beat the Kaiser by buying Liberty bonds."[8]

A troupe of over-exposed cabaret girls in town for a show caused some controversy. They were driven through busy downtown streets for several days in an open truck hawking bonds. A $500 certificate would earn the generous patriot a kiss from a girl of one's choice. There is no record of how many kisses were dispensed, but the practice elicited at least one objection from the mother of two soldiers who branded the gimmick as degrading. Instead, she believed the nation should be "safeguarding our boys from all temptations and opportunities for lowering the American ideals of manhood."[9] If similar letters of protest came from men, they were never published.

The zeal displayed by the local chapter of the National Woman's Liberty Loan Committee was a deciding element behind the success of the effort. Under the leadership of Mayor Behrman and the War Finance Brigade, they created and placed publicity banners all over town; volunteered to give patriotic speeches at theaters, concerts, and park events; and even canvassed door to door for subscriptions. Speakers from each of the Brigade's regiments were assigned to streetcars to confront any passenger who had not yet contributed. In neighboring Jefferson Parish, the names of anyone not subscribing were made public. A permanent "Altar of Liberty," dressed in American flag bunting, was constructed on the sidewalk in front of Werlein's music store to accommodate patriotic speakers and bands for the several drives. Silent film star Marguerite Clark, soon to wed a New Orleans native and Army lieutenant, sold bonds in front of nearby Maison Blanche at a "bank" built at the store's entrance. The ubiquitous promotional devices and solicitations were impossible to ignore.

One especially inventive promotion kicked off the third drive. The committee erected an enormous thirty-five-foot-tall sign extending for three blocks above four retail stores on Canal Street. Said to be the largest sign in America, it spelled out, "Buy Liberty Bonds." Beneath it strutted a promenade of marching bands, a phalanx of flags, and men and women wrapped in billboards urging all to do their duty. The pageant was preceded by a stunt worthy of the movies. Pilots dropped sacks of flour from the open cockpits of their planes in a mock bombardment of the downtown area. Then the fire department dashed through the streets, bells clanging loudly, pretending to put out the "fires." It was quite a show.

Local organizers were overjoyed when they learned that Douglas Fairbanks would visit the city to encourage bond sales. And the most beloved celebrity of them all would also be in town for the premier of *A Dog's Life* at the Strand Theater on Baronne Street featuring the beloved "Little Tramp." Charlie Chaplin also made a live appearance at the Fair Grounds to raise enthusiasm for the drive. And raise it he did. As he mounted the stage constructed for him and a backup orchestra, the estimated herd of ten thousand went wild. Prowling back and forth on the stage, waving and blowing animated kisses out over them, he finally convinced the adoring mass of people to settle down so he could speak. This would be quite exciting—hearing Chaplin speak! It was here that they discovered that the "Little Tramp" could be quite an orator. "I am only a moving picture actor," he told them, "but I want you to understand that I am speaking seriously.... Money is nothing. If you don't give it now," he thundered, "they [Germany] will take it from you later, so come on and subscribe! We have had too much of the waving of the Stars and Stripes. Let's get down to business!" A hand waved in the crowd interrupting the actor. Identified only by his last name, Viccaro wanted to be the first to pledge—for $10,000. Chaplin's face immediately illuminated. He ripped off his jacket, threw off his derby, bounced high in the air as though the stage was a trampoline, and then scrambled in a flash to the bandstand to direct "Stars and Stripes Forever" with enough comical gestures to make Souza blush. The thousands roared in approval.

He followed that stunt by leading three lusty cheers for the military and the president, punching the air vigorously with his fist with each *hoorah!* The *Picayune* described the noise as "deafening." Then an usher shouted out excitedly that another had promised $10,000. Chaplin vaulted into the air again, this time falling to his back, raising his legs, and doing a perfect headstand. This produced another thunderous roar.

More pledges followed—for $5,000, $2,000, and another for $25,000. Each time, Chaplin performed a different acrobatic stunt. Vicarro, clearly swept up in the emotion of the moment, wasn't finished. He stepped forward to pledge another $10,000 and then once more for $15,000—$35,000 for the day. That's what star power can do. Sweating from his frenetic rushing and tumbling across the stage, the star bounded to the bandstand to lead everyone in the singing an energetic "Over There" for his finale. The police struggled to wedge him through the mob as he made his exit, kissing babies and shaking hands left and right. In one hour the campaign secured over a quarter million dollars in pledges during this remarkable performance.[10]

The fourth Liberty Loan drive began on September 28th, 1918, two days after the launch of the largest assault in US military history, the Meuse-Argonne offensive on the Western Front, helping to break the back of the German lines and ultimately bringing the war to an end. It would be the most systematic and intensive fund raiser ever conducted in the city's history. Five hundred businessmen, professionals, and civic leaders joined what was hoped to be a final push from the War Finance Brigade. (A fifth drive would be mounted after the Armistice.)

Coming just six months after the previous drive, which collected $15 million in pledges, the task to coax more dollars from a public already weary of these overtures would not be easy. Organizers sensed the onset of "appeal fatigue." Furthermore, the influenza epidemic flared just as the campaign was launched, which not only reduced the Brigade's manpower by a third but also affected the shrinking pool of people who might buy the bonds.

Organizational and update meetings had to be canceled under orders from health officials, who warned that crowded, enclosed spaces encouraged the disease to spread.[11] The city's quota seemed insurmountable—just under $29 million—about one-fifth of the combined deposits of all of the city's banks. To open the fourth drive, three military bands ushered yet another Saturday afternoon parade from Lee Circle, snaking its way to City Hall, where it was given a proper salute by Mayor Behrman. They played the national anthem and the inevitable "Over There." One would think that New Orleanians would have had their fill of parades and patriotic music by now, given their frequency, yet a mob of people still raised their voices under the mock direction of the mayor. Before the parade resumed its march to Canal Street, there was one more piece to play. Rebel yells erupted as the trumpets announced the surefire "Dixie," the inimitable crowd pleaser.

As the bands marched off in the procession, they were followed by a river of military units from the Algiers and West End training stations, Army quartermaster units, flag carrying Boy Scouts, businessmen and women sporting banners coaxing bond sales, and Red Cross units led by a statuesque nurse on a white stallion. Several dozen French Foreign Legionnaires, entertained later that night at Antoine's restaurant, attracted even more attention and applause, particularly from the female spectators. Uniformed African American stevedores partnering with a ragtime band danced the castle walk in time with the music.

They passed in front of Canal Street store windows adorned with aggressive, hard-sell posters that were sure to unsettle even the most impassive: "What Kind of An American Are You?" asked one directly. In another, a giant, gnarly Marine pointed his bayonet, growling: "Come On, Buy More Bonds." It was enough to frighten a small child. A few were cleverly worded—"Liberty Bonds or German Bondage" and "Come Across or the Kaiser Will." The government printed nine million of these posters along with five million stickers and ten million promotional buttons. In the midst of the parade participants, a huge float rumbled slowly down the street recreating German and allied trenches opposite each other, each manned by a uniformed "soldier." "Hand grenades" hurled by the "Hun" toward the American line were blown to pieces by the Yank, an expert rifleman firing from his trench—a kind of public skeet shoot. With each shot, the throngs erupted with loud approval.[12] Later that week, the Brigade's publicity committee conjured up several more original stunts certain to tempt even the grumpiest citizens to open their wallets and purses. In one, the manager of the Orpheum Theater was "rescued" from the Werlein's Music Store. As he screamed "fire" from a fourth-story window, a fire engine rushed down the street on cue, deployed its long ladder, and sent a fireman scurrying up to assist the "victim" down to safety. As they descended, a large banner was unfurled, revealing a message to the surge that gathered to view the spectacle: "The fire is out but the war is not out—Buy Liberty Bonds!" Barnum and Bailey could have taken notes.[13]

Much of the drive's success can be attributed to major Canal Street merchants who fully participated in the effort. The entire half-block display window of Maison Blanche devoted itself to the cause. There, a lifelike statue of President Wilson faced out to the sidewalk. Behind him were five models of the cracked liberty bell, two labeled with $50 signs, two more with $100 signs, and the largest with $1,000. At the statue's feet a placard read, "Wilson says, 'Which One Are You Going to Ring?'" Further down the street, the owners of White Brothers jewelry store constructed an elaborate stage decorated with plants and flags, which protruded onto the sidewalk. Performances by orchestras and patriotic speakers entertained crowds at noon each day of the drive. Meanwhile, traffic halted to make way for the daily march of the "sandwich men," roughly a hundred of the city's most prominent businessmen and professionals who agreed to carry sandwich boards over their shoulders, each painted with the identical message, "Buy More Liberty Bonds."[14]

But there was more to the drive than simply sales pitches. Bulletin boards on ten street corners downtown allowed newspapers to update breaking news. And the *Item* did its part by distributing what it called a free "newsboy special" edition on October 7th. Printed diagonally across the front page were the words, "Pray Tonight for Victory—Buy More Bonds for Safety." Businesses, professional offices, civic and religious groups, elected officials, and the press—all united in a single goal. It was an extraordinary display of planning, energy, and sacrifice.

An impressive sum was tallied during the city's five Liberty Loan drives, easily eclipsing assigned quotas. While these campaigns were the most important, the city had to brave twelve other fund raisers during the nineteen months of US participation in the Great War—about one every forty-five days. In addition to two different Red Cross drives, the YMCA and the YWCA each conducted their own appeals. There was a War Savings Stamps campaign and a drive to raise money for the War Camp Recreation Fund. (See Appendix D.) Additional smaller solicitations were conducted for the Salvation Army, the Boy Scouts, the Knights of Columbus, Jewish refugees, and for the needy in Belgium and elsewhere. Black and white societies, civil and religious, raised money within their own organizations as well.

During some of these fund raisers, the intent was to shame or embarrass rather than to elicit nationalism or compassion. "An Appeal to All But the Heathens," read the banner of one of the Brigade's ads in the weekly *Herald*.

Another was equally brusque: "Every wage earner is expected to save in the next six months at least $20 in War Savings Stamps. . . . Every man or woman who can do this and does not is a slacker. . . . He is unpatriotic."[15] Governor Pleasant was equally gruff. Anyone who is able but refuses to invest in a bond, he insisted, is a "coward" equal to a deserter on the battlefield.[16]

Then there were confrontational house-to-house solicitations. Residents were asked to sign a statement reading: "I, whose signature appears above . . . now own ___ Thrift or War Savings Stamps." Further down the form was a request for further purchases for the $4.12 stamps.[17] All were warned that they might be asked to display their stamps to the volunteer door knockers in order to prove the purchase. Letters of complaint from some of the victims of the hard-selling solicitations were mailed to the *States*. One was a widow of very modest means who had two sons in the military. In spite of this sacrifice, the volunteer warned her that a yellow "slacker card" would be posted on the front of her home if she did not make a purchase. Another woman, a struggling dressmaker with a son in the service, was likewise threatened with a yellow card despite her destitute condition.[18]

Still more antagonistic was the decision by a Brigade "commander," a local business leader named Crawford Ellis, to post to a large "slacker board" conspicuously displayed in front of the prestigious Boston Club on Canal Street, the names of anyone who had not contributed, or not contributed enough. He intended to make sure that "those who are able to give in thousands are not permitted to escape by contributing hundreds" and warned, "we shall see that men of wealth . . . shall be subjected to the scorching light of publicity."[19]

Many poor wage earners were also forced to endure the disgrace, willing but unable to buy the government bonds. An American Federation of Labor organizer expressed his frustration at their condition. After spending several days in the city investigating, he indicting New Orleans hotels and restaurant owners for lacking patriotism, "satisfied" that it was they who were "assisting the Kaiser" as there were "no waiter or waitress who can afford to buy War Saving Stamps . . . or Liberty Bonds."[20]

These zealous petitions for money, however pushy, were successful. In each of the bond campaigns, the city exceeded its goals. A stunning $103 million was raised, $12 million over the quotas ascribed to them. Behrman, who contributed $7,000 himself to various causes, was effusive:

> No finer spirit of loyalty was ever exhibited before by any body of citizens in behalf of any cause. . . . No Southern city compared with New Orleans, either in the amount of money subscribed to Liberty Bonds and War Stamps or . . . in the amount contributed to war relief

funds. . . . [The successes of the drives] disclosed to us our unlimited capacity for cooperation . . . and our unflinching loyalty and love of country. We remember [too] . . . how glorious was the conduct of our women . . . how devoted . . . how zealous, how untiring, and how modest [they were]. . . . The inestimable service rendered by this element . . . is a tireless theme of admiration and compliment.[21]

Chapter 8

"FIRST I WANT TO HANDLE REVERSE GEAR"

By recognizing the key role played by women in the Liberty Loan drives, the mayor was reminding the city of how eager women were to forfeit their time, resources, and muscle to meet his challenge. They were making a significant impression on a population that remained divided on the fermenting suffrage issue. Bowing to Behrman's appeal to husband the city's energies behind the AEF meant much more for New Orleans women. The war hoisted them into a much higher profile, validating the claim that they deserved to be given the right to vote.

Opportunities to contribute were inexhaustible, and women capitalized. Hundreds from New Orleans enlisted for military service. It was the first time in US history that regular Army and Navy nurses would serve overseas and the first time women other than nurses were accepted into the Navy and Marine Corps. (The Army did not officially allow women to join but welcomed them as civilian volunteers.) Many jumped at this opportunity to challenge society's etiquette, but most simply wanted to do their part to assist in the war's effort, despite being denied rank and veterans' benefits.

The Salvation Army attracted dozens of female volunteers, some of whom signed up for service in France to build and maintain trench "hutments"—small sanctuaries behind the lines. In these shelters socks were cleaned and replaced, hot coffee and doughnuts were served by "doughnut dollies," and even religious services and concerts were held—sometimes within range of enemy artillery. In France, the hospital at Nueilly welcomed volunteers from the New Orleans chapter of the United Daughters of the Confederacy, who helped to manage beds there. Less well known were locally formed groups who focused on relief efforts. One was *Secours Louisianais de la France*, Louisiana Relief of France. Its efforts raising money for the support of French families during the war was recognized by the French government. Two of its members were even decorated with medals by the French government.

There were other women who had a unique opportunity to join the Yanks in France. Because of the crucial role of telephone communications, the shortage of switchboard operators near the war zone, and the archaic French telephone system, General Pershing ordered his Signal Corps to recruit American women who could fill these positions of need. Newspapers in large metropolitan areas ran appeals for applicants who spoke French fluently. New Orleans was one such city where French linguists might be found, so the *Times-Picayune* was asked to run an appeal to go "over there."

The response in Louisiana was impressive, but the parents of most all of them refused to part with their daughters. One French-speaking New Orleans girl did make the cut. Josephine Davis, 24, who had no brothers eligible for the military, wanted to contribute. "I am hoping for a chance to get a line to Berlin," she wrote to a friend while still training, "so I can ring the Kaiser's head off."[1] Eventually 377 "Hello Girls," as they were called, were selected out of the roughly seven thousand applicants. (Pershing called them "switchboard soldiers.") Davis and thirty-two other young women were sent to France in the first contingent where, in Tours, their fluency in French was put to good use for $60 a month. All volunteered despite being denied the right to vote, veterans' benefits, or even honorable discharges—the latter awarded to survivors only in 1979. And they were required to purchase their own uniforms of blue jackets, long skirts, and high-top shoes.[2] There is little doubt that these women in uniform helped to convince many that the time for equal political rights at the ballot box was long overdue.

There were other signs of changing mores. An Emergency Motor Service was created and staffed entirely by uniformed women in their personal vehicles willing to drive officials or carry supplies to military encampments. They were warned, however, by their superior at the outset of their service, "No matter how good looking the officers may be, you will be compelled to await and go where ordered. . . . Real discipline is imperative."[3] Bernice Jalenak, an employee at a music store in town, shared a personal perspective with an *Item* reporter while seated in the driver's seat of a delivery truck. "We women have got to learn to do almost anything. . . . Between time when I'm not selling phonographs or learning to drive this thing," she said as she gripped the steering wheel, "I'm getting the hang of the store elevator. I'm just about ready," she assured the newspaper man, "to give either the elevator boy or the truck driver to my country." Then she added with a smile, "But first I want to handle reverse gear."[4]

Women were clearly attracted to motor-car driving, so much so that the Grunewald Hotel's garage became a classroom for any society women interested in operating and maintaining these vehicles. At a time when it was rare for any woman to be seen driving, dozens were not only doing so but were now in garages on their backs, in male clothes, under chassis changing the oil and operating piston vices, and trading their *chamoisette* gloves for those made of thick leather. Classes, conducted by a woman, filled up so fast that they were forced to larger spaces.

At Thompson's two restaurants, women replaced men in heretofore masculine jobs as waiters and stood in for boys as dishwashers. The trend continued at the Orpheum Theater, which was flooded with applications for ushers. Three were hired there to substitute for former employees who were off to war.[5] More and more banks became comfortable placing women as bank tellers. Several dozen African American women were hired at a bag factory, filling vacancies that opened after the second draft. Bell girls became the norm at the city's best hotels, and female elevator operators were commonplace by 1918. Marks Isaac's department store employed four women, earning the same pay as the men they replaced. The city's branches of the United Cigar Stores brought in upwards of sixty eager women to make up for shortages of men. Lunch counters and even positions as clerks at men's clothing stores were staffed by women despite the initial shock to customers.

Age often did not matter. In the search for employees, newspaper ads enticed girls as young as fourteen to leave school for available openings.[6] It did not seem to matter much that many of these jobs were repetitive and tedious. The seductive adventure of being a pioneer was itself part of the attraction.

These opportunities were a godsend for the women of New Orleans, but there were those who were worried about what these experiences would bring over the long haul. "The girl who dons overalls and whose face is begrimed with grease and . . . whose work begets a roughness," cautioned a YWCA spokesperson, "needs some influence to pull her back into line with all femininity." They will need help, she promised, "in observing the womanly ideals so important to homemaking and motherhood."[7] A writer to the *Picayune* agreed, concerned that some of the work they were doing was "barbarous and inhumane." Elevator operators, for example, were forced to "drag those big, heavy, iron doors," opening and closing at every floor throughout the day. Could the newspaper please help do something about this situation?[8] But the arguments fell flat. There were dozens of opportunities from which to choose, and women feasted on the openings, even though they may have only lasted for the war's duration. Besides, their country needed them.

Civic activist Elizebeth Werlein and her League of Women's Services acted as a kind of ad hoc advocacy group for the elimination of wage or salary discrimination based on gender. Service workers were often victimized. Hotel waitresses in 1918 New Orleans, for example, were paid on the average of $30 a month. Men in the very same positions made $10 more. Working conditions, she claimed, were unreasonable, demanding that hotels with women employees allow no more than a fifty-four-hour work week (from the current average of sixty hours), better food, the removal of the requirement to pay for uniform cleaning, and so on.[9] Werlein's League was tinkering with a smoldering social issue that lay only barely beneath the war effort. The war did not interrupt. Rather, it helped build momentum for Progressive ideals, like gender equity, which had been emerging for over a decade.

Aviation was in its infancy, and its role in combat appeared to be yet another male only sphere. Some women, however, pushed hard against this maxim. Werlein, among her other interests and activities, was a licensed pilot and ached to fly for the Army. That never happened, but her unique skill pushed her to the front when help was needed to identify the most suitable aircraft landing fields throughout Louisiana. She did so at the request of Governor Pleasant and military authorities. Werlein was perhaps the most qualified to do so and was awarded a set of wings by the New York Aero Club, the governing body of American aviation, for this service. She proudly wore this pin for the rest of her life.[10]

More famous was aviatrix Ruth Law Oliver, who held a number of records, including flying nonstop for 590 miles from Chicago to New York State. A tremendous attraction and in great demand all over the country, she commanded $1,000 a day for her performances.[11] Here was one occupation that could be pursued by adventurous women, for no law or regulation existed banning them from being pilots. Once the war began, Oliver lobbied unsuccessfully to allow women to fly combat aircraft, although she was authorized to wear a regulation army aviation uniform—which she always did. In New Orleans for its annual farm fair in November of 1917, the New Englander promised to attempt to break her record of flying sixteen straight "loop the loop" stunts in her biplane. This was sure to hike attendance. None would guess, however, that during her stay in the city, she would receive more publicity on the ground than she did in the sky.

A few nights before her public appearance, she was invited to dine with three fair organizers at Maylie's restaurant on Poydras Street. The place was known for its long communal tables and its strict, male-only policy. This did not dissuade Oliver, who may have suggested it purposefully. Meek she was not. The aviator tucked her brown hair into her wide-brimmed campaign hat and entered clad in her khaki uniform and brown leather puttees with her hosts in tow. Oliver never removed her hat at the table, hoping to hide her long braids, but this in itself attracted the attention of Maylie's proprietor. But by the time her ruse was revealed, she had already begun eating her first course. Oliver completed her dinner leisurely and left without incident.[12]

Unquestionably, these well-publicized activities served as catalysts for women. No longer were they buried entirely behind the achievements of their spouses, fathers, or brothers. They were certainly not the first women to claim a respectable position in society, but those numbers had always been comparatively small. The war, however, acted as an agent of change, a stimulant, an opening for thousands of women to work outside traditional roles, thrusting them into the public arena. Given the shortage of men due to military service, women were in demand, and they became impossible to ignore. Their extraordinary service was transformational—on the brink of something big.

Shouldering much of the responsibility for the mobilization of this ready resource for industrial work was the women's division of the Department of Labor. During a fifteen-day period in the summer of 1918, a massive campaign was launched nation-wide to entice women to apply for jobs off-limits to them before the war. Interest was high in New Orleans. Eighty African American women, for example, were placed in lumber yards driving trucks for a most attractive salary of $3 a day. Others, both Black and white, found work with scrap iron companies, freight yards, bottling works, and manufacturing plants.[13] The Women's Committee of the Council of Defense, also active in job placement, reported at the war's end that it had found good jobs for over four hundred women.[14] Good pay (outside the service industry) contributed to a newfound independence and a higher status for women who filled these positions, even if it was on an interim basis. The experience emboldened many to demand that the government recognize them as citizens just like their male counterparts, beginning with the right to vote.

The Red Cross in New Orleans, fifteen thousand strong, was especially active both in the city and overseas, and its nurses, while only part of one department in the organization, were quick to assert themselves. One was noted writer Natalie Scott, a 1909 Tulane graduate and a native New Orleanian. Scott would receive the French *Croix de Guerre* for her intrepid service at a field hospital near the warfront, the only American nurse to be so honored in the war. Then there was Katherine Dent, who gave her life while serving in France.

The importance of the Red Cross cannot be overestimated, for the organization's Nursing Service furnished almost all of the Army's Nurse Corps during the war.[15] Many witnessed the horror of combat up close. Aletta Horn, a nurse's aide from New Orleans, volunteered to serve in an army hospital in Paris, making the dangerous crossing of the Atlantic twenty-three times and always paying her own expenses. Even after the fighting ended, she remained with the hospital until it closed three months afterward, such was the depth of her loyalty to the patients and staff. Horn reported to her hometown newspaper that she and the women she worked with "lived through frightening times . . . with all the terrible and hellish long range guns." Her shifts were from 9:00 a.m. to 9:00 p.m., and "things were beyond description." During the American offensive of July 1918, an overwhelming number of wounded soldiers, over three thousand in just two days, were brought in for treatment, "shot to pieces." She went on to say that the men had nothing more than temporary dressings on their wounds administered at field hospitals. "It was scorchingly hot, and how these poor boys suffered," Horn bemoaned. "I literally waded in blood for days," and "bombs have dropped all around us," but she thanked God that she was able to help through the ordeal.[16]

Red Cross work was reinforced by young women from Newcomb College, who created their own chapter on campus. The college's gym became a large workspace. First-aid classes replaced basketball games. "The gym looks like a hospital clinic," read the *Newcomb Arcade*. Tables covered the court, and "practically every" student used her free time to come there to knit sweaters, socks, and roll bandages.[17] More volunteered for positions in a Women's Ambulance Unit and in hospitals. Other students later demanded and finally received permission to form a rifle company for 150 women who were trained in marksmanship—perhaps as much a sign of the rapidly cascading role of women in society as it was of their patriotic zeal.[18]

The first of six local chapters of the Red Cross was formed in 1916 under the leadership of Laura Penrose, a widowed member of the New Orleans café society. The chapters would be made up entirely of whites. However, according to Red Cross regulations, auxiliary units could be established composed of people "associated through ties of race, work, or common interests." This meant that African Americans could belong to a chapter's auxiliary, but it would, of course, have only a subsidiary status.[19] Sadly, an independent chapter for Blacks was disallowed. In spite of this rebuke, three African American nurses in the city, Sarah Hall, Viola Dominique, and Louise Ross, motivated no doubt by patriotism as well as by the drive for "racial uplift," were determined to and finally did form two auxiliary branches—one on each bank of the river.[20]

Their organizational meeting in May of 1917 was at the Pythian Temple on Gravier and Saratoga Streets, ground zero for the movers and shakers in the New Orleans Black community. Later it established its headquarters on the Temple's first floor and operated a canteen there for soldiers of their race. Since most of the tasks would be performed by women, here was a rare opportunity for gender independence and decision-making. They promoted public health, first aid, hospital work, or aid to dependent families. Their work helped to elevate the standing of African Americans in the eyes of New Orleans's whites by demonstrating citizenship and sacrifice.

Both branches made fervent appeals for members. On the west bank of the river in Algiers, a "colored" membership rally and parade in May of 1918 was described as one of the largest mass meetings of its kind ever witnessed there. African American branch leaders reached out to their white friends to "urge their colored help" to join, and Mayor Behrman joined speakers from both races for support.[21]

Red Cross work also was important in promoting African Americans' sense of self-worth. The movie short entitled "A Trooper of Troop K" was shown to the auxiliaries' members not only to inspire, but also to emphasize the bravery and devotion to duty soldiers of their race had displayed during the recent Mexican border dispute. Black cast members depicted "the unflinching bravery of negro troopers under fire." Based on a true story, it featured the "heroic rescue" of their white commander while braving heavy machine gun bursts.[22]

Yet activities like these were merely fleeting reminders of the significance of their contribution. Simply becoming part of a military organization with twenty million members nation-wide brought with it a profound sense of dignity. Too, there existed the immeasurable, positive impact on these African American citizens of simply participating in the city's numerous parades—dressed proudly in the same uniforms as their white counterparts and in front of the mostly white crowds. While they may have been in separate formations marching behind their white Red Cross cousins, they still received the same cheers.

Despite the inferior station of the auxiliaries, white chapter officers intentionally assumed a low profile during Black-themed events by only sponsoring or co-chairing them. This was done so as not to upstage the leadership role of these Black auxiliaries—quite extraordinary given the city's solid reverence for white superiority. White-owned city newspapers also afforded these branch events a fair amount of publicity and praise. And in a further example of racial harmony, the movement of the first party of three hundred African American draftees from New Orleans to depart the city for training on October 7th, 1917, was covered on the *Picayune's* front page. Their destination was Camp Pike, Arkansas.

Chapter 9

"NEITHER HYPHENS NOR SLACKERS AMONG US"

An estimated multitude of twenty thousand boosters came out for a parade to honor the city's African American conscripts just before they boarded their train for boot camp. Among those cheering on the sidelines were prominent Black pastors and civic leaders instrumental in promoting draft registration and enlistments, like businessman Walter Cohen and J. Madison Vance. It was October 7th, 1917, "Afro-American Day" in New Orleans, and naming the day as such was in itself a hint of racial fellowship. Included in the procession of three hundred was an honor guard of African American veterans of the Spanish-American War, various uniformed social groups from the Black community, and former Civil War soldiers whose leader proudly carried a battle-scarred Confederate battle flag. No one seemed to notice the irony. One particular oddity was the presence of white draft-board members who marched with the men they had selected from the different wards of the city.

Mayor Behrman furnished his own tribute to them, appearing on the steps of Gallier Hall under its Tuckahoe marble columns to salute them as they filed by, smiling, waving, and clapping like a proud parent. His appearance gave him credibility on the streets, betraying the narrative of racial divide by demonstrating the entire city's recognition of what these men were poised to do. Tipping his derby each time the American flag fluttered by, he may have wondered if the African Americans before him knew that they were pacing in front of the very building where Confederate president Jefferson Davis's body lay in state less than three decades before. Behrman was no revolutionary—no agitator for racial equality. On this day, however, the mayor stood out among other southern leaders.

Few other communities took the trouble to organize a salute to their Black conscripts as they departed for basic training. In other corners of the South, resentment surfaced. Donning the same uniform as whites was racially leveling, a fact that did not go unnoticed by many Republicans during the

Civil War who clamored for the enlistment of freed Blacks. The *Shreveport Caucasian* went a step further. It complained harshly that the army was an inappropriate place for a Black American. "Instead of being a trooper, he should be assigned a hoe and a plow and held in the fields where he has been provided by nature for such labor."[1] In order to make up for the absence of official civic send-offs, Black churches or fraternal groups across the nation hosted banquets, dances, or ceremonies for these men.[2] Elsewhere, many would have to quietly board trains without any fanfare. Not so in New Orleans where the city administration opened its heart for its overlooked citizens.

One Black Red Cross auxiliary branch handed out boxed lunches provided by the Boston and Pickwick Clubs, just as they had done the previous month for the white conscripts when they departed. Whites attending the parade even distributed snacks, cigarettes, and clothing to the men as they marched along. A journalist commented on the crowd's behavior, writing that there was evident "a determination on the part of the white citizens to give way to the Negroes," stepping back in order to provide "vantage points for the Negroes that they might get their full share of the entertainment." Whites "giving way" to Blacks during the era of Jim Crow? The reporter went on to say that the police recorded no incidents of racial conflict despite the estimated twenty thousand people on the parade route. The *States* commented similarly.[3] Noting the absence of any discord suggested an expectation of unrest between the races. Yet none occurred.

The anxiety expressed by these newspaper reporters was probably a consequence of the deadly race riot that erupted in East St. Louis three months earlier, when a policeman was shot by a Black man. An incensed mob of several thousand whites responded by assaulting the "Negro belt." Somewhere between one hundred and two hundred African Americans were murdered, lynched, or burned to death.[4] On top of this horrible event, there was more racial strife in Houston in late August when soldiers from the Black 24th Infantry, hearing a rumor that a Black soldier was killed while in police custody, marched on the outskirts of town and began targeting whites with gunfire. In two hours, seventeen people lay dead, including five police officers and two soldiers who were shot mistakenly by members of their unit. Nineteen soldiers were hanged and sixty-three received life sentences in federal prison for mutiny and murder.[5]

Perhaps patriotic fervor had transcended fear and racial suspicion, at least for this one day in New Orleans. Perhaps there was a recognition within the white community that Black soldiers were risking their lives in the defense of a society that perpetuated racial discrimination. Never fearing that the status quo would be jeopardized once the fighting ended, whites likely did not find it inappropriate to cheer the Black recruits, to back off and allow their relatives and friends the best "vantage points" to witness the parade. It was only a blip on the screen, but for a few hours on Afro-American Day in New Orleans, its Black citizens were treated with a bit of humanity.

Given how recently the two riots had occurred, it is no small wonder that the sendoff was genuinely warm. This point was made the following day in a *Picayune* editorial that crowed about the "kind and friendly relations" that prevailed between the races in the South. Ignoring the Houston incident, the editor claimed that the "bitterness" which surged in East St. Louis after its "disgraceful" riots could not happen in the South "under existing conditions."[6]

Mayor Behrman had been uneasy for some time about the large numbers of Black and white family members and friends who would push and shove in a tight crowd at the train terminals to see off their loved ones, particularly when emotions would already be very high. There was no precedent for this kind of cramped mingling. During Mardi Gras Black and white spectators had always lined the parade routes in separate locations. The races separated instinctively, locating their own viewing space. Still, this was not Mardi Gras, and law enforcement viewed the troop departures as a tinderbox. The decision to order different parting dates for Black and white troop movements was designed in part to avoid the potential for trouble. There was none.

Plenty of tears, of course, intermixed with the cheers at the terminals, recreated the scene when their white counterparts entrained for camp. Families and friends edged as close as possible to the cars for one last glimpse of their darlings. The luckiest poked out their heads from the train's windows for that final kiss, then pulled back for another to take his place. Finally, the train jerked backwards, stopped, and then lurched forward with a jolt. On this cue, the swarm of people immediately responded. They stood waving caps and hands for several minutes until they could see the train no longer, transferring their loved ones over to the war gods. Returning home, families were disconsolate—yet heartened by a profound sense of pride that would be sustained for the rest of the war in the Black community.

Only three weeks after Afro-American Day, however, the sentiment of racial unanimity was marred by the shooting of an eighteen-year-old African American oyster truck driver named Fred Johnson, who snatched the hand purse of a white woman while walking home from a downtown movie house. Her loud cries alerted a nearby barber, who dropped his razor and gave chase. A dozen men formed "an impromptu citizens' posse," according to the *States*, and began to pursue the thief as he ran from street to street, ducking in and out of saloons and alleys. The "posse" grew to roughly two hundred.

Several of them drew pistols and fired at Johnson who finally jumped into a canal carrying two bullets in his body. The police then appeared and pulled Johnson from the water. He died before the ambulance arrived, the woman's purse in one of his pockets. Johnson was identified by one officer as the man he had arrested recently for stealing a bicycle.

The gravity of this shooting in no way approached the immensity of the racial crises in East St. Louis and Houston. Still, Johnson's death ignited neither rioting nor violence. And there exists no evidence of denunciation from the African American community even though deadly force was used by the presumably all-white posse on an unarmed Black man in flight. The *Picayune* reported that the police "so far" had been unable to identify which man in that posse fired the deadly shots.[7] The silence (or indifference) from Black leaders in New Orleans was likely an acknowledgment of their grudging acceptance of the status quo and the powerlessness they felt in 1917 New Orleans, resigned as they were to their tyrannized lives.

Fred Johnson was not alone. While there were none in New Orleans, four African Americans were lynched in Louisiana during the two years prior to the war declaration (nine in Mississippi), and pressure built on the governor to respond.[8] In response to a petition begging him to act, Pleasant called a conference of Black leaders—ministers, professionals, and businessmen—to discuss the problem. They were hopeful that he would at least strongly condemn the violence and push local authorities to be aggressive in identifying the murderers. Pleasant was inept, reminding whites that "lynching is not a good thing at any time." Then he withdrew into the safe harbor where southern politicians had hidden for decades, blaming lynching on the victims and encouraging the attendees to go back into their communities and "teach" their people not to commit crimes that inflame whites.[9]

RACIAL UPLIFT

The War Department struggled mightily with trying to decide where African Americans would be sent for training. Southern Congressmen, unsurprisingly, recommended that camps in the North be set aside for them. They did not relish thousands of these men walking the streets on leave in their towns. Northern Blacks were considered more "uppity" and more likely to resist the customary racial barriers that existed in Dixie. But "vigorous protests" from a number of communities near the potential camp locations in the North arose, which likely convinced Secretary Baker that there may be a greater danger of more serious racial disturbances north of the Mason-Dixon Line.[10]

Both Black and white New Orleans conscripts were ordered to Arkansas's Camp Pike, just eight miles from Little Rock, where the government promised them identical housing, food, and equipment. They were both paid the same as well, earning $30 a month and a stipend of $15 more if they were married—$25 more if married with one child. But the races would be strictly segregated on post whether they were shooting pool off duty in their day rooms or qualifying on the rifle range.

Black men entraining to their army encampment had little expectation that their subordinate role in white society would be transformed simply because they wore a uniform. It was not. Racial oppression was institutionalized. Of the thousands of African Americans sent to France, only the Black 92nd and 93rd Infantry Divisions saw combat. The great majority—roughly 80 percent—were assigned to the Army's Service of Supply units—essentially labor battalions that operated allied ports and built wharves, train depots, and the warehouses that sheltered food and military hardware. It was somewhat akin to playing right field in Little League—picking clovers while others on the team got to actually touch the ball. Moreover, they also were selected to perform undignified work—digging and maintaining trenches, cleaning horse stables, or if they were sailors, waiting tables in the officers' mess. Many more served as stevedores on docks, loading and unloading cargo meant for the front—jobs not dissimilar from those that they held as civilians. African Americans from New Orleans were especially familiar with this work. A battalion of one hundred of them were among the very first to land in France.

After the Armistice, six thousand African American troops were ordered to prepare graves for twenty-three thousand of their comrades, but none marched in Paris's victory parade.[11] With the exception of the 92nd and 93rd, it was their strong backs that were tested—not their courage under fire. Despite their meritorious conduct in both the Civil War and in the Spanish-American War, the perception persisted that Blacks were incapable of being reliable fighting men.

Not only were African Americans saddled with that stubborn stereotype, but there also existed a deeply rooted suspicion that members of their race were vulnerable to German propaganda efforts to turn them against the government and the war. The supposition conjured up the historic fear, particularly in the South, that certain whites might stir thoughts of rebellion in the Black community. Memories of unscrupulous Reconstruction-era carpetbaggers who manipulated gullible African Americans remained strong. Days before Congress declared war, for example, it was reported that a Black settlement in North Carolina may be a base of operations for German agents intending to incite Black field hands on tobacco farms against the government. Their activities were said to have even spread to cotton belts in four other southern states.[12] News also surfaced that two Black men were arrested in Alabama for seducing members of their race to support Germany, and Black labor agitators in Tennessee were found labeling the war as a white man's fight.

According to historian Mark Ellis, these and other stories gave currency to what he called a "racial spy scare" in 1917.[13] The anxiety was later exacerbated by the training and arming of tens of thousands of Black troops. In some still-unreconstructed corners of the South, this was an unthinkable action. A climate of uneasiness blanketed those places not unlike that felt by their ancestors after abolitionist John Brown attempted to arm enslaved Virginians in 1859 at Harpers Ferry. In 1917, the arming of large numbers of Blacks remained an intimidating image.

The notion that African Americans were being preyed upon and influenced by German agents was difficult to dispel. Black activists who worked against racial injustices were automatically believed to be inspired by the long tentacles of Berlin's espionage agencies. Hundreds of investigations were conducted by the Bureau of Intelligence to determine the existence of any scheme by German agitators on US soil to soften African American support for the war. None of them found anything substantive.[14] But it did not seem to matter that proof of a German conspiracy was lacking, for it made perfect sense that it was much more likely for African Americans to be less patriotic.

The task of squelching German evangelism was much more difficult in the trenches of France, where leaflets dropped from planes somersaulted into American lines with the hope of at least placing doubt in the minds of African American soldiers. One such letter used a common-sense approach to stir discontent, questioning why they were fighting the Germans and reminding them of the injustices of institutionalized racism in their country. Entitled "To the Colored Soldiers of the United States Army," it read, in part:

Fighting the Germans. Why? Can you go to a restaurant where white people dine, can you get a seat in a theater where white people sit, can you get a Pullman seat or berth in a railroad car, or can you ride in the South on the same streetcar as white people? Now all of this is different in Germany ... where they do treat them as gentlemen and not as second class citizens. . . . Come over and see for yourself.[15]

Rumors among the troops were difficult to smother. One was that since Germany was the champion of the Black race and no color line was drawn there, they were open to equal rights, including marriage with white German girls. Another was that the bodies of Black troops were exhumed from their graves by the US military to be used in the production of soap.[16]

Congress addressed the suspected threat at home by attempting to squash the distribution of literature that might have promoted disloyalty. This included, of course, messages directed against what was believed to be the most impressionable segment of the population. The Espionage Act of 1917 criminalized the conveyance of any "information with intent to interfere with the operation or success of the armed forces of the United States or to promote the success of its enemies." The post office was given wide authority to confiscate such material. In addition, the government's propaganda arm, the euphemistically named Committee on Public Information, directed the nation's four-minute men to speak out against possible "Negro subversion" in their talks.[17]

In order to dampen this potentiality further, one southerner suggested that trusted whites should be encouraged to speak at Black church services and schools, teaching them about American war aims and explaining how African Americans were a valuable resource, especially as farm hands. His commentary testified to the widely accepted belief among whites that rural Blacks lacked probity—their hands needed to be held to protect them from the enemy's toxic ideas. As one commentator wrote, Negroes were "here to stay, 'part and parcel' of us. As a race, I believe they are loyal to the country, but they need guidance."[18]

It would be a difficult sell. Surely the African American population would be less inclined to support a government that prevented them from enjoying full citizenship. How could the president's rallying cry to "keep the world safe for democracy" be embraced in Black communities, especially in the South, when they were still struggling under laws that denied them suffrage? The war would expose the irony of men in uniform being asked to fight for a nation that did not uphold its promise to all its citizens.

Still, with no visible exception in Louisiana, African Americans in New Orleans magnified their claims of fealty to the cause of the war, perhaps overcompensating for the resolute rumbles of disloyalty. Black fraternal organizations repeatedly came to the defense of their race. One week after the war declaration, a crowd of over a thousand citizens met at the center stage for Black community leaders, the eight-year-old Colored Order of the Knights of Pythias Hall. There, they roared an absolute endorsement of Wilson and the war. After speeches and a patriotic parade, scores of men lined up to sign a resolution to be delivered to the War Department promising that they would enlist whenever the order came. "Certain evilly disposed persons have . . . circulated rumors," read the statement, "that the Negro was not loyal to the flag." This was "wicked propaganda." The "colored citizens of New Orleans . . . offer our services unreservedly." [19]

Largely Creole, educated, and civic minded, the Pythians and similar Black organizations, along with the Black clergy, worked tirelessly for racial uplift. This could only be accomplished, they trusted, by disassociating themselves from the more objectionable elements of their population. Meanwhile, they resolved to align with white leaders and their politics, as much as was plausible in the era of Jim Crow, to attain that elusive approval and recognition from the white community. There were areas of kinship within which the Black middle class and progressive white leaders could work, such as church affiliation, the arts, social grace, education, moral turpitude, and respect for the law. Music too was a common denominator. Many Creoles who grew up on an exclusive diet of classical music denounced jazz as crude and lurid, thus linking them with the respectable white elite. Both equated the new musical form with the lower classes, sinful dance, and rebellion.[20]

In 1917, however, another huge area of commonality was now available—the president and the war. In this they were informed by the most respected Black periodical of the day, W. E. B. Du Bois's *The Crisis*, which also promoted the mutuality of war policies and aspirations between the races. There was little politicizing in his magazine. The journal nurtured a mild and cooperative attitude—keeping its eye on the ball—despite the volatile context in which African Americans lived.

It was the very same approach taken by the New Orleans *Southwestern Christian Advocate*—distancing itself from controversy, parroting the conventional white press. Support the war declaration and the draft, castigate the isolationists, decry all slackers, take part in war bond sales, participate in conservation efforts, sponsor patriotic events—this was the best strategy to destroy the German army. And as a bonus, Jim Crow might be weakened. *The Vindicator*, a publication of the New Orleans Branch of the NAACP, followed suit. The war, it wrote, was "the race's greatest opportunity since emancipation. The race is on trial, and it is up to us to prove ourselves equal to the task."[21] Their collective fingers were crossed.

It was the hope that displays of support would tamp down the suggestions being propagated that they were vulnerable to enemy intrigue. While cooperation with the white community during the war was paramount, organizations like the State Negro Civic League of Louisiana never failed to remind the public that their race was denied rights—even in their own place of birth—rights which their white German and Austrian neighbors enjoyed.

That was clearly the most humiliating slight for African Americans, and it was the war that italicized the discrimination. Despite this grave inequity, the group insisted that there were neither "hyphens nor slackers among us."[22]

Local African Americans involved in the music profession used their artistry to demonstrate solidarity with the crusade overseas. Two of the most well-known wrote and published "America, They Are Both for You" in 1917. Armand Piron, a classical violinist and music publisher, who composed the music for this piece, was the leader of one of the city's most coveted smooth jazz society orchestras in New Orleans. Samuel Perrault, also a native, collaborated with Piron to write its lyrics:

> My only son who is twenty-one,
> For his country's sake will shoulder a gun.
> And a daughter too for her nation first,
> Will do her bit to help you as a Red Cross nurse.
> I'm proud to know they both will go,
> For "My country tis of thee,"
> America—they both are for you. [23]

Music professor William Nickerson, who once taught Jelly Roll Morton, composed both the music and the words for "The Colored Soldier Boys of Uncle Sam: We're Coming." Also published in New Orleans, the cover of the sheet music read, "Dedicated to the Colored Soldiers of the U.S.A." Its words were equally nationalistic:

> Loudly our country calling
> To arms its men of might,
> Into the ranks they're falling
> To battle for the right.
> We're coming, we're coming.
> We're loyal to a man.
> They'll be no stop till we're over the top.
> We're the colored boys of Uncle Sam.[24]

First performed by a Black chorus at an outdoor patriotic rally in October of 1918, the song was a huge hit with the racially mixed audience.[25]

Black churches in the city were loudly cheerleading for the war too. There was "no stop till we're over the top." At the Wesley Methodist and Episcopal Church, its pastor cried out to his congregation to answer the country's call to the colors. Race, he said, should not enter into the current discussion at all. Parishioners at St. James AME Church sang "My Country Tis of Thee" with great gusto at their first service since the April 6th war declaration. No race could sing this hymn "with more heartfelt earnestness and meaning than the Negro," proclaimed Pastor Rev. Edward Wittenberg. "His ideals," he preached, "are American. And in the present crisis . . . , he will shoulder a rifle and do his part."[26]

Letters from Black citizens echoed these pastors, consistent in their assurances that they would proudly continue to respect the flag just as they had done in previous wars, most recently the border incident in Mexico. A rash of them were sent to the *Picayune* as the country braced for war. One by L. A. Clark was typical: "No member of my race will take up arms against his home. . . . He is loyal to his country regardless of prejudice; he is ready, willing and waiting to come to the colors."[27] Black citizens, wrote another, had never produced a Benedict Arnold from the beginning of US history.[28]

Several white citizens did step forward in their defense, convinced that the threat of disloyalty was entirely exaggerated. "There is not one Negro in a thousand," maintained a New Orleans correspondent just after the war declaration, "that can be induced by Germany . . . to do anything against this country."[29] The point was made by another writer that German administration of its African colonies had been characterized by brutality, showing them to be "the harshest and most cruel of masters and rulers." There was no chance "conspiracies of this kind [would receive] the slightest encouragement among the Negroes of the South."[30] And the white *St. Tammany Farmer* printed the story of Aunt Jenny Goff, a local 102-year-old former slave, who sponsored a benefit for War Savings Stamps.[31]

Once a cease-fire was imposed in November of 1918, anxiety about the return of uniformed African Americans heightened. The War Department was sensitive about the potential for disruptions. Would there be a shift in attitudes about their subservient role in American society? How would they be received by white Americans once back home? To what extent did German propaganda affect the Black soldiers? And if African Americans in France became acclimatized to the relatively unbiased treatment given them by French civilians, would this stir in them a unified resistance to Jim Crow in America once they returned?

It only followed that the post-war racial climate would worry officials everywhere given how careful the government was about African Americans each step of the way: their registration and the draft, the location of their training cantonments so as to avoid contact with whites, their possible susceptibility to German propaganda, their interaction with white US soldiers—and with French women. To Mississippi senator James Vardaman, they would continue to be "French women ruined niggers."[32]

Concern was widespread that discharged soldiers strutting around with impudence in their uniforms and chest ribbons might lead to racial violence. After the shooting ended, several Black combat units were assigned to occupy Germany, yet they were returned to France and were quickly transported to the US by January 1919. Black labor battalions were ordered to move away from populated areas. Meanwhile, Washington sent conservative African American leaders like Robert Moton to France in order to investigate the condition of soldiers of his race and to speak to them before returning home after the war.[33] He urged them to conduct themselves in a "straightforward, manly, and modest way" and to be careful to avoid behavior that discredited the character and bravery they displayed during the war.[34]

Jim Crow, dressed in a doughboy uniform, was dragged across the ocean to Europe, where it continually diminished the honor of the African American soldier. Everything was racially segregated, from the combat units to the barracks, mess halls, and YMCA huts. Only hospitalized Blacks escaped the humiliation, although there were instances where white doctors or nurses refused to treat any nonwhite patient. White enlisted men commonly refused to salute Black officers at Camp Pike, seriously undermining respect for military rank and transgressing the very basis of military discipline.[35]

General Pershing would never have risked reducing the combat readiness of his army by advancing social justice for his Black soldiers. It would have been too disruptive to the business at hand for him to engage in any sort of army wide flirtation with desegregation. Moreover, he and his staff took a dim view of Black troops in general, underestimating them time and again. His bigotry led the commander to attach four infantry regiments of the Black 93rd Division to a French unit, reducing the possibility of an ugly racial incident under his command. At the time of this troop transfer, Pershing made clear his racial bias in a 1918 order to his French counterparts. In it he explained that while these Black soldiers were US citizens, they were regarded by white Americans as "inferior" and subject to vices that were a "constant menace to the American who has to repress them sternly." He therefore expected the French military to pay deference to Jim Crow while African American soldiers were under their command. He ended the order by outlining several segregation laws as they were written. And after the conclusion of the war, strict orders were issued to minimize contact between Black troops and French women.[36]

Besides the trials of segregation, other evil forces were at play. African American men in uniform had to regularly endure verbal abuse and mockery from white soldiers. Jokes invoking stereotypes derided them. Many were more than cruel, capitalizing on their unpolished vernacular and accents. It was part of white culture to wring humor from Black dialect—even in the sober newsprint of the local press. A 1917 Meyer-Israel clothing store advertisement in the *Picayune*, for example, included the head of a smiling, dark-skinned African American male. Beneath this image was printed the following: "E-heh! Th' boss jes guv me a suit o' his old clo'es, an' dey got th' Meyer-Israel label in 'em! E-heh!"³⁷

During the war the YMCA published a nationally syndicated newspaper called *Trench and Camp*, which partnered with the *Times-Picayune* and other dailies across the country. It was inserted within the regular newspapers' pages once a week but with its own banner. Published in order to help raise morale in the camps, it was also meant to give civilians a personal glimpse of what the men were doing on and off duty. The four-pager was printed in different editions for each camp so that the gossip, intramural sports stories, pranks, and articles about specific soldiers at that camp were more interesting to them and the readers back home—the equivalent of a school newspaper.

One issue ran a particularly tasteless joke that lampooned Black street talk. It provides a good example of the disregard whites had for the comic Negro-in-arms who often became the butt of their mockery. Entitled "Dixie Darkies in France Meet New Brand of Kin," it began as two Black soldiers were sitting on the steps of a YMCA hut when several dark-skinned Moroccan dockworkers passed them. "Say, Bo. Wha's dey, anyhow?" asked one. "Doan ast me," came the reply. "I never saw no niggers like dey befo'." They also talked funny. "I got it," said one with confidence. "Dem ain't no ordn'y niggers. Dem's Mystic Shriners, an dat talk . . . is religious services."³⁸ Phonetic banter such as this was rare in the three major dailies in New Orleans, but it could be found enough times to establish that this derisive caricature raised few eyebrows.

There was hope that if African Americans quietly suffered through the ridicule, it would pay off by earning a newfound respect from the white community. Perhaps their ordeal would help to split open the thick walls that sequestered them. Black churches reinforced this hope, preaching that the Lord would not overlook their devotion to country. The message was that the quiet, redemptive suffering they weathered in uniform would ease the path to true liberty. This was the same position taken by many Black preachers in the antebellum South—earthly trials would surely be followed by heavenly rewards.

Robert E. Jones, perhaps the most distinguished and influential Black religious and civic leader in New Orleans, devoted his life to racial unification.

In the *Southwestern Christian Advocate*, a powerful forum for his thoughts, Jones was predictably moderate in his tone, steeped in the Christian belief in turning the other cheek. He called it "the supreme challenge for the Negro race." Jones implored his readers to "pray for our enemies" and "those who despitefully use us." "It will take a great deal more courage to carry out this program than to be a bully or a swagger." But it can be done because the Negro "is a big man who can forget for the time being his group sufferings ... and run up the flag of truce."[39]

W. E. B. Du Bois suggested as much in *The Crisis*. He lent support to the war effort in spite of the obvious hypocrisy of his nation fighting Teutonic tyranny abroad while simultaneously persecuting his race at home. "Let us ... forget our special grievances and close our ranks shoulder to shoulder with our own white fellow citizens and the allied nations that are fighting for democracy. We make no ordinary sacrifice, but we make it gladly and willingly with our eyes lifted to the hills."[40]

In a letter to the *Item* two weeks after the Armistice, an African American wondered about the future of his people. Would the Great War be the beginning of opportunity? He would not let the public forget that thousands of his people served with honor in both the military and in war-related industries. "They have given all that they had to give," he noted, "even life." But what will be their compensation once back home? "Will they be given a chance that they can be good citizens who deserve just wages and fair treatment, or will they still be jailed without provocation and lynched without trial? "All we can ask," he added, "is a fair chance."[41]

The legacy of Black servicemen on the Western Front did little to weaken the pulse of Jim Crowism. In some white quarters, seeing them in uniform only served to intensify a perceived threat to America's values. African Americans, however, were not alone. During the war, a parallel, bitter conflict was taking place in America against the enemy within. Much less gallant than the one overseas, this war would lend more substance to the false narrative that the world was being made safe for democracy.

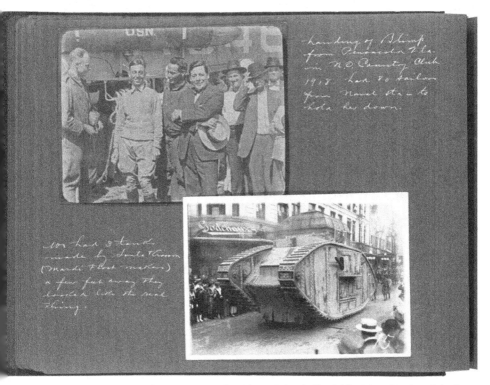

oat reproduction of a British Mark series tank rolls down Canal Street during the Fourth Liberty Loan Parade on Saturday,
ɔtember 28, 1918 (The Historic New Orleans Collection, gift of Arthur R. Bedient, 91-11-L.1)

Over seventy-five thousand African American soldiers served in World War I, but they were rarely depicted in popular magazines or songs. This piece, by the New Orleans African American composer William Nickerson, provides an exception. (The Historic New Orleans Collection, 94-832-RL)

The "Champs-Élysées" of Storyville, where the most opulent and expensive brothels were located, was Basin Street. The she
ter for Southern Railway's Terminal was just steps away on Basin's median. (The Historic New Orleans Collection, Gift of Mr.
Albert Louis Lieutaud, 1957.101)

This map displays the location of the entire "restricted district" as it was known in polite society. (The Historic New Orleans
Collection, Gift of Mr. John Churchill Chase and Mr. John W. Wilds, 1979.167.21a)

tators line up to watch sailors march in a Liberty Loan parade in 1917 on Canal Street. (Charles L. Franck Studio ction at The Historic New Orleans Collection, 1979.325.4084)

Rooftop view of the Terminal Station's entrance on Canal Street. Storyville is hidden behind the large building to the left of the entrance. (The Historic New Orleans Collection, Gift of Waldemar S. Nelson, 2003.0182.177)

A huge Liberty Loan sign blankets two stories of the iconic D. H. Holmes department store on Canal Street's busiest block. (The Historic New Orleans Collection, Gift of Waldemar S. Nelson, 2003.0182.181)

White-shirted daredevil Bill Strothers, standing on a platform before his stunt, draws a large crowd in downtown New Orleans. The "human spider" would scramble up three of the city's tallest buildings with no safety gear. Strothers was one of many attractions hired to create excitement during Liberty Loan drives. (The Historic New Orleans Collection, Gift of Waldemar S. Nelson, 2003.0182.193)

A poster for the silent 1918 Screen Classics Productions film "To Hell with the Kaiser" is displayed on an unknown location in downtown New Orleans. During its run, the Kaiser was hung in effigy near the theater where it played. (The Historic New Orleans Collection, Gift of Waldemar S. Nelson, 2003.0182.185)

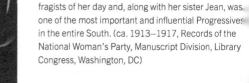

Kate Gordon, 1861–1932, was one of the leading suffragists of her day and, along with her sister Jean, was one of the most important and influential Progressives in the entire South. (ca. 1913–1917, Records of the National Woman's Party, Manuscript Division, Library Congress, Washington, DC)

Mayor Martin Behrman, posing at his desk, held the office for sixteen years, longer than any other in the city's history. (The Historic New Orleans Collection, Gift of Mrs. Jeanne Rabig, 1994.115.16)

Hardly a citizen of New Orleans was ever deprived of seeing their mayor, Martin Behrman, in person. Here he delivers a talk at a children's festival at St. Roch playground. (The Historic New Orleans Collection, Gift of Waldemar S. Nelson, 2003.0182.269)

ıglielmo Marconi in an Italian naval officer's ıiform standing among a small group of men near ıllier Hall. Marconi invented wireless telegraphy ıd received a Nobel Prize in physics in 1909. ı came to New Orleans in 1917 as a member the Italian government mission to the US. (The storic New Orleans Collection, Gift of Waldemar Nelson, 2003.0182.261)

paganda posters like this reinforced stories of ıman savagery in Europe and helped to inflame ılic opinion against the German "Hun" both ɔad and at home.

GET-READY
NUMBER

Life

PRICE 10 CENTS
Vol. 67, No. 1737.   February 10, 1916.
Copyright, 1916, Life Publishing Company

BARBARIANS

Nagasenttle · Heliener · Von Papen · Hoch · Bismarck · Heinenpolis · St. Karl

Boy-Ed City · Achdenn · Salalakesburg · Schevann · Omahoch · Kaiser Bluffs · Prosit · Schlauterhaus · Rassmir · Kruppsburg · Trombourg · Koblaplatz · New Potsdam

JAPONICA

Wilhelmplatz · Hohenzollern · Denverburg · Zweisten · Hindenberg · Heidelbergapolis · New Berlin

San Slake · Ach Dooey · Starhberg

PRUSSIA

Yokohanpolis · Wienerschnitzelplatz · New Bingen · Cape Lightfellness

AMERICAN RESERVATION · Desert · Kaiserkase · Gotterdammerungham · Karltown · Cape Backwater

Nietzsche · Van Hindenburg · New Hamborg · TURCONIA · Bagdad Corners

AUSTRIANA · New Breslau · Constantinople Junction

New Vienna · Barthaw · GULF OF HATE · Panllaha Beach

PROVINCE OF MEXICO

Mackensenilla · Wolf Today · STRAITS OF HORROR · WEST INDIE LAMPE

Benropolis

VON TIRPITZ OCEAN

"MY COUNTRY, 'TIS OF THEE"

This image of a US map appeared on the cover of the February 10, 1916, cover of *Life* magazine, a year before the US declaration of war. Entitled "MY Country Tis of Thee," its intention is clear. New Orleans is renamed New Hamborg on the map. (Courtesy of Cornell University—P. J. Mode Collection of Persuasive Cartography)

Roman Catholic clergy in procession after a mass on the first Sunday after the Armistice at St. Louis Cathedral celebrating the end of the Great War. Reverend A. E. Otis, President of Loyola University, delivered the sermon. (The Historic New Orleans Collection, Gift of Waldemar S. Nelson, 2003.0182.147)

The scene at the intersection of Saint Charles Avenue and Canal Street on November 11, 1918, after news was announced earlier in the morning of the war's end. Businesses along the downtown side of Canal Street from the 700 through the 900 block are shown. The photo was taken at 1:30 p.m. when the celebration was waning. (The Historic New Orleans Collection, Gift of Waldemar S. Nelson, 2003.0182.135)

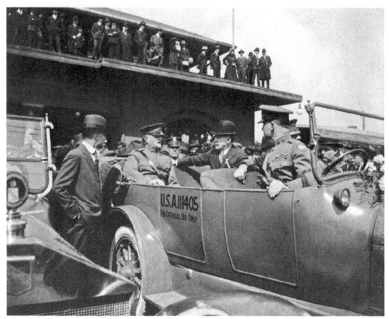

General John J. "Black Jack" Pershing (1860–1948) upon his arrival to New Orleans at Union Station, 1001 South Rampart Street, seated in an army vehicle with Frank B. Hayne (derby), chairman of the committee to meet Pershing. A welcoming crowd is seen trying to get a view of Pershing. The general came as a guest of the city to witness the 1920 Mardi Gras. (The Historic New Orleans Collection, Gift of Waldemar S. Nelson, 2003.0182.235)

The Victory Arch, designed by architect Charles L. Lawton, was erected in 1919 at McCarthy Square in the Bywater neighborhood as a tribute to the men of the Ninth Ward who fought and died in the war. Funded by residents of the ward, it was the first permanent WWI memorial in the nation. (The Historic New Orleans Collection, Gift of Waldemar S. Nelson, 2003.0182.247)

Chapter 10

"WE WERE AMONG WOLVES"

"The Germans are ruthlessly destroying this great work of art because they are what they are . . . because they are Germans, just Germans. There is no name to call anyone that could be worse."[1] Thus read a letter, printed in its entirety in the *Picayune* on page one, from the Catholic Cardinal of Reims to a New York fundraising group, distraught over the wanton German artillery shelling of one of the world's great architectural jewels, the medieval Reims Cathedral. This atrocity was another in a list of barbarities committed by the Kaiser's forces, this time against a magnificent structure with no military significance whatsoever. It underscored the belief that the Teutonic hordes were as fiendish as their popular namesake, the Huns. And the decision to print the Cardinal's words points to another important piece of the calculus that produced so much fury against innocent German Americans. Reports materialized—one from a New Orleanian living in London, accusing enemy soldiers of tying Allied bodies together with wire and boiling them in order to render fat and grinding up what remained of the corpses to feed poultry and swine.[2]

Washington's propaganda arm during the war bore the chilling, Orwellian name of the Committee on Public Information. Among its functions was the publication of materials that would keep citizens staunchly behind the war effort, so worried were some that the nation was not entirely clear about why its sons were going into combat thousands of miles away. One such publication was entitled "German War Practices." Part I, addressing the Germans' treatment of civilians, was a collection of quotes from enemy military doctrine, proclamations, and soldiers themselves all reinforcing the characterization of the enemy as creatures of uncivilized evil. In the 1902 *German War Book*, for example, officers were told to guard against "excessive humanitarian notions," for "certain severities are indispensable to war . . . and that the only true humanity often lies in a ruthless application of them." Another quote included parts of a speech by German general Moritz von Bissing defending the extreme measures in 1914 taken by his army in Belgium. The innocent "cannot be spared, and if isolated houses, flourishing villages, and even entire towns are annihilated, that is assuredly regrettable, but it must not excite ill-timed sentimentality."[3]

Other tales, mostly British in origin, told not only of mass rapes and murders, but also of the horrific mutilation of their victims by the sadistic Huns in their orgies of horror—celebrations in Berlin after the *Lusitania* incident, the crucifixion of wounded POWs, and the use of saw-edged bayonets to more brutally tear flesh. Stories such as these abounded in the press.

This was a different enemy—insidious. Devious and cunning. The playlist was long. Its U-boats ambushed combatants and noncombatants alike, cloaked by the sea, invisible and deadly. Allied ships were cowardly mugged from behind, cold-cocked in the shadows. Ghostlike, 650-foot-long zeppelins hovered menacingly over England, Belgium, and France dropping thousands of explosives from moonless skies on population centers. Poison gas slunk deep into trenches and gagged soldiers' throats.

Political cartoons depicted spike-helmeted German soldiers as sneering brutes carrying away defenseless girls on their shoulders or as monstrous man-apes or grinning skeletons bayonetting the unprotected. Nothing here was new. Cartoonists had jeered America's enemies in previous conflicts. But the volume of the messages was unprecedented during WWI, for it was a government-roused industry in itself. The campaign's effect on American public opinion was impossible to minimize.

New Orleanians were not protected from the hailstorm of print profiling the "Bestial Hun" as morally squalid. It did not matter whether the reports were well documented exaggerations based on some truth or simply innuendo elevated to an extreme. Readers believed them. As expected, Germans living in the city were victimized regardless of their feelings about the war. The 1910 census reported 6,115 native Germans living in New Orleans, 22.1 percent of its ethnic population—the city's second largest.[4] (Italians were first with 29.1 percent.)[5]

As early as 1914 before the storm of propaganda became really ugly, nine German priests in New Orleans were moved to write a letter of protest to Archbishop James Blenk, a native German himself, about a report in the local Catholic newspaper, the *Morning Star*. In it, the "horrors perpetrated by the Germans" were described by an eyewitness in Belgium who claimed that they tore old wooden statues from church altars and converted them into torches "to light their crimes." These "savages," who "rage against God" and dare to "invoke at every moment the name of God, attack Him in his temples and in the sacred presence of women and children."

The priests insisted that the letter was filled with lies. They understood how this "unfounded" report would find its way into the mainstream press, the "hirelings" of British money, but were "astounded and deeply wounded" to see it in the *Morning Star*. Blenk replied to the priests immediately, agreeing with them that the report reproduced in the newspaper was "slanderous" and promising to have the editor "blue pencil" anything not entirely impartial and accurate.[6]

Many Germans were highly recognized and in the foreground of the city's economic engine, like Adolph Ricks, Joseph Reuther, and William Franz, all of whom were bank presidents. Rudolph Hecht and Rudolph Krause were the owners of a large dry-dock company and lumber business respectively. Albert Weiblen created a nationally known stone manufacturing business, and Peter Blaise's Standard Brewing Company produced one of the city's most popular beers. Several were also active in politics and education. Reuther and Franz both served on the Orleans Parish School Board, the latter honored by the naming of a new school after him. Congressman Charles Buck ran unsuccessfully for mayor against Behrman in 1904. Ricks was on the city's Commission Council during the war years. Conrad Kolb was one of the most respected restauranteurs in the city.

Among the most esteemed of this group was William Edenborn, owner of the Louisiana Railway and Navigation Company. One of the wealthiest men in America, he became the largest landowner in the state and was a leader of Louisiana's German community. Each of these men was born in Germany. With the exception of Edenborn (following chapter), there is no evidence that they were in any way traitorous to their new home in America. Yet it could not have been an untroubled nineteen months for them or their families while the US was at war with the nation of their birth.

The *Neue Deutsche Zeitung*, the local German-language weekly, was beginning to agonize. Editorializing a week after the *Lusitania* sinking, it determined that the burden of living in a country at odds with the Fatherland was "part of the sacrifices that have to be made for Germany and her allies before they can emerge victorious." As long as the US was able to stay out of the conflict, their position was uncomfortable but not perilous. Newcomb College history professor and German citizen Heinrich Maurer addressed the issue at a celebration of Bismarck's hundredth birthday in 1915, assuring his audience that German principles could be easily reconciled with American values—as long as Americans stayed true to those values.[7]

In February of 1916, another episode bubbled up that did nothing but sharpen distrust for German residents of the city. Dr. Paul Roh, the German consul in New Orleans since 1909 and president of the city's foremost German fraternal organization, *Die Deutsche Gesellschaft* (the German Society), scribbled a short message of condolence to Franz von Papen, the German military attaché in Washington. Von Papen was expelled for being complicit in acts of sabotage by German agents in America. On his way back to Berlin, von Papen was searched at Falmouth, England, where Roh's message was discovered by British officials and promptly printed in newspapers across the country. "I don't suppose that you are very unhappy to be able to shake the dust of this unfriendly country from your feet," Roh wrote, expressing regret for his countryman's dismissal.

A guest slandering his host would not sit well with the American people, particularly on the heels of the *Lusitania* sinking. But it was this next sentence that was so controversial: "May the day of reckoning come and our government find again that iron determination with which alone one can make an impression here." Was the "day of reckoning" the beginning of military aggression against the US? The letter was signed "Roh," although the signature was somewhat illegible. The doctor at first denied writing it, but when the penmanship was compared to documents in New Orleans written in his own hand, he admitted that he was indeed the author.

The New Orleans business community as well as the French consulate were outraged and immediately circulated petitions to be delivered to the State Department to recall the consul, but no action was taken since his words were in a private correspondence.[8] Roh never made a public apology and left the presidency of the German Society in 1917, bemoaning "the pressure of political circumstances" and the "increasingly deteriorating situation of the times."[9]

Internationalists warned that insidious Germans like these could soon be controlling America if the US government continued to sit on its neutral hands. That frightening thought was vividly communicated by a controversial map of the US that appeared on the cover of the February 10th, 1916, issue of *Life* magazine, entitled "My Country 'Tis of Thee." "New Prussia" was scrawled across the forty-eight states in large print, the Atlantic Ocean was labeled as the "Von Trippitz Ocean" (after the chief builder of the German navy), and major cities were renamed. Washington became "New Berlin," Chicago was cleverly called "Schlauterhaus," and New Orleans became "New Hamburg." One year later, the American ambassador in Berlin, James Watson Gerard, reinforced that image by repeating a bogus warning given to him by a German official that there were 500,000 Germans living in the US poised to lead a revolt if war broke out. Gerard returned the salvo—there were 501,000 lamp posts to hang them from.[10]

Three days after the president delivered his war message to Congress, the *Picayune* editorialized rather naively that it did not anticipate a bumpy relationship with the city's German population. "We feel confident," the column began, "that there will be nothing done during the war for which we will have reason to apologize or explain; that there will be nothing in our treatment of the ... thousands of peaceable, friendly, and law-abiding Germans ... that can be complained of." An overwhelming number of them are "as loyal as any born American.... The city must remember, it continued, that their position will be "awkward ... for they have many friends and relatives in the German army or navy; but for this they are in no way responsible."[11]

Unfortunately, many paid little heed to the editorial's expression of magnanimity. Rumors swirled that bombs had been found stored in Kolb's restaurant, a fixture in the local German community, and that Conrad Kolb had been arrested. Although the *States* attested that the story was entirely false, Kolb felt obliged to buy space in the city's newspapers addressing questions about his citizenship. "When I took my oath of allegiance to the United States," his commentary read, "I meant it, and I still mean it."[12] Kolb would spend the rest of the war as one of the largest benefactors of the Red Cross and was a pillar in the city's Liberty Loan drives. He regularly donated the profits made by his restaurant to several war-related charities. Yet the skepticism endured. The wife of one of Kolb's cousins later remembered hearing that he was once hanged in effigy on Canal Street during the war.[13] There is no evidence that this ever occurred, but the persistence of this hearsay decades later within the family suggests the plausibility of such acts. Kolb and his fellow Germans had to be on their guard.

The *Neue Deutsche Zeitung*, of course, was much less buoyant than its big brother, the *Picayune*, recognizing that its readership was besieged, trapped inside a nation their Fatherland was fighting. It made its position known in its April 15, 1917, edition, predicting that the coming days would be difficult for their estranged community. There would be "terrible days of conflict between duty toward our country and natural sympathy for the land of our fathers. There cannot be any question as to which of the two, duty or sympathy, will prevail. For perfidy is not a German trait."

What the newspaper did not address was how they would now be treated as they confronted this personal dilemma. No one knew how deep-seated a German's devotion would be to his bloodline. The purchase of US government Liberty Loan bonds to help finance the war effort was the litmus test of loyalty, and by May the *Neue Deutsche Zeitung* began to advertise their sale while insisting that even though it still printed in German, it was certainly an American publication.[14]

Anxiety intensified, and local Germans began ducking for cover. Business-es changed their names. The Commercial Germania Trust and Savings Bank became simply the Commercial Trust and Savings Bank, and the German-American Homestead Association was renamed the Liberty Homestead As-sociation.[15] The German Society of New Orleans even removed its sign from its entrance as if it were going into hiding, and the *Neue Deutsche Zeitung* quietly ended its operation in August of 1917.[16] No wonder. They could hear the footsteps. The language itself was under attack. The legislature further criminalized any statements determined to be "disloyal" or "abusive" to the US. Further, it was made illegal for anyone to "knowingly or maliciously" display the flag of the nation's enemies.[17]

Churches felt the sting of hatefulness as well. A Lutheran church in nearby Abita Springs removed German inscriptions from its altar and replaced them with English translations.[18] The Salem Evangelical Church ended services in German "owing to the war conditions"; several other German churches dropped "German" from their names and began displaying the Stars and Stripes.[19] Henry Weyer from Gretna, Louisiana, a close suburb of the city, remembered hearing about those tense days. "Someone in the family got the idea that those [church] members born in Germany would probably be deported. And one of the thoughts was, 'let's burn the birth certificates. If they don't have that, they can't check us out.'"[20] The Southern District of the Lutheran Synod, meeting in New Orleans in the spring of 1918, voted to make English rather than German the predominant language in its schools.[21] Doris Ann Gorman's parents spoke their native German, "but it was always indoors in a quiet tone." "They were suspicious that people would hear them speaking German in their home."[22] Sadly, people simply stopped speaking the language of their birth country to each other in public. It just became too risky.

No public event was spared from the tone of militancy—even at construc-tive affairs like Liberty Loan rallies. Incendiary orations received the loudest approvals. "Ninety percent of the Germans born in the U.S. are unfaithful to the country," announced City Attorney J. J. Reilley at one Lafayette Square event, "and 100 percent of the German-born are unfaithful." No matter that he was wrong and presented nothing to substantiate his feckless charges. His audience demanded none, feasting on the hostility. The rhetoric and timbre of his voice secreted hatred. And he wasn't finished. With the throng of two thousand cheering wildly, Reilley, in booming baritone, made it clear and simple: "The German people and the Kaiser are one and inseparable, and I believe every German alien should be interned."

The next speaker, an officer in the Canadian army, took it up another notch, continuing with more weaponized words to the delight of the aroused listeners. "Germans have done every damnable thing they could think of, and it would give me no hard feeling if you would hang every pro-German and," pumping his chest, "make me the hangman!"[23] Fortunately, his provocation was followed by a flag presentation from a Boy Scout troop and a sensible appeal for generosity by the mayor—or else the audience might have become unglued.

Martial music contributed to the infectious venom at another raucous patriotic gathering, also in the Square. It would not take much to provoke an incident. One inebriated man in the audience screamed at a speaker soliciting government bond purchases, abruptly interrupting him: "I guess you're getting a pretty good graft out of that!" Several people nearby instantly overheard him and shouted, "Let's mob him!" If not for the several policemen present, he would have been pummeled. The twenty-five-year-old was held for federal authorities.[24]

Unsurprisingly, a string of fraternal organizations began to screen its members to sanitize their rolls of the unfaithful. Rotary Clubs throughout the city sent out loyalty questionnaires. The Young Men's Gymnastic Club expelled ten of its members when they were accused of disloyalty. Every member was required to answer questions on what it called "loyalty cards." Questions included, "Do you pledge absolute loyalty to the government of the U.S.?" and "Were you born in a foreign country? If so, where?"[25] The prestigious New Orleans Chess, Checkers, and Whist Club approved a resolution stating that "any member of this club who issues a guest card to an enemy alien shall be immediately expelled."[26] And when Pickwick Club member A. Baering, a German citizen, refused to sign a pledge to support Wilson and the war, he was asked to resign.[27]

Theo Schlitz sensed the city's temperament. The eminent German lumberman could often be found staying at the Grunewald Hotel while on one of his frequent business trips to New Orleans. But now he was carrying more documentation than usual—a folder filled with testimonials that he had been collecting from Americans attesting to his loyalty to the United States, including one from the mayor of Hattiesburg, Mississippi, where his business was located. One could not be too careful. In an interview with a reporter in the hotel's lobby, the entrepreneur felt a need to make clear his devotion to his adopted country: "I am an American, the U.S. is my country, and I want all my friends to know it."[28]

Another example of the extent of the Germanophobia that ruptured the good sense of the city's citizenry was the move to rename Berlin Street, a nondescript residential road that sliced through a quiet uptown neighborhood. The street ran parallel to a collection of other streets all commemorating

Napoleon's victories over Germany. The emperor's triumphant appearance at the Brandenburg Gate in 1806 was memorialized by naming Berlin Street in his army's honor. No matter the irony. All it took was a letter to the *Picayune* from a reader who thought it was unpatriotic, and the idea snowballed. Suggestions were made to change the name to Columbia Street or Wilson Street, but most seemed to prefer to give tribute to the AEF commander. The *Picayune* editorialized against it, but the mayor grabbed hold of it and personally introduced an ordinance to the city council in May of 1918 to re-name the street Gen. Pershing Street. (The general sent Behrman a cablegram thanking him for the tribute.)[29]

One writer for the *Picayune* had fun satirizing the foolishness, reporting that a recommendation had been made to Behrman to change his Germanic name as well. It was quite inappropriate and an embarrassment to the people of his city! "The mayor is working under strain," answered an "unnamed" City Hall spokesperson, "and has not had much time to select a name. The trouble was that almost every name has already been taken. Moreover, it would be difficult to find a name to fit his occupation. There are Goldsmiths and Shoemachers, but no "Mayorsmiths." As long as he can continue to "induce the banks to honor checks with the good old name of Martin Behrman, . . . the mayor will try to worry along with the name his ancestors gave him."[30]

Retail merchants and property owners were not immune from the ran-cor against anything that smacked of Germany. A druggist on St. Charles complained that many of his customers were unreasonable. If they find a bar of soap with a German name, he exclaimed, "What a raking I get!" They rant about the Germans "and all that has to do with the Germans." "No wonder I hate the Kaiser." The tenants of the Audubon Building on Canal Street argued that theirs was the only building visible that was not flying the flag. They demanded that the manager explain. (A flag was hoisted later that day.)[31] An *Item* reporter took time to count 297 homes along St. Charles Avenue between Lee Circle and Carrollton, but "only" 156 of them flew flags. "Won't somebody please come forward," he wrote sarcastically, "and organize a society for the purchase of American flags for millionaires on St. Charles?"[32]

Mayor Behrman himself was targeted for not doing his part, even though he was too old to enlist and his only surviving son was an Army captain on active duty. One writer to the *Picayune* asserted that it wasn't enough to simply wear an American flag pin or sing the national anthem. "Carrying a rifle in the trenches" is real patriotism, so he challenged elected officials to "lead by example and enlist."[33] Enlisting would, however, not be so easy for Albert Kaiser, a resident of St. Ann Street. He may have been the only American to ask for an exemption to the draft because of his name. "If I am sent to an encampment, the other boys will immediately make it hot for me."[34] He was probably correct, but he received no sympathy from his draft board. In some respects the hysteria is understandable given the incessant messages in the press that inflated the dangers people had to face. One especially fierce gladiator for the government was former New Orleans district attorney St. Claire Adams, chairman of Louisiana's division of the militant, far-right American Defense Society (ADS). He did little to help smother the alarm, telling a reporter that the enemy's spies were everywhere, using dynamite to destroy America's industries and poisoning its food and water supply.[35] The ADS paid to have inflammatory alerts periodically printed on the pages of newspapers across the nation. One read:

American Defense Society Warning
Every German or Austrian in the U.S. . . . should be treated as a potential spy. Be on the alert. Keep your eyes and ears open. Take nothing for granted. Energy and alertness may save the life of your son, your husband, or your brother. The enemy is engaged in making war in this country . . . and in spreading peace propaganda. . . . Whenever any suspicious act or disloyal word comes to your notice, communicate at once with the police or with the local office of the Justice Department. [36]

While the story of Hans Halle, the bomb maker who was arrested in New Orleans in late 1914, was not far from memory, there had been no other incidents of this magnitude since. It was wise to remind citizens to be on their toes while rumors circulated that enemy U-boats were operating in the Gulf near the river's mouth. But these continual threat warnings ratcheted up the level of zealotry for many, moving them off the spectrum of good sense and sending many into a state of excessive intolerance.

A syndicated column called "The Enemy Within," regularly featured on the editorial pages of the *Picayune* for thousands to absorb, was penned by dyed-in-the-wool Germanophobe Robert Bowen. His words were tough and jingoistic. "A half allegiance," he preached, "is no allegiance." Bowen called German aliens "the scum in the melting pot" who were "poisoning" America's safety. They were "serpents in our bosoms," yet Americans treat them with a velvet glove, "extending the bitten hand to the fangs that have repeatedly lacerated it."[37]

This kind of combustible rhetoric was becoming commonplace in the local press. Neither the *Times-Picayune* nor its rivals, the *New Orleans States* and the *New Orleans Item*, had ever been students in the school of yellow journalism. But the decision by the *Picayune* to carry "The Enemy Within" was revealing. So too were the editorial cartoons that always depicted the demonic Hun as bloodthirsty, cowardly, and sub-human. While the editorial essays of the three newspapers remained mostly sober and restrained, reporters could not parse the volatile words of speakers who lashed out at Germans, loyal or not.

Belligerence was in the vernacular. It was inherent in everyday conversations on the streets, at family dinners, and within the city's business offices. The rare had become the norm. The inappropriate, acceptable. German-owned businesses were shunned. Longtime neighbors who were once friendly stopped speaking. Public displays of patriotism were the expectation, often translating into anti-German hostility.

This incendiary atmosphere provided a perfect ignition for violence. Fistfights were especially common. One altercation began when a man at a saloon in neighboring St. Tammany Parish boasted how the Germans were set to invade the British Channel Islands, capture Paris, and then New York. Another man at the bar took exception and knocked him down. The incident descended into a brawl involving several more bar patrons, resulting in injuries to a draftee and a New Orleans cop. The *St. Tammany Farmer* predicted vigilantism, warning law enforcement that "if . . . no punishment is inflicted, it is probable that some organization of citizens will be formed for dealing with such cases."[38]

Mrs. Renee Samuel Bear, a member of the Women's Council of Defense and resident of St. Tammany, remembered in a 1975 interview that the home of a German in her town, William Oswald, a prominent electrical engineer and inventor, was burned down by anti-German elements some time during the war. There were rumors, according to Bear, that he was operating a wireless radio from his home.[39] While the suspicious fire cannot be blamed on the bar brawl or the provocative editorial, the charged atmosphere could have been an accessory to this crime. The story of the fire that destroyed the property of an important business leader went mysteriously unreported, a real curiosity given that news of much less import would commonly be found on page one of the *Farmer*.

The strain for a few Germans became too great. Sixty-year-old German national John Schroeder threw himself out of a window from the second floor of his Magazine Street apartment. "I tried to dash my brains out on the pavement," he told a reporter. The rattled dockworker explained later that he believed the government was trying to kill him. His fears intensified when he read the signs posted at the city's wharves warning aliens not to approach the ship terminals without identification.[40] Fellow German national Martin Elkan reached the limit of his tolerance by hanging himself from his bed post. Elkan had abruptly lost his job as an interpreter for the St. Charles Hotel and was also said to be distraught over the war. Having already been arrested and released for disloyal talk, he likely succumbed to the malice and suspicion that steadily pursued him.[41]

Hollywood made a contribution to the hysteria as well. Movies like *The Claws of the Hun*, a silent film about German saboteurs in America, played in New Orleans and helped to shake the cage. *The Little American* with Mary Pickford realistically recreated the sinking of the *Lusitania*. Mary's character survives the sinking and, while serving later in the war zone, is barely saved from rape by a squad of snarling German soldiers. In the promotional poster for *The Kaiser, The Beast of Berlin*, two women and a child are huddled together in fear as a German soldier approaches. The Kaiser, standing nearby, orders the soldier to "kill the Belgian swine."[42] *To Hell with the Kaiser*, sponsored by the Elks, was on the marque at the Strand for a week and stirred moviegoers to hang the hated emperor in effigy, helmet and all, from a tall pole erected at Canal and Baronne Streets. When the Elks band on the street teased the frenzied mass of spectators with "Dixie," the hurrahs echoed back and forth down the famous thoroughfare. Hats flew into the air as "Berlin's Beast" was raised on high.[43] Messages like these bombarded the public from these films and from dozens of other sources, as incessant as artillery barrages on the front. The demonizing was impossible to escape.

Following the lead of other states, the 1918 Louisiana legislature passed a law outlawing the teaching of the pernicious German language in both public and private institutions, elementary through college.[44] The New Orleans school board preempted the state with its own prohibition, beginning in the fall of 1918.[45] The legislation was widely hailed, the *Picayune* opining that "Teutonic leaders" were using their language to seduce and pervert the American republic. But the editorial then pulled back a bit. While demonstrating support for the law, it reminded its readers that most German residents were loyal to America. Many of them, it went on, were among the most active in suppressing the German tongue in America.[46] A spokesman for the American Defense Society was not nearly as gracious, insisting that the study of German was initiated more for political than educational reasons, "Teutonizing" America's children. "To speak German is to remain German," wrote Ludwig Fulda, a German playwright who validated the society's fears. "To cause others to speak German is to make them into Germans."[47] It was more than simply cultural chauvinism to some. It was a conspiracy.[48]

An even higher wall was erected in Baton Rouge—disallowing the sale of German merchandise in the state, restricting the German language in advertisements and signs, and halting the distribution of German publications or any other that painted Germany and Austria in a favorable manner.[49] It passed easily with a vote of 85 to 12. Legislators had already produced bills in 1917 requiring the registration of German and Austrian aliens and prohibiting them from possessing firearms or explosives. Not one vote was lodged against any of these. Representative William Zaunbrecher, the only German-born member of the House, was absent for one of these five roll calls but voted with the majority in each of the others. A resident of the small German community of Roberts Cove, Louisiana, Zaunbrecher had been a strong advocate to preserve his beloved language. Despite his convictions and difficult as it must have been, he succumbed to the pressure to conform. But he did not run for reelection.[50]

These initiatives were loudly applauded. One citizen had written the *Picayune* grumbling that "pan-Germanism, with its abominable *Kulture* ... stripped of religious morality ... is partly the result of teaching the language in our schools."[51] Another reader maintained that the world "can flourish and be happy and scholarly too without the German language. We don't want it. Neither do we want their music. The Germans have fallen too low in the scale of decency."[52]

"Poisonous" material was identified and stricken from textbooks to protect the city's young from the Prussian proselytizers. School board superintendent J. M. Gwinn issued orders to all principals to purge two pages from a reference book on New Orleans used in area schools, which extolled Germany's contribution to the city's growth. The section in question, entitled "Pre-Eminence of Germany in City Planning" with a sub-heading that read, "Some Causes of German Success," was considered objectionable by some teachers who brought it to the board's attention. So too was a photo of an attractive new school in Germany found in fourth-grade textbooks with a caption that read, "How would you like to go to school here?" Gwinn ordered it removed after a complaint from the local chapter of the National Security League, ready as always to agitate against anything associated with German culture.[53]

A school board committee also recommended replacing the classics with "patriotic selections" in high-school literature classes, and a high-school course entitled "Democracy Today" was launched, accompanied by a textbook with patriotic documents from history. In addition, the board saw fit to publish a chilling pamphlet entitled "Why the U.S. Is at War with Germany," to be distributed to all students. Germany, it said, "has filled our country with spies" and "has paid them to destroy our property and to try and influence our people to plot against the government." We must insure, it stated, that they "shall not conquer the world."[54]

Much more troubling was the fear that the enemy was infecting students with its insidious propaganda through schoolteachers. In April 1918 the Orleans Parish school board voted 5 to 0 for a resolution that dropped from its employment rolls every teacher and staff member who was a citizen of Germany or Austria, regardless of his or her record, in order to address "the aggressiveness of certain teachers in spreading German propaganda."[55] The NSL wanted coaches to be vetted as well "lest there be any man or woman in charge of the youth of our country whose thoughts or expressions might be tinctured with the slightest trace of disloyalty."[56]

At its January 23rd, 1918, meeting, Tulane's board of administrators also resolved to immediately remove enemy aliens from its faculty and to require that all new hires "furnish satisfactory evidence of unreserved loyalty to the Government of the United States." For these people, it was guilty until they proved their innocence. That same meeting produced a more volatile decision. Because it was the "fundamental duty of American universities to teach love of country and loyalty to its institutions," each faculty member was immediately required to state his or her country of citizenship and then to sign a loyalty oath to "uphold the Government of the United States in the prosecution of the war against Germany and her Allies." Refusal to sign was "construed . . . as an act of disloyalty of an American citizen or an enemy alien."[57]

The mandate, predictably, was not well received by the Tulane faculty. Some were openly incensed at the board's hardline stance, and a few simply refused to sign. Charlton Beattie from the law school quit his professorship with a sharp rebuke on February 4th, stating how insulted he was as a descendent of men who fought in the American Revolution. (See Appendix C.)[58]Three others, all physicians on the faculty of the medical school, also ignored the oath. Two of them, however, were listed on the faculty roster years after 1918. There exists no record of what action was taken against the third. Three more who agreed to sign the oath either resigned or did not have their contracts renewed after a board-appointed committee investigated rumors of possible disloyalty. Two were teachers at Newcomb College, the women's school closely associated with Tulane. The other, George Beyer, was a veteran biology professor at the university.

The vote not to extend another contract to them was 11 to 1. The lone dissenting voter, Charles Rosen, believed that each of them should be granted a hearing before any action was taken. All were denied that privilege. A resolution from the student body at Newcomb protesting the dismissal of German citizen Heinrich Maurer, their popular history professor, was introduced to the board. It read, in part, that his firing was "arbitrary and inconsiderate" and an "irretrievable wrong" committed against a man who "contributed materially to the curriculum and the spirit of the college."[59]

The petition did not move the board members. They slammed the door on it, deeming it "unnecessary to reply to the communication."[60] It did, however, develop suspicions that the Newcomb student body might itself be pro-German, the protest being judged as too compassionate. Consequently, Newcomb's Alumni Association felt compelled to issue a proclamation declaring support not only for the government's war efforts, but also for the board's decision to remove the professor.[61]

Professor Beyer's case was especially tragic. He wrote a letter to the board begging it to reconsider, given his long service to the university and his unswerving loyalty to the US. A thirty-seven-year resident of the US and a naturalized US citizen, Beyer, German-born, admitted making statements before US entry into the war that might have seemed disloyal to some, but they "assumed a meaning and significance unintended." Since he was never informed about what those statements were, however, he could not properly defend himself. He wrote that he had never been a member of any Germanic society, was married to an American who worked for the Red Cross, had a brother-in-law serving in France, and was a proud Liberty Bond holder. "My aspirations and ambitions and interests are all completely American." The professor closed by digging deep: "I am now fifty-six years old; twenty-six years of the prime of my life has been lived in loyal, devoted, and unremitting service to Tulane University. My happiness and my life have been my work at Tulane. Today, that has been blotted out." He implored the board for the simple opportunity to appear before it in order to make his case. After "a lengthy discussion" at the July board meeting, a motion was made and seconded for Beyer's letter to be received and recorded in the minutes "without action." The voice vote on the motion again passed almost unanimously except for one—Rosen again voting nay, objecting to the denial of due process.[62]

The busy Camp Street office of the NSL was alerted, most likely from a student or a parent, about a Newcomb German- and English-literature teacher, and an investigation of her "disloyal" statements was launched in April of 1918. Miss Anna Veters, according to the report, raised eyebrows when she remained in her classroom during a flag raising ceremony on campus that all faculty members were "expected" to attend with their students. The report went on to say that Veters had once before stigmatized flag raising as a "war dance." In another instance, she admitted to six students (their names and addresses were listed) that her heart was "not with America because my mind is against it." And according to several seniors, when they asked her to write a note and sign their yearbooks, she said she would as long as they allowed her to do so in German.[63] Given that she was a German teacher, this should not have surprised anyone. But because of the uneasy climate hovering over the campus, she too was dismissed.

German social groups, also struck by the backlash, slowly vanished as the date of US entry approached. Before then, those organizations were active in support of German and Austrian military relief agencies for military dependents and other war-related charities. In the spring of 1915, *Die Deutsche Gesellschaft* sponsored its most elaborate high-profile affair—a two-day bazaar at the Athenaeum to raise money for the German and Austrian Red Cross. In return for the twenty-five-cent admission, German bands, choral groups, food, and, of course, beer awaited them in Bavarian decorated halls lined with dozens of booths. It was quite a success, clearing a $7,000 profit.

One unique feature offered was the showing of authentic footage of German infantry in combat. The film, sanctioned by Berlin, included an actual assault on a French village with graphic scenes of the dead and wounded, a French airplane being shot down by camouflaged German ground fire, and the shelling and destruction of a French fortification. There were also scenes of German soldiers distributing food to Belgian refugees. The *Picayune* reported that the crowd "showed much enthusiasm" when the Kaiser appeared on the screen inspecting an infantry formation. The German Society's president, Hans Forscheimer, estimated that the swollen audience numbered four thousand, including many "full-blooded Americans," who were "literally pressed together" in the festivities. The propaganda film was so popular that it opened at the Crescent Theater later in the week to more overflow crowds. Notwithstanding the profits generated, Forscheimer maintained that the event was a milestone of another kind. Perhaps revealing his annoyance at having to live in the shadow of the French fleur-de-lis, he wrote in the afterglow of the festival that the German presence in New Orleans was "appreciated for the first time."[64]

The bazaar would prove to be the swan song for the German Society. Nine days later twelve hundred civilians would die when the *Lusitania* was torpedoed, and along with that liner sank any promise resident Germans may have had to improve their increasingly tentative relationship with the rest of the city's population. When war broke out in 1914, the society's fidelity to its homeland was clear. "We are confident that Germany," the president wrote in his annual report, "in the power of her manhood, and loyalty to the emperor and the empire, will, with its allies as before, repel the enemies," and will "emerge victorious from the unjustly imposed heavy struggle."[65] But as the US crept closer to war, membership began to dwindle.

Charitable fundraising continued under a newly formed German Red Cross Aid Society. Members conducted a Christmas festival in 1916 similar to the German Society bazaar held the year before. Auctions were conducted for dozens of different items, including everything from postcards depicting scenes of Germany to two tickets for a cruise to Cuba. At the end of the evening, three five-hundred-mark German war bonds were offered. In comparison to the 1915 bazaar, there were no references to the German war machine.[66] After the US war declaration, however, events like this would be unthinkable.

Die Deutsche Gesellschaft was compelled to assume a much lower profile once hostilities began. Then in 1918, another setback—the society's president Hans Forscheimer, following the resignation of his predecessor Paul Roh, was also forced to resign. Forscheimer and three other wealthy lumber exporters were arrested, accused of violating the Espionage Act. The society's annual report attempted to conceal the magnitude of the incident, stating that their leader was "forced by the circumstances" to leave office. But the statement could not camouflage the facts from the newspapers.[67]

The four, who arrived in New Orleans shortly after the war began, had been in regular telegraphic contact with the former German ambassador to the US., Johann von Bernstorff, who was himself suspected of leading a spy ring before his ouster in 1917. It was believed that Forscheimer and the others were sent by Bernstorff to the city for nefarious purposes. Letters from Paul Roh, the former German consul in New Orleans, were also discovered, lionizing the businessmen for being "pillars of Germanism" and suggesting propaganda methods for them to use. Investigators believed that Roh, after resigning in 1917 in disgrace from the German Society's leadership, maneuvered Forscheimer into the presidency even though the organization's bylaws required officers to be US-born. Moreover, one of the four men, an officer in the German Red Cross Association of New Orleans, corresponded with former Professor Heinrich Maurer of Newcomb College, implicating Maurer as being in league with the culprits.

Forscheimer and the other enemy aliens were detained after weeks of undercover work stemming from seized personal effects and documents found, with the help of a safe expert, in Forscheimer's office. A hidden dictophone was planted behind a bookcase, which revealed more evidence of propaganda activity directed from abroad. Several wagonloads of evidence were recovered from the men's homes. As further proof of their pro-German sentiments, it was said that the foursome gathered the night of the *Lusitania* sinking for a celebratory dinner. Division Superintendent Forrest Pendleton of the Justice Department called the men some of the "most dangerous

Germans . . . in the U.S." He also stated that the arrests were handled in secrecy so as not to arouse the public, yet word had somehow spread that the four were sequestered at the DeSoto Hotel until charges were filed. They were then locked up at the House of Detention, but fear of mob retribution forced them to be moved in an unmarked car to a more secure facility at Jackson Barracks. Pendleton admitted to the "great public sentiment in this city against these men and threats of lynching have been heard."[68]

Stunned by the accusations, remaining members of the society discussed suspending or even closing their organization entirely. But they finally decided to "remain actively alive" despite the crisis, especially since the US Immigration Service enlisted their help in the so-called Americanization movement meant to integrate native Germans into the American mainstream, already an ongoing mission of the society since its inception.[69] Its efforts now took on new meaning and importance. By husbanding their resources to this end, it would not only be doing a service to the recipients, but, remaining members hoped, it would also provide them with some defense from scrutiny and suspicion. As for Forscheimer and his partners, they and thirty-one other enemy aliens detained in New Orleans were eventually escorted under heavy guard to the internment camp at Fort Oglethorpe, Georgia. Once the Armistice was concluded, they were released.

The German Society's work to assimilate its fellow Germans into the local culture may well have been sincere, but the arrest of its president, the society's second to be connected with the enemy, shattered any hope that the organization would escape the public's conviction that it could not be trusted. Not surprisingly, the fraternity became another victim of the war with these arrests. Two of its recent presidents, Roh and Forscheimer, were both found to be colluding with the enemy. How many more of its members were disciples of theirs? Its minute book from April, 1918, to November, 1921, is blank, signaling a three-year period of dormancy for the once respected organization.

By the war's end, German ethnicity, for the most part, had been gutted from New Orleans. What remained of the tightly knit community was devastated by cultural genocide. Dr. H. A. Gabert, president of the postwar German Society, resigned his post in 1921, citing reasons of health. But in a written statement to the members, he bitterly laid bare the true reason, perhaps more comfortable with his revelation in 1921 than he would have been in 1917 or 1918.

Three years after the war, the wounds were yet unhealed. Anti-German sentiments continued to linger. Gabert identified the spoken sound of the German language as the "red cape" that intensified the wrath against them.

They were "surrounded by spies," he wrote, and "everyone who was anti-German was a secret service man and practiced his patriotism by laying all possible roadblocks in front of the Germans." They were constantly under siege, suggesting that the German people in New Orleans were playing a survival game. In an extraordinary statement with significance beyond the surface, he intimated that the German community's public persona of loyalty to the US during the war years—its participation in Liberty Loan drives, its effort to wear American patriotism on its sleeves—was merely a ruse of survival. Once the war ended, the "masks" fell away and they were able to reconvene with their German souls. "We were among wolves," he admitted, "and had to howl with them."[70]

Chapter 11

HUNTING WITCHES

The American Protective League

Since the 1915 Lusitania attack, public opinion began tilting more noticeably in the direction of the Entente allies of Britain and France. The 1916 explosions at New Jersey's Black Tom munitions facility, magnified thereafter by the accumulation of mysterious incidents at defense plants in Kingsland, New Jersey, and Eddystone, Pennsylvania, and a number of suspicious fires on ships headed for Europe, did nothing to temper the outrage directed at Germany—this despite a lack of evidence at the time linking Berlin to these crimes. Many voices, like that of the idolized xenophobe, former president Teddy Roosevelt, became more convinced than ever of the Kaiser's long western reach. His fist-pumping oratory, vilifying Wilson's policy of caution and warning of the collapse of western democracies, was reaching a wider and wider audience. Examples of Prussian *schrecklichkeit* or frightfulness on the Western Front blotted the front pages of the nation's newspapers day after day, no less so in New Orleans, whose three major dailies promoted military readiness. After the publication of Berlin's Zimmerman Telegram, threatening war with the US through its proxy Mexico, the city's residents were wired and worried. The contagion of fear was spreading.

Emotions were already high even before war was declared. In New Orleans, for example, one man received twenty-nine days in jail for standing in front of a residence that displayed the American flag, screaming out that it was "a dirty old rag" and making derogatory remarks about the president. The forty-eight-year-old was jailed for twenty-nine days, charged with disturbing the peace. Still, the judge was infuriated, wishing he could have given him a year or more in the pen.[1]

Once Congress declared war, the nation's intelligence agencies began to rapidly expand. Because of the anticipated surge in German subterfuge at home, however, US attorney general Thomas Gregory urged Americans everywhere to act as "volunteer detectives," and district attorneys were told to accept reports of "even the most informal and confidential nature" so that "citizens should feel free to bring their suspicions" to authorities. After all, the barbarians—the Huns—were at the gate. Appeals like this coupled with the need many had to profess their patriotism led to an enormous response. In one month following the war declaration, the Justice Department was receiving one thousand accusations of disloyalty from around the country each day, and in May of the following year, that number had grown to fifteen hundred a day! Gregory was no fool, dismissing the great majority of these reports as "utterly worthless," coming from "hysterical" people who were motivated by "malice and ill-will."[2] Yet the response itself, whatever the motivation, revealed a vigilantism lodged deeply in the American psyche that would exhibit itself throughout not only the rest of the war, but also early into the next decade.

Albert M. Briggs, a wealthy, forty-four-year-old pro-war advertising executive in Chicago, wanted to do his part. In February of 1917, no doubt hearing Gregory's appeal, he offered to help local Justice Department officials search for questionable German nationals in the Chicago area by providing agents with cars and volunteer drivers to augment their poorly funded department. Encouraged by this program's success, the portly businessman traveled to Washington to pitch the idea of a nationwide extension of his project to Gregory and Chief Bruce Bielaski of the Bureau of Intelligence (BI), later the FBI. The plan was to create an adjunct organization to Bielaski's bureau, made up of hyperpatriotic deputies of good character, who would assist the BI in providing intelligence on German spies or saboteurs throughout the country.

It seemed a reasonable proposal, given that the Bureau employed fewer than three hundred men at the beginning of the war with little hope that Congressional funding would improve thereafter. Besides, an alliance between government and civilians was an attractive strategy and one that mirrored the American tradition of mutual self-defense, beginning with the minutemen militia during the Revolution. Safeguarding the nation from a threat was, for ruggedly individualistic Americans, a civic responsibility stamped on their souls—thus the concept of a "citizen's arrest." The romantic notion of frontier justice was reawakened.

Wilson was sensitive to the charge that many people were only lukewarm in their support of the war. Widespread volunteerism from ordinary people would counter the claim that US participation in the war was a top-down affair driven only by the White House and a divided Congress. The president and his cabinet therefore approved the project, so Briggs and two friends, Victor Elting and Charles Frey, passionate patriots themselves, dropped their business obligations in Chicago and moved to the capital to open the headquarters of the newly named American Protective League (APL) as its unsalaried directors.

In March of 1917, the organization was ready to recruit its home-front posse, armed with an introductory message to local Bureau chiefs from Bielaski, which vaguely outlined the role of the APL in obtaining useful intelligence. The exact functions and limits of this free manpower, however, were not stipulated. Bielaski's cover letter simply assured the chiefs that the APL footmen would be ready to assist them "in any work you may assign to them."[3] America's self-anointed "guardians of the flag" were locked and loaded, ready to assume their first mission, even if it was unclear what they would be asked to do. But it hardly mattered. Their country called.

It did not take long for thousands to apply. Soon the League would become the largest intelligence gathering operation in US history. By July 1917 there were already 112,000 League trackers working in 600 cities and towns across America.[4] Many who joined were middle-aged or older, politically conservative white men already engaged in law enforcement or civic work. Others were deferred from the draft and wanted to contribute to the war effort by becoming operatives, often on a part-time basis. Their membership was kept secret, allowing them to function efficiently simply by listening while employed in their normal jobs.

By the war's end, over 260,000 Americans became APL deputies working in 1,400 local units.[5] They were issued ID cards, code numbers, and rather pretentious badges, purchased for 75 cents, with "Secret Service" engraved in large letters in the center. Treasury Secretary William McAdoo, whose office managed the Secret Service, was understandably furious. In a harsh letter to Gregory, copied to the president, he protested that the badges deliberately deceived the public and was "astonished" that the AG sanctioned the APL. In the same letter, McAdoo compared the League to the Revolution's Sons of Liberty, which "committed grave abuses and injustices." The League, he determined, "contains the same evil potentialities." The APL soon issued new badges, replacing the words "Secret Service" with the less pompous "Auxiliary to the Department of Justice."[6]

The badge itself, resembling those the police wore, undoubtedly attracted many to the League. Most were well-meaning men who wanted to play-act as detectives, their authority backed by the flash of that small but exclusive piece of metal in their wallets. The organization also boasted a letterhead that read, "Organized with the Approval and Operating under the Direction of the Department of Justice, Bureau of Investigation." All of this seemed very official and enhanced the status of the volunteers who, while paying their own expenses, considered themselves the nation's second line of defense against conspirators. Vigilantism, it appeared, was now sanctioned by the federal government.

Briggs, along with Frey and Elting, envisioned that information would be collected on the activities of foreign government contractors or persons, native or otherwise, unfriendly to the US. They quickly recommended that the local offices create divisions whereby agents would specialize in hunting spies in areas like industry, utilities, banks, hotels, transportation, finance, or education. The amateur detectives were ideally placed in the divisions where personal connections were already established. It was in the workplace where they could keep their ears to the ground without causing suspicion.

Specific instructions were lacking as to how to collect the intelligence, how to distinguish hearsay from solid information, or what exactly to do if they witnessed an act of disloyalty in progress. Charles Weinberger, a New Orleans business and civic leader and chief of the New Orleans division, admitted that the "exact purposes and nature of some of the League's activities were not thoroughly understood by the membership."[7] The nation, therefore, was rife with tens of thousands of unqualified, ardent laymen who implicated and detained forty thousand civilians and instigated an astounding three million loyalty investigations during America's nineteen months of war.[8] Some self-important sleuths undoubtedly continued to identify themselves as members of the Secret Service, exploiting the ambiguity of their roles. Wide latitude was allowed to the investigators, making the League a dangerous loose cannon in a country where personal liberties were embedded in the Constitution.

While Bielaski never specifically allowed APL members to arm themselves or make arrests, he blinked whenever understaffed local police forces gave permission for them to do so. More mixed signals. And if any of them tried to detain someone, enter a house to ferret for evidence, or open personal mail, all of which happened repeatedly, they, as volunteers, could not be disciplined. Dictaphones for surreptitiously recording conversations were often issued to them along with cameras for photographing documents. Permission to use these devices were supposed to be obtained through the local superintendent, but because the APL was so decentralized, proper use of this equipment could easily be overlooked. Badges were often used improperly as well, acting in New Orleans as a sort of permanent voucher for French Opera House seats, streetcar rides, or maybe a free cold beer at a saloon.[9] The badge packed a punch.

No training was provided, however desperate the need. Nor was there any Congressional oversight of their activities. Briggs and the League directors did not even possess a complete list of who had joined his organization![10]

Here was plain evidence of the organization's lack of discipline and its haphazard recruiting. Its officers at its headquarters in Washington, along with local APL directors, were nothing more than dislocated administrators rather than supervisors. The League depended on home-grown, autonomous chiefs to monitor the activities of their own lieutenants. This was often impossible, or the local bureau chiefs were simply indifferent to unacceptable behaviors, excusing illegal acts in the interest of national security while using the rhetoric of democracy even though the civil rights of hundreds were violated daily.

The war pressed everyone hard for conformity, and most prudent detractors of the APL were muted in their criticisms, afraid to raise their heads too high for fear of being labeled as unpatriotic. No League agent was ever prosecuted for making a false arrest. Forty years later, this same paralysis would bedevil many Americans once again during the McCarthy era.

It was not simply the absence of training that percolated these problems. In the beginning, there existed no screening process, oddly, for prospective employees. The application for membership could be completed in one minute or less. There were a mere five questions requiring a simple yes or no answer. The applicant was asked if he was married, if he was a military veteran, if he spoke a foreign language, if he objected to leaving his hometown, and whether he understood that there was no monetary compensation. If the application was approved, an oath was signed swearing allegiance to the Constitution.[11]

At first there was no query about a prior criminal record, no educational or age requirements (women were eventually barred from membership), and no résumé was requested. It was a fast track. Very fast. Once one applied and received an identification card and number, he was ready to hunt down those who threatened the flag. The more people out in the street listening, the more intelligence could be collected. This speedy procedure was amended somewhat in September of 1917, when background clearances were finally mandated after state APL directors complained that standards for membership were too low for their hungry sentinels.[12] But training was never forthcoming.

An agent either typed his report on a standard form or on a plain sheet of paper before delivery to the office of the APL and then to the Justice Department's desk, if warranted. There was clearly no training given about what should be included in a report or how it should be formatted. Often they were unsigned with only the operative's code number listed. Occasionally, the name of the person under suspicion was identified in the report. Instructions to maintain confidentiality were either not spelled out or ignored. Facts about the suspect's age, occupation, or background were accompanied by the agent's own judgement concerning his conduct—even when the report identified no specific law violation. Many of the documents were nothing more than a summary of hearsay from a second party.

The first issue of the *Spy Glass*, the official organ of the APL, outlined and applauded the provisions of the Espionage Act, which punished anyone who interfered with the military or supported the nation's enemies. Its new cousin, the infamous Sedition Act, laid harsh penalties on anyone found guilty of making false statements interfering with the prosecution of the war; insulting or abusing the US government, the flag, the Constitution, or the military; or agitating against the production of war materials.[13] No distinction was made between the native-born and the alien in either piece of legislation, the bulletin emphasized. It was the action itself that violated the laws and not the perpetrator. Further, it instructed, in order to convict someone of sedition, one did not suffer the burden of proving intent. "Like murder or burglary, espionage and sedition are positive crimes." More latitude would now be allowed for the APL to perform its work. "For the first time we have an inclusive law from which to operate," the bulletin gloated, "a law broad enough in its scope and classification to cover and define as serious crimes a multitude of offenses which were classed as minor by our peace-time code but actually offered serious hindrances to this country's military operations and preparations."[14]

With these new weapons in their holsters, the APL's leaders urged that "prompt and aggressive enforcement . . . is of the highest importance in suppressing disloyal utterances and preventing breaches of peace." That was all the encouragement needed. Badges began to flash. By 1921, 2,162 individuals were tried under these laws. Nearly half—1,055—were convicted.[15] Particularly troublesome to the willing deputies were conversations that lauded the German war machine or criticisms of the government or the draft. But then there were the more innocuous statements that nevertheless drew attention from the rank and file. Anyone critical of the Liberty Loan drives or even those who made sarcastic statements about a patriotic song or parade were fair game.

That is exactly what happened to the wealthy seventy-one-year-old William Edenborn, the German-born railroad magnate and New Orleans resident. In April of 1918, as a leader in the German American community, he was asked to make a few remarks at an Americanization rally in town meant to prevail upon immigrants to conform to Washington's war policy. In his speech, he assured the audience that Germany would never launch an attack on US soil. "It would take a maritime nation to do that because America is surrounded by water." He continued in a thinly veiled reference to England that she, not Germany, was more likely to invade the US because of her navy.[16]

Those lines created a furor. Mayor Behrman condemned his words in an address to Moose Lodge members, saying that it didn't matter how high one's standing was in the community. No one should "stand on a public platform in this city and criticize any of our allies. Speaking with punctuated deliberation, he promised "to know where everybody stands on this question of loyalty in New Orleans."[17]

The nationalistic American Security League (ASL) immediately issued a resolution outlining Edenborn's "seditious treason" by propagandizing Germany and "breathing the arrogant spirit of Prussianism" in a most "cunning, insidious, and demoralizing manner." There was more. Edenborn, it stated, had both an "open and covert" relationship with Hans Halle, an alien earlier arrested in the city for manufacturing bombs intended for allied cargo ships. Also included was what the ASL believed was proof of his disloyalty—his contribution to the YMCA's war fund was but $2.50, an insult considering his great wealth.[18] The Pickwick Club's governing board expelled him the next day in a unanimous vote, ordering that any dues he had paid for the unexpired term be returned to him. Behrman was present at their meeting when the resolution passed. He asked the gathering to tone down its public rebuke of him, worried that it may incite mob violence.[19]

Edenborn also made the mistake of naming one of his rail stations "Wilhelm," although he quickly insisted that it was not named after the Kaiser and that it was the only German name on his lines. But a letter to the *Picayune* by an alert resident revealed that there were actually twenty-one German names (each one published in the newspaper) on the railroad's timetable, including Manheim, Emden, and Essen. The writer hoped that they would be replaced with "good Anglo-Saxon names."[20] Edenborn responded that he had no problem renaming the stations and that his purpose in doing so was to distinguish them from those names already in use elsewhere. That was hardly a satisfactory answer in the charged environment surrounding him. Claiming that he had named them before war was declared did not blunt the furor.

As tensions rose, word spread on the streets that "something would happen" to the railroad tycoon after arriving in town from a meeting. Would he be taken away for retribution? Sure enough, a large crowd waited at the Terminal Station on Canal Street for the train to pull in. But they would be disappointed. In order to avoid an incident like others across the country where angry mobs dealt cruelly with those suspected of treason, the feds arrested Edenborn at a station just outside of the city. He was handled in secrecy, the police using a fake name when processing him. The millionaire soon posted $10,000 in bail, insisting that he was never disloyal "to his country" and that he never knew Hans Halle. A grand jury later refused to indict him after three days of investigation.[21]

The Edenborn saga merited press exposure across the country. Other "seditious" arrests received much less attention, but they do serve to clarify how one's freedom of speech was marginalized during the war years. A young railroad flagman named Gerdes was arrested at his home on Burgundy Street for returning a questionnaire, perhaps sent by his draft board, with these unacceptable remarks: "I won't answer any of these questions, and no one can make me answer them. I am a free American, and everyone else can go to hell. Hell is where your President Wilson should be. I would rather fight for the Kaiser.... Put this in the papers and me in jail if you like. I don't care." That's exactly where he was sent, with no bail, to await a grand jury.[22] An informant, presumably an APL member, reported to the US Attorney's office that a man named Kliene was "extremely bitter" in his denunciation of the US and was trying to solicit fellow Black workers to support Germany, even betting $10 that the Battle of Verdun would be a German victory.[23] There is no record of Kleine's disposition after the report.

The hysteria continued. Well-intentioned but overly alarmed letters sent to the APL were often too frivolous even for its eager agents to consider. One wrote that the German keeper of the Chalmette Cemetery just "didn't look right" and could be "abrupt." Another accused a Catholic priest of concealing an iron cross on his person.[24]

A particularly diligent New Orleans APL member wrote two one-page reports on June 4th, 1918, on two different suspects. One was named Krist, known to be vocal in showing his support for Germany before US entry, although the agent admitted that "he did not recall exactly the nature of his remarks, except that they were in his opinion, seditious." It was signed simply, "#849." The second report was a summary of a conversation between #849 and the suspect who worked as a camouflage painter in a government shipbuilding yard. Nothing in the report indicated why the report was written. Nevertheless, #849 ended his narrative with this: "I full [sic] believe that the Subject while not overly Patriotic, is not as Loyal as he one should be, in view of his being associated with Government work and receiving the remuneration . . . as a result of this."

Two months later, #849 sent to headquarters a profile of a building contractor named John Henry who was having a home completed in Waveland, Mississippi. When work concluded, the laborers proudly hoisted an American flag on the property as Henry was visiting the site, but "the subject did not take off his hat." This apparently angered the workers who hauled down the flag, forced him to kiss it, and eventually compelled him to leave his home in New Orleans. #849 attempted to harvest more information from those who knew him, but nothing substantive turned up.[25]

Sometimes the accused resisted. The APL was alerted when, at a party at a Baronne Street home, the hostess gave vent to several cheers for the Kaiser. One of her guests must have taken exception and called upon the APL to intervene. She was pulled from her home and taken in hysterics to League headquarters. After arriving, she reportedly became unhinged and began to break furniture, holding fifteen League men at bay and defying any one of them to touch her. None was bold enough to do so. Police reinforcements had to be called in before the combative woman was finally subdued, bound, and held for federal authorities.[26]

While the *Spy Glass* rejoiced over the passage of the Espionage and Sedition Acts, there were snares to avoid. Both of these laws were vague and therefore dangerous as they could be interpreted however one wished. This was especially true of the Sedition Act. Lacking years of jurisprudence, injustices were inevitable within those gray areas. Gregory understood the hazard of allowing the brigade of APL provocateurs carte blanche in helping to scout for violators of these controversial laws. The attorney general urged discretion, searching for that elusive sweet spot between stimulating the APL soldiers to continue their mission and releasing them to run amuck over the Constitution. In order to temper the League's most overzealous rogues, he issued this warning: "It should not be permitted to become the medium whereby efforts are made to suppress honest, legitimate criticism of the administration or discussion of government policies; nor should it become a medium for personal feuds or persecution.... Protection of loyal persons from unjust suspicion and persecution is quite as important as suppression of disloyalty."[27]

Here was a plain defense of the First Amendment. Yet by the very act of creating the APL, a person's freedom of speech was almost certain to come under attack. At the very least, the Sedition Act silenced many who may have wanted to make derogatory or sarcastic remarks about the government but were unwilling to chance it for fear of being overheard by guardians of the nation's conscience. The warning statement may well have been the politically correct thing to write, or it could simply have also been a veiled attempt to establish plausible deniability if Briggs or the League office came under attack from civil libertarians. In spite of these noble remarks, monitoring the loosely managed officers was impossible. Even Assistant Attorney General John O'Brian was dismayed with the ambiguity of the legislation, which covered, he lamented, "all degrees of conduct and speech, serious and trifling alike," and "gave the dignity of treason to what were often neighborhood quarrels or barroom brawls."[28] Sacrificing these liberties was the price the US must pay, it was thought, to win the war.

Scores of New Orleanians daring (or foolish) enough to express contempt for the war were dogged relentlessly by the League's Praetorian Guard. A salesman who sold rifle covers to soldiers was "obnoxiously pro-German in his expressions," and a "dangerous individual." The suspect apparently said that the US had no business in the war. "Damned shame America is fighting for Wall Street." He was brought in for interrogation. A St. Charles Avenue tailor's rather vague "pro-German remarks," whatever they were, and his refusal to employ anyone with French heritage, was disclosed to Weinberger's office. Often a report was triggered simply for possessing anything printed in German.[29]

Imprecise accusations often led to combing through a person's residence or office—without a search warrant. An APL agent, allowed by the manager to unlock and forage through an apartment on Magazine Street, found incriminating material—a postcard photo of the Kaiser on the mantle, a magazine called *The Fatherland*, a similar publication entitled *The Deutsch-Amerika*, and a book, *What Germany Wants*. The man claimed under questioning that his mother had sent him the postcard and that the periodicals were subscribed to before the war. During questioning, the individual's boss robustly defended him, and he was exonerated. Another landlady provided the key to an apartment occupied by her tenant so it could be searched, claiming simply that he was "acting suspiciously."[30]

In the absence of any instruction in the complex art of counterespionage, the *Spy Glass* attempted to furnish the League's deputies with a few simple tactics in intelligence gathering. It was easy enough to establish trust with coworkers or acquaintances, but gleaning intelligence from strangers was another matter entirely. It recommended, therefore, that its operatives pose as salesmen, newspaper reporters, or school truancy investigators, creating a pretense for conversation. Building trust was essential, so patience was needed. The newsletter recommended that a dossier be built on the witness or subject under suspicion before turning it over to the local APL chief.[31] Most often, however, the information collected was typed in a short report before delivery, for it was eventually determined that thick files were unnecessary—there was little or no enemy espionage activity to report.

Briggs had originally conceived of his organization as a vital adjunct to undermanned federal sleuths seeking to harpoon German spies. But by the end of 1917, he and his associates realized that they were chasing phantoms. They had taken their lead from President Wilson, whose war message to Congress on April 2nd announced to all that the enemy was in the nation's midst. "From the very outset of the present war," he claimed, "Germany has filled our unsuspecting communities and even our offices of government with spies and set criminal intrigues everywhere afoot . . . against our industries and commerce."

It was an irresponsible charge, for there was no evidence that communities were "filled with spies." They were not. Nor was there any indication that governmental agencies were being compromised by the enemy. By mid-1917, Wilson's alarmist words may have been devised to create a sense of urgency, maybe even fear, among the members of Congress where isolationist sentiment still ran strong. The administration had hoped that a vote on a war declaration would have had as few dissenters as possible, serving to broadcast a communion of purpose between the two branches.

Hyperbole or not, the speech indeed fired a shot that was heard loud and clear in the APL headquarters. One APL chief wrote to Attorney General Gregory in frustration, "There is quite a good deal of hysteria in the country about German spies. If you will kindly box up and send me one to a dozen, I will pay you very handsomely for your trouble. We are looking for them constantly, but it is a little difficult to shoot them until they have been found."[32]

Rather than concede that his growing membership was becoming irrelevant, Briggs shifted his agency's initiative, repurposing the considerable muscle of the APL toward targets less seductive than espionage. During most of 1918, therefore, Briggs pledged assistance in rationing food and war materials, suppressing vice near military installations, and unearthing disloyalty. The League was a rapidly evolving organism.

Weinberger received a mountain of tips from his scouts who were becoming, in essence, the food- and fuel-conservation police. Bakeries, cafes, and hotel restaurants appearing to be in violation of the nation's food management guidelines were reported. So too were businesses and residents who hoarded coal. Keen eyes spotted Sunday pleasure drivers who were told to save fuel. By his own estimate, 1,471 cases of hoarding or wastefulness occupied Weinberger's small army of men for the duration of the war. (See Appendix A.)

In January of 1918, Weinberger's New Orleans division included only thirty-eight members. At the war's end, however, it boasted a robust office consisting of 2,097 staff members and field enforcers deployed into three branches. The local APL's Bureau of Investigation was responsible for enemy alien issues, disloyalty, sedition, and pro-German propaganda. Hotels, restaurants, banks, shipping, and retail businesses were surveilled by APL volunteers who searched for conservation violators. There was also a Selective Service Bureau whose mission was to help with draft investigations, appeals, and reclassifications. Four APL members occupied chairs on the draft boards themselves.[33]

Gradually, however, enforcement of the Sedition Act demanded most of their energy. In fact, the New Orleans office alone handled 2,952 cases labeled propaganda, disloyalty, and sedition. (See Appendix A.) Weinberger and his men were bombarded with letters from well-intentioned folks who had seen or overheard something that they believed may be disloyal. They were encouraged to do so by groups such as the militaristic American Defense Society whose honorary president was the waspish former president, Colonel Roosevelt.

Often, African Americans were specifically targeted. One agent, for example, was sent to learn more about an upcoming meeting of the Negro Civic League in New Orleans whose agenda had fallen into the hands of the APL. The planned discussion topic, "Better Treatment of Enemy Aliens," begged for an investigation. Weinberger wanted the names of the discussion's facilitator and any who were in attendance, thinking that the topic may generate seditious talk. Another anonymous League investigator reported that two white ladies were apparently attempting to organize a union for Black cooks and restaurant workers in town. Challenges to authority were believed to be outside the boundary of patriotism and therefore fair game for further examination.[34]

More thoughtful leaders in Washington hoped to stamp out the burglarizing, slandering, and other embarrassing APL behaviors. The Louisiana Council of Defense hastened to help, devoting two bulletins in July 1918 entirely to the problem, even though its particular mission—coordinating industry and resources—had no direct connection to matters of civil liberty. Suppression of disloyalty must only be achieved by "arousing" patriotism, announced John Marshall, secretary for Louisiana's branch of the COD. In the two publications, Marshall wisely insisted that loyalty can never be encouraged by "forcing a show of patriotism." Unlawful actions against those who may simply be apathetic toward the war were "deplorable." Care must be taken, the secretary instructed, "to distinguish between . . . misunderstanding or legitimate differences of opinion" and sedition.[35]

Marshall was blessed with willing companions in the New Orleans Association of Commerce and the Louisiana Suffrage Party, for each was savvy enough to advocate a "honey rather than vinegar" blueprint for grooming Louisiana's German nationals. The suffragists set aside their primary goal of a voting-rights amendment to assist the Red Cross, train women to farm, and facilitate the placement of qualified women in jobs vacated by men called to military duty. It also promoted Americanization as one of its missions, preferring this strategy over the ironhanded methods of the APL. The party recognized how difficult it would be for aliens to see the war through an American lens, a situation, it predicted, that would insure a state of intolerance and antagonism. With this in mind, members offered to teach classes to willing aliens in order to nurture a better understanding of the nation's war motives and assist them in the naturalization process.[36]

Suspected acts of sedition were also handled by military intelligence personnel if the matter was directly connected to active-duty service members. A December 1918 lecture at Camp Beauregard to Black troops awaiting discharge ended badly. Speaking at a YMCA facility on post, a Dr. Ira Landrith was invited to speak to an African American labor battalion on their approaching return to civilian life, but he "went off on a tangent." A report confirmed that Landrith told them that once they returned home, they should "take orders from no one," free as they would be from white authority. Moreover, since prohibition was imminent, they should "get drunk now" before it became the law. The YMCA's invitation to him at first seemed innocent enough, but his talk "had a most unsavory effect" on the battalion's morale and discipline, the men refusing to obey orders and threatening to riot or "desert in squads." Nothing happened, but innuendo throughout the South continued to associate African Americans with tepid support for the war. These and other incidents were indications of how racial tension and doubt continued to be a flash point throughout the war and into the years which followed.[37]

The post office in New Orleans was another useful tool in the suppression of words that might incite racial disorder. Its censors were quite vigilant, intercepting and holding without delivery, for example, a newspaper that printed a story about the National Colored Liberty Congress, an organization that pressed for a federal antilynching law, the abolition of Black disfranchisement, and what it called "caste discrimination." The government, it opined, "is strangely indifferent to the many wrongs and injustices done to our people." Inspectors also opened a letter from a "Clarise" on Pitt Street to her aunt. "German propaganda," she determined, "is not lacking here, the city being full of spies who make the blacks believe that they will be put back into slavery after the war." She went on to claim that the majority of them "refused to work for white people." The censor noted, however, that her claim was entirely specious.

That same theme arose in another letter seized for analysis, this one to a brother from his sister on St. Ann Street. Moaning that they were "having an awful time here," she wrote that "if things keep up, the negroes are going to rule the whites, for they are making some awful remarks about what they intend to do when the whites go to war." The message went on the say that the streets are unsafe. "It looks as if they are taking all the good ones and leaving the no-account ones here." An intelligence officer commented that this was the second such letter he had seen that alluded to Negroes threatening whites or refusing to work, but "so far as I am informed, there is no such feeling here in New Orleans." A letter coming through New Orleans from Mexico addressed to Marcus Garvey's leftist newspaper, the *Negro World*, invited suspicion. Inside, a poem was discovered that postal inspectors found seditious. It read, in part:

> We will endure the taunts no more.
> Turn us loose on Africa's shore.
> There we'll find freedom.
> Where is the negro with soul so dead
> Three hundred years with a heart of lead?
> Look! You can't see that embellished light
> And know for your rights it is time to fight?[38]

Another responsibility premiered for the League in the last nine months of the war—identification of "slackers" who attempted to evade the Selective Service. In February of 1918, Provost Marshal Enoch Crowder, who managed the Selective Service system, and Attorney General Gregory asked the APL to cooperate with them in locating deserters and delinquents—those who had not registered, failed to appear for the physical, ignored orders to report for training, or not been employed in a vital occupation. This next task—to tag slackers, became the toughest test of the League's endurance, for its members eventually would conduct more than three million such investigations for the BI.[39] APL evangelists were now reduced to hunting for males without draft registration cards. Nevertheless, the order provided the APL with a wider scope of functions, albeit its most controversial one. League officers learned to establish more rigid guidelines for its agents in this new endeavor, including the requirement to always include a federal or local police officer in slacker "canvasses." The *Spy Glass* recommended that information on suspects could easily be mined from homes displaying the American flag. Those proud residences often had a family member in the service, so there was little hesitation on their part when asked to finger a slacker known to them.[40]

In the New Orleans office, roughly twenty thousand slacker investigations were processed. That was an extraordinary number—about ten per agent. The responsibilities of the intelligence community—the BI and military intelligence—would never have been met without the assistance of the APL. "It is safe to say," Gregory crowed in his annual report to Congress, "that never in history has this country been so thoroughly policed as at the present time."[41] Others argued that this excessive surveillance was a dangerous shortcut to despotism.

Civil libertarians began again to complain of illegal apprehensions by fervent APL headhunters with no authority to arrest and, contrary to APL mandates, without the accompanying law officers. And after being spirited away without a warrant to a detention facility, the suspects were sometimes held for days or even weeks until their draft boards could confirm whether they had indeed registered. Trapped in the momentum of the moment, hundreds of innocent citizens were illegally detained.

This time, however, the transgressions invited severe criticism on Capitol Hill and in the national press. Still, Congress failed to produce any legislation that would clarify the League's ambiguous legal status. In a letter to Briggs published in the *Spy Glass*, the attorney general felt compelled to reiterate to League members the warning to be careful not to make independent arrests of men simply because their registration or classification cards were not on their person. He quickly tempered the wrist slap, however, by assuring them that the APL continued to enjoy his department's "hearty endorsement."[42]

By the spring of 1918, as Pershing was preparing to mount an American offensive, the attorney general inaugurated an aggressive new approach to the growing numbers of men who had avoided the call of conscription—a national dragnet whereby large numbers of deputies would storm haunts where suspected draft delinquents might gather. Called "slacker raids" by reporters, swarms of cops and US marshals swooped down on theaters, pool halls, offices, and even private residences. The League and even a good number of uniformed soldiers and sailors assisted them by providing willing and earnest manpower.

One such operation in New Orleans corralled over four hundred men from every ward in the city who were not carrying their draft cards. Word spread quickly, however. As cars sped into some neighborhoods, dozens of men were already grabbing for wallets to display their cards as agents spilled from their vehicles. Ever so vigilant, the force even boarded the Mississippi River steamer *Sidney* after a moonlight dance cruise. Several men were unhappily separated from their female partners when they were unable to produce their draft cards.[43] Wagonloads of suspects were taken to the post-office building on Canal Street, where Superintendent Forrest Pendleton of the Justice Department had his office. Most had alibis for not carrying the required cards and were released, but fifty or so were put behind bars.

A much larger and even more systematic manhunt in April of 1918 involved up to three hundred League deputies in teams of four to six men assigned to different geographic areas of the city looking for those who had not registered. Each team, bunched together in sixty privately owned vehicles, crisscrossed around town targeting "loafing places" where African American men might be found at night—cabarets, pool halls, saloons, clubs, and "every man they saw on the streets."

The well-orchestrated, two-hour raid was directed by Weinberger from his headquarters on Camp Street. Once the bird dogs scoured a locale, they telephoned the chief to report how many they had nabbed. Vehicles were then sent to assist in transporting the suspects to the APL office. By 9:30 p.m., practically the entire city had been covered resulting in the detention of 250. Only one of those men was white. After questioning, sixty-six of them were sent to the parish jail, including the lone white man who confessed that he had not registered. Oddly, his was the only name printed in the *Picayune*'s story. The remaining suspects were released. According to the reporter, the examinations were conducted by the foot soldiers of the APL, "assisted by Justice Department personnel."[44]

In October of 1917, having received word that some members of the New Orleans APL were stretching the limits of their law enforcement parameters, Bielaski wrote to Superintendent Pendleton ordering him to look into these reports. Clearly, some of the two thousand card-carrying APL commandos who patrolled the city were bullying innocents. Weinberger was thereupon notified that arrests by his men were absolutely disallowed and raids could never be conducted without being accompanied by a US marshal. Pendleton replied to Bielaski that he had "cautioned Mr. Weinberger and several members of the APL against making arrests or permitting members to conduct themselves in any way other than in a courteous manner."[45] In order to insure that League activities were more carefully managed in this untested political minefield, Gregory ordered that an assistant DA, a Justice Department agent, and at least one US marshal be assigned to each APL office across the country.

Weinberger always denied that his men were conducting arrests while they were on raids, stating that they simply asked suspects to accompany them to headquarters for questioning. He added that he was sure that New Orleans had a smaller percentage of draft dodgers than other city, so the incidence of abuse could not be very high anyway.[46] Tell that to the young man who was innocently walking his date home one night a month before the Armistice. Suddenly, a Comet sedan pulled over and stopped the couple on the street. Out popped two APL detectives, who flashed their badges and ordered the young man to produce his registration and classification cards.

When he was unable to do so, he was placed in the car and whisked to League headquarters for further investigation. His young female companion was left there, forced to walk home alone despite her tears.[47]

This was just the sort of incident that created scorn for the League, more so because of the breach of etiquette shown to the young woman than, perhaps, for the age-profiling performed on her male chaperone. Yet the APL was about to invite even more contempt when it eagerly sought to help enforce the government's assault on vice.

Chapter 12

NEW ORLEANS—NO "PURITAN MOTHER"

In 1902 the Louisiana legislature, following the lead of other states, had passed a local-option law that allowed voters in parishes or cities to decide whether they wished to restrict the sale of alcohol. Precedents were being established, and parishes further north, where support for temperance was strong, opted one by one to become dry.[1] Reform legislation from the state capital continued with the approval of a law that criminalized betting on horse racing in pool halls. Public opinion in New Orleans was slowly becoming conditioned to expect limits on some of its favorite pastimes.

Progressives, twentieth-century reformers, were relentless in their march for political and economic equity, women's suffrage, and the Social Gospel. Each of these noble goals required a movement in its own right, so huge were the roadblocks. But the lines between them were blurred. There was a commonality—a commitment by these mostly middle class, urban activists to provide better lives politically, socially, and economically for the common citizen.

Progressive legislators in 1908 had produced the controversial Gay-Shattuck law,[2] which addressed one area overlooked by Jim Crow. Blacks and whites could no longer be served alcohol in the same establishment, an indication that racial intermixing in saloons was not unusual in the city. Liquor-license holders would now have to declare whether their customers were white or Black, and the renewal price for those licenses tripled. Further, women and minors, whether they were employees or customers, were prohibited from any business selling liquor. Musical instruments and gambling devices were also barred. So too were the "table girls" who hustled drinks from male admirers. (An exception was made for places like cafes and hotels where prepared food was served.)

The legislation was extraordinary, for it forced a modification of another familiar enterprise on the city's landscape—the combination grocery store and bar. The law required that there must be a ground-to-ceiling partition separating the bar from the grocery, with separate entrances for each so that diners would not mingle with barflies. Additionally, public entrances to bars could only open from the street.

Gay-Shattuck was calamitous to the vice industry in the entire city. That was its intent. Historian Karen Leathem concludes, however, that there existed a hidden agenda. Many legislators hoped that the law would help to delay an outright prohibition of alcohol.[3] If the regulations were severe enough, the thinking went, it would be unnecessary to go further. People sensed that the national mood was drifting in favor of the abstinence zealots. But that mood did not afflict most New Orleanians, whose significant Catholic population of French, Italian, and Irish was raised on alcohol, and whose notorious tolerance of drinking could be traced back to the city's 1718 origin. Enduring the harsh demands of Gay-Shattuck would be worth it if it fended off alcohol's death penalty and kept alive the city's renowned permissiveness toward drinking.

To many, restrictions like Gay-Shattuck were being imposed by state legislators, particularly those from north Louisiana's Bible Belt, who did not understand the city's mores or history. The same was true for the various national pressure groups who drummed up support for prohibition. Organizations like the Woman's Christian Temperance Union, the Church Temperance Society, and most importantly the Anti-Saloon League were seen by some as interlopers fueled by Protestants bent upon colonizing New Orleans with their unwelcomed ideas—a kind of cultural or even religious imperialism. This bred resentment and an inclination to resist these alien forces, who were attempting to redirect the wayward toward the path of godly righteousness—without the consent of the governed.

The dark ages of prohibition may have been imminent in 1917, but the thousands of young recruits at military camps during the war years were not about to embrace the message of its enthusiasts. In between drilling and inspections, drinking continued among the troops and sailors. It was just what one did. Efforts to quarantine the men from its allure had historically been futile, particularly when the men were in garrison. Selling liquor to soldiers may have been illegal, but because the demand was so great, vendors always found a way to make it available.

This was so at Camp Beauregard near Alexandria, Louisiana, where many recruits from both Louisiana and Arkansas were stationed. A heated war of words erupted when the governor of Arkansas, Charles Brough, in an address at Hot Springs to an audience of Progressives, charged that the sinful sauce in "unlimited quantities" was finding its way through the gates at Beauregard and threatening the piety of Arkansas's native sons. "They didn't even have to buy the stuff. It was handed out to them as fast as they could dispose of it."

Brough indirectly accused the city of Alexandria for permitting this, contrasting the situation in Louisiana with Camp Pike in Arkansas, where his "soldier boys" were sufficiently protected from all dissolute influences.[4]

Saloonkeepers and cabaret owners were facing a serious hurdle after Gay-Shattuck. Whiskey, women, and song did more than simply fertilize vice. They were its essence, its vital organs. The proprietors targeted by the law would not go away quietly. Adjustments were rapidly made to exploit a loophole in the law that allowed hotels and restaurants to continue operating as usual. As long as food was served and rooms were rented, the law would not apply.

One dancehall on Customhouse Street provided an example of what others began to do. Known for the bawdy behavior of its clientele, the owner constructed a tamale and hotdog stand on site while the women held "high revel" in a rear room, where music continued unabated.[5] Other places affected found much simpler means to sidestep the law. Cabarets pretended to lease makeshift bedrooms using bogus signage to dodge arrests. Some decorated tables and bars with recycled sandwiches, eyewash for the benefit of the police. These "blind tigers" contributed to the uneven enforcement of Gay-Shattuck.

Six long years after the law was enacted, the loophole had still not been sealed. To expose this, a writer from the *Item* pretending to be a patron walked casually into a nightspot that he suspected had always eluded the law called the Haymarket in the Tango Belt, a micro-neighborhood in the French Quarter. Between 11 p.m. and 2 a.m. he counted about fifty male and female customers coming and going, drinking at the several tables. A single bologna sandwich, which none of them ate, was served at one of the tables along with the drink orders, but then it was transported from one table to another as people moved around. "Somewhere in the shuffle," he joked, "one of the sandwiches lost its bologna ... but was not retired from active service." When the journalist finally ordered food, the waiter told him that they were out of everything.[6]

In the absence of a reformer in City Hall, arrests for violations would continue to be intermittent despite lip service designed to placate civic minded groups like the Progressive Union. Philip Werlein's pro-business organization held that the city's reputation for permissive behavior made it unlikely that it would ever be a beacon for investment and commercial advancement as long as Storyville, particularly, was humming. With willing allies from the clergy, Werlein, always passionate and steadfast, ramped up his attack on the district he so loathed using the city's major dailies as his mouthpiece. His Union produced a resolution calling for the shuttering of Storyville using a different angle, one that he knew would strike at the tenderloin's most exposed nerve—interracial sex. In its crosshairs was Basin Street because of its proximity to the Southern Railways Terminal Station, the tip of the funnel for many guests coming into town. "The situation is calculated to prejudice the casual visitor," the resolution stated, "against the sacred tenant of the Southern people—racial purity." Even those who shrugged at Storyville's debauchery found this to be a particularly repugnant feature of this playground of sin. And while its visibility was somewhat occluded, it was a well-known commodity and becoming increasingly untenable. The resolution insisted that Louisiana's standing anti-miscegenation law should be strictly enforced within the district's footprint, with jail terms for violators.[7]

Other allies in the battle against immorality were local activists Jean and Kate Gordon, the latter taking time from her work for women's suffrage to attend community meetings concerning the proliferation of brothels, which had pierced the restricted district's boundary only to nest in respectable neighborhoods. At one such meeting, she read from a letter sent to her from a whistle blower who plied her occupation at one of Storyville's cathouses. In the letter, the woman listed addresses of over fifty resorts, alleging that they operated with impunity beyond Storyville.[8] Years after Storyville's birth in 1897, the experiment to confine the commercial sex trade was not working.

GAY-SHATTUCK RETURNS

After sending mixed signals about the city's commitment to prosecute crimes of the flesh, public safety commissioner Harold Newman finally unleashed the kraken. After a meeting with his police superintendent in early 1917, he ordered a massive "clean-up" campaign against prostitution and vice, promising to enforce Gay-Shattuck's provisions with vigor. The commissioner's initiative paralleled the work of the American Protective League's agents, who had by then shifted their attention to many of the same gremlins. In their initial sortie into the underworld, the police shuttered over sixty illegal brothels outside of Storyville. Cribs inside the district were also targeted by requiring the girls who rented these tiny spaces to live in them instead of renting them nightly.

One unfortunate result of the aggressive campaign was the unemployment of several hundred hustlers. With no place to go, many were forced to scatter and beg from pedestrians. One cluster of them brazenly trolled for dimes and quarters on St. Charles Avenue. "Say, we are up against it," they shouted. "Can you give us two bits?"[6] Another report had seventy-five of the newly displaced girls booking space on a steamer headed to Panama's Canal Zone hoping for a more accommodating locale to ply their trade.[9] This presented a dilemma for the Progressives, who, as social engineers, had sought these

moral maneuvers for years but now had another problem on their hands—
caring for large numbers of the newly displaced.

One local woman expressed her concern for those "branded with the
scarlet letter to be victimized, hunted, and hounded." How could a Christian
community stand by and permit "the merciless searchlight to be turned only
upon those poor outcasts of society?" The religious theme continued in other
letters to the *Picayune*:

- "These unfortunates," one enlightened writer sympathized, were left
  with little choice. "We hear so much of freedom, liberty, and justice,
  but let us stop and think how little of that goes to the masses who
  are struggling for an existence."
- And another: "Are the human derelicts affected by this propaganda to
  be scattered and driven to slow starvation? Has any provision been
  made for their succor and practical redemption?"
- "There can be no Christian sincerity in any concerted effort ... which
  does not carry with it that divine spark of sympathy for the fallen."[10]

In another sweeping blow, Commissioner Newman's cleanup disallowed
cabarets and saloon owners inside and out of Storyville from renewing their
licenses. And until their current licenses expired, their music permits were
revoked—whether they served bologna sandwiches or not.[11] The decree revoked City Hall's current policy, which gave a pass to live music venues in
defiance of a long-ignored provision of Gay-Shattuck. Cabaret owners in
particular who contributed to the Old Regular machine had always been
immune from enforcement.[12] Just as the jazz craze was beginning to blossom,
the police and their APL ally hoped to dig up the taproot of New Orleans
culture while quarantining servicemen from the dens where cheap whiskey
flowed and delinquent women strutted.

This last edict was a signal that Newman had had enough of the Tango
Belt, with its seedy cabarets, seedier saloons, and assorted immoralities. It was
as though Storyville was bleeding, with some of its worst elements seeping
out and infecting its sidekick nearer the river. Something had to be done to
stop the escalation of evildoing, he believed, even if it meant that dozens
more would lose their jobs. One disgruntled citizen complained angrily to
the *Picayune* that saloon owners were put in jail and treated as criminals for
little or no cause, expressing a viewpoint that he likely shared with hundreds
of others. "What has he done? Nothing but trying to make a living."[13]

There were plenty of others, however, who ignored the impact on business
and were ready to assist in the social purification of the city—whether invited

by government leaders or not. The problem begged for a hands-on approach. Between twelve hundred and fifteen hundred attended a rally sponsored by the Citizens' League, an assertive civic group headed by William Railey, to hear speakers keen to maintain pressure on the police to do its duty. The creation of an organic committee of one hundred was announced, composed of those willing to assist the APL in tilting the city toward godliness. The announcement was met with vocal approval, but the loudest applause followed the stinging remark of Rev. Dr. Hosley Werlein, when he tagged his hometown as "the most sin-saturated and politically misruled city in the union."[14]

SUNDAY—THE DAY OF REST OR RESISTANCE?

There was much to be done. While it was not technically a provision of the Gay-Shattuck law, the previous century's Sunday closing law was a close cousin to it. For Newman, that statute was perhaps an even greater challenge—bringing to a halt the sale of alcohol and tobacco on the Lord's day. But there was more to the law than turning off the tap on Sunday. Retail outlets, barber shops, and groceries were also forced to close, though the latter's proprietors could erect stands on the sidewalk to sell bread, milk, and vegetables. Fish markets, drug stores, and butcher shops were also immune, for none of these sold the offending spirits. And unlike some other urban areas where streetcar service, soda stands, and perishable food sales were prohibited, theaters and other places of amusement were left untouched. But the law was hardly enforced—the city following a policy of "unobtrusive non-observance." For the past decade, there had been no dry Sundays, no interference from police. During the entire year of 1913, for example, only thirty-six people were arrested for operating on Sundays.[15] Businesses remained open carte blanche.

Newman planned to change all that in 1917. Exception was made for restaurants that served wine with dinner, but not beer or whiskey. The commissioner warned that his officers were wise to tricks, like waiters serving cocktails in coffee cups. He thought his police would be up to the task. It appeared they would be, at least on February 4th, the first Sunday after the initial announcement of tighter enforcement. The *Picayune* reported the next day that the city's finest conducted the Sunday surveillance "with unwonted zeal." Thirty-two were arrested, most of them for saloon infractions. But even criminal minutia could not escape the dragnet, which continued through February. Several men playing a mechanical racehorse machine in a pool hall attracted the attention of a cop who took the owner into custody. One nineteen-year-old was brought in for shining shoes at a bootblack stand on Canal Street, and another man for selling a pack of cigarettes for a nickel out of a café window.[16]

Reactions to the Sunday crackdown were mostly positive. The press seemed generally to be behind it. The Woman's Club of New Orleans was another important bellwether of public opinion and, presumably, could be counted on to endorse any plan to scrape away the city's infamous impurities and be relieved of the incubus of vice. But there were divisions in the ranks. Feminists were concerned about the large number of women who had been employed at the cabarets but were now dependent on public charity.[17] More than a few concerned citizens also held that any intervention against the sex trade was certain to fail unless the male clients of the city's soiled women were also criminalized.

One subscriber to the *Picayune* contributed a sentiment that he felt represented most New Orleans natives. The "radical" cleanup, he submitted, was erasing the distinct identity of his place of birth, "dulling the local color and impairing the individuality of our town." It would be a mistake, he believed, if New Orleans was judged by the same template of etiquette that was used elsewhere. Its distinct culture must be respected, and this meant the preservation of its European roots, however unsavory they may be to some. "Our city is not a Puritan mother. . . . We took our cue from Paris." "Let our city be conducted to express the intimate notes of its individuality."[18]

The Citizens' League had lobbied hard for action, alleging that enforcement of the Sunday Law had stalled for years because of collusion between the city machine and the booze industry. Now there appeared to be movement. Yet several months into the offensive, its militant leader remained unsatisfied. "It is evident," William Railey proclaimed, "that tremendous pressure has been brought to bear by the liquor interests . . . to have the town run wide open, . . . and it would appear that the mayor has thrown the weight of his influence in that direction." And then, with emphasis, "How much longer can right-thinking people of New Orleans endure the order of things?"[19]

The moral warriors of the Citizens' League were as vigilant as APL investigators, patrolling the city, taking notes not only on liquor and Sunday-closing-law infractions, but also on gambling operations and prostitution, forwarding information to the police. It was the group's contribution to the war effort and Mayor Behrman's cry for civilian collaboration with the military's mission of a vice-free fighting force. Railey was so persistent that he once persuaded the police department to deploy officers with him on one of his taxi searches around town to prove that the law breakers his men had identified were indeed worthy of arrest. Nothing turned up on that particular inspection. From then on Railey had difficulty convincing the police that his group was anything more than a nuisance, continually criticizing City Hall for its dalliance. To assure the public, the department announced that cops who closed their eyes to the violations would be punished. Still, Railey continually pressed the police to do more, even demanding at one point that every police officer should be ordered to inspect three saloons each Sunday to ensure they were closed for business.[20]

Commissioner Newman, to whom the police superintendent answered, would not be moved. He kept Railey at a distance, insisting that the Citizens' League reveal the names of their members who witnessed the offenses so that their testimonies could be substantiated. This sounded like a reasonable demand on the surface, but given the historic foot-dragging by the police in attending to the city's vice problems, Newman's refusal to accept the intelligence gathered by these citizens appeared suspicious. He blasted the Citizens' League's Sunday patrol with ridicule, mocking them for being cop pretenders. "The utter absurdity and ineffectiveness of the amateur police methods of our local Sherlock Holmes aboard a taxicab, and only minus a brass band, was strikingly demonstrated."[21]

Railey refused to disclose the names of his investigators, citing worry about their safety and anonymity. He may have had a point. There existed an undercurrent of fear that those who pushed the envelope would be asking for trouble. Several members of the Citizens' League indeed had been involved in altercations which, they stated, were ignored by police.[22] Newman himself seemed displeased at the pace of the cleanup, insistent that the Sunday law could never be effectively policed unless plainclothesmen were used to help scout the streets. Whenever a uniformed cop was spotted, it was too easy for cabaret managers to clean up and reshuffle things in advance of an inspection. This was certainly the routine, and the police reported this to their superiors in frustration. It was futile, Newman complained, to expect proper surveillance with over two thousand saloons in the city to inspect and only 212 patrolmen to do so.[23] Newman needed the help of undercover officers if the cleanup was to work. Without them, he claimed, police details on Sunday were practically a waste of time.

Mayor Behrman flatly refused to allow this practice. Like other campaigns initiated against vice in the past, he gave his tacit approval for anticrime crusades, saying all the right things in order to quell the public's clamor. But he expected these initiatives to subside once a few days of arrests were reported in the press. That is exactly what had happened in 1908 immediately following the passage of Gay-Shattuck. Newman's 1917 cleanup, however, was persistent, and aside from leaving Storyville mostly untouched, the police were making arrests each weekend. It was a legitimate police action. But the mayor believed that using plainclothes cops was going too far.

A break between the two men was inevitable. Rather than keeping a lid on their differences, Behrman publicly debated the issue with Newman, claiming that undercover police would in effect be used to "spy" on businessmen and invite officers to abuse their police privileges. Never known as a civil libertarian, the mayor nevertheless stated that since many groceries that sold beer also served as the residences of the proprietors, their homes and privacy might very well be invaded. There was truth to his objections, but it still led many to wonder whether Behrman was fed up with cleanup.

Newman, feeling handcuffed, shocked everyone and resigned in June over the issue.[24] It appeared to be the honorable move. Was not the commissioner simply trying to do his job effectively? And was not the campaign working? In the first three months since the launch of Newman's crusade, there were 129 Gay-Shattuck arrests, nearly four times as many as in all of 1916. While convictions were notoriously low—under 10 percent—Newman was vacating the office on a high horse.[25] Legitimate doubts remained about why he was leaving. Newman's spotless reputation as an honest reformer was difficult to ignore, so his abrupt departure seemed to reinforce the notion that Behrman's public support of the Newman cleanup was merely a facade. And did Newman resign, or did Behrman fire him? The perception persisted that City Hall's political machine was less than sincere in conducting any initiative that would interdict the stream of money coming from these tawdry sources.

The optics of his withdrawal were made worse because of its timing. Just four months earlier, Hugh O'Donnell, the editor of his short-lived newspaper, the *New Orleans American*, published a sensational, detailed account of police corruption. "Everybody knows that graft in New Orleans is colossal," he began, "but few have taken the pains to figure out anything like the exact figures." O'Donnell claimed that a total of $3,200,000 annually stuffed the pockets of city leaders. He then listed the vice pits, his estimates on the numbers currently in operation, and the amount of money each operator spent to grease the palms of policemen. The figures were printed on page one in the *Item* on January 27th. For example:

Device or Activity	Estimated #	Weekly Payment in Dollars
slot machines	600	10
lotteries	200	15
baseball pools	150	10
saloons on Sunday	2200	5
unlicensed liquor vendors	600	10
legal prostitutes	723	10
illegal prostitutes	500	30

These payoffs, he continued, percolated their way up the ladder to "higher ups," that is, to Mayor Behrman, the commissioners of public safety and of police, and their principal lieutenants. The editorial then provided the names and addresses of twenty-eight women who held liquor licenses in violation of the Gay-Shattuck law. "The grafting ring," said his editorial, "is eating the vitals of the civic body like a cancer."[26] And from where did O'Donnell arrive at his figures? From "men in the know" who had been forced to pay these tributes. Of course, the names of his sources were not revealed. There was no need to validate the numbers. Given the existing theory in the public's mind that city government was on the take, O'Donnell's words simply reinforced that conclusion.

Sam Stone Jr., the architect whose firm built the Athenaeum, the Maison Blanche building, and the Shriner's Masonic Auditorium on St. Charles Ave., replaced Newman on the Commission Council in the aftermath of these allegations. Behrman never commented on the charges, but he and Stone both tried to assure the public that the Sunday law would continue to be rigidly enforced. That was quite an exaggeration. Even Newman had made it clear to saloon and cabaret owners that they would only attract the attention of the police if they were conspicuously selling adult beverages on Sundays. There was one difference. In the past, owners would merely have to drop a curtain across their doorways to conceal their regulars at the bar. Now, front entrances had to be closed and exterior lighting had to be turned off. In other words, there had to be no "flagrant" indication to passersby that drinks were still available there after midnight on Saturdays. Police were told not to peek through windows if these conditions were met.[27] Inside, neighborhood friends were still able to gather as was customary, laughing, no doubt, at the stupidity of these restrictions.

Despite the noble remarks made in the press, the entire arrangement was obviously designed less to end the practice of drinking the devil's brew on Sunday than it was to pacify those who were outraged at the saloons for openly nose-thumbing the law. Much like the paradigm of Storyville, if vice was kept out of view, then it could be tolerated. Moreover, very few violators of the law were ever punished. In the seven months between January and the end of July 1917, only 15 people were convicted out of the 280 cases that made it to trial. The other 265 cases were either discharged by the district attorney or dismissed by judges, mostly because of insufficient evidence.[28] The highly publicized program to scrub down and purify the city had failed.

CLOSING STORYVILLE

Given the Progressives' impulse to launder the city of its disreputable enterprises, Storyville's existence was becoming increasingly tenuous. Washington's
Commission on Training Camp Activities, created to provide a "clean and
wholesome" environment for servicemen, was especially troubled. One of its
members labeled Storyville "the Gibraltar of commercialized vice . . . given
over to human degradation and lust." Raymond Fosdick, its leader, called it
"one of the most vicious red light districts I have ever seen" and "a Mecca"
for young men in uniform. Suggesting that it was an economic windfall for
the city's political machine, he referred to the district as "the last stronghold
of the old regime."[29] Besides, Camp Nicholls and the Algiers Naval facility
were inside a "moral zone" of five miles, within which such establishments
were disallowed.

Most of the casualties suffered during WWI were caused by the ongoing
influenza epidemic. Venereal disease, however, was close behind. This was
both intolerable and avoidable, so the pressure was on to insulate the ranks
from the most likely incubators—immoral houses. But this pressure was not
coming from New Orleans newspapers. None openly agitated for Storyville's
closure, though their voices were growing weaker as the iron arm of local
churches joined the Civic League and the War Department in this holy,
patriotic battle.

Behrman did exactly what he should have done. He enlisted the commanding officers of each service branch in the area to station military guards
in the district to augment the local police in keeping out any uniformed
service men. This was only minimally effective, however, as many borrowed
civilian clothing to get through the checkpoints. According to a February 1918
APL report, one tailor in the French Quarter rented clothes to the men at the
rate of a dollar for three hours of action.[30] Taxi drivers especially nourished
the caper. For a fee, they provided several sets of civilian clothes in their
vehicles for visiting servicemen. The enterprising drivers also solicited them
on the street, selling bottles of whiskey and rides to the sporting houses of
their choice for five dollars. Other common practices were for saloon girls
to escort young men to private rooms and to sell booze from rear doors.[31]

The military's full cooperation in helping law enforcement curb these
activities did not dissuade Fosdick from sending the head of the Commission on Training Camp Activities' enforcement division, Bascom Johnson,
to survey Storyville in person. Johnson had previously been instrumental in
forcing the closure of San Francisco's red-light district, the Barbary Coast.
But his New Orleans mission would prove more difficult. Behrman was

worried when he learned of the probe from this Washington outsider. As expected, Johnson's report concluded that the district was "intolerable from every point of view."[32]

At the completion of his surveillance, Behrman asked Johnson to meet with the local service branches before he left town in order to validate the mayor's claim that Storyville was indeed being properly monitored. When he refused, Behrman became incensed. In a statement issued to the press, the mayor found Johnson to be arrogant—projecting a "dictatorial manner." Johnson, he divulged, even declined to be briefed on the subject. When Johnson ordered the district's closure, Behrman told the CTCA inspector that he would do no such thing until he heard directly from Secretary of War Newton Baker himself.[33] This refusal ignited local criticism from Progressive circles that the mayor was stalling. On the defensive, the "King of the Tenderloin," as his detractors called him, wrote later that he was only "doing what I thought was in the best interests of the soldiers, sailors, and Marines and the city."[34]

In August Behrman trained to Washington to plead his case to Secretary Baker. In order to bring more heft to his proposal, he was joined by both Louisiana senators and Rep. Albert Estopinal, who represented New Orleans in Congress. Their argument was that illicit temptations would be tempered if they remained surveilled and confined within Storyville's perimeter. If not, dozens of Storyville's "social ladies" would scatter throughout the city, taxing the manpower limits of the police and contaminating prim neighborhoods. Baker, a former mayor of Cleveland, was empathetic, reluctant to dictate his will on local government. He bowed to the delegation's plea and promised to delay a definitive order until the results of Behrman's compact with military police could be further examined.

Returning home in high spirits, Behrman thought that he had won a stay of execution for the twenty-year-old neighborhood. Unwilling to occupy the sidelines, Kate Gordon, the city's most vocal Progressive fixture, surfaced to blast the mayor for his latest political machinations and, she claimed, his effort to keep Storyville vital and intact. Responding directly to his nemesis, Behrman insisted that his visit with Baker was only meant to maintain orderliness in his city with an eye on protecting servicemen. "I am at a loss to know just how Miss Gordon acquired her knowledge of what occurred at an interview at which she was not present," he countered.[35] Equally idealistic was Kate's sister Jean, who reinforced Kate's barrage, hurrying a letter directly to Secretary Baker pleading relief from her hometown's millstone of sin: "We have seen these plague spots closed everywhere else, Newport, San Antonio, Alexandria, but to our surprise and disappointment, the conditions in New

Orleans . . . are daily growing worse, as the women from these other cities which have been closed are fleeing to our city."[36]

A victory for the mayor was not to be. While Baker retreated, Congress extended to the Navy Department authorization to enforce the Selective Service Act's provision prohibiting sexual commerce near military bases. In September, the governor's office received an order from the puritanical North Carolinian, Secretary of the Navy Josephus Daniels, copied to Mayor Behrman, that Storyville's doors had to be shut tight. Included in the letter was a copy of Bascom Johnson's report, which noted in detail the addresses of the brothels and the dates when he saw servicemen there.[37] Noncompliance meant removal of service personnel from the city. If Behrman did not act, all military facilities in the city would be closed, including the Algiers Naval facility, an economic boon to the mayor's own beloved neighborhood.

Despite City Hall's public insistence that the security around Storyville was tight, most knew this was fiction. One local madam said that the invasion of clients from their camps reminded her of the gold rush of 1849. "Fornication," she declared, "became epidemic."[38] A police spokesman admitted that his force was incapable of keeping servicemen from the district. According to him, an average of fifty a week were being detained for drunkenness or disorderly conduct.[39] The pursuit of nightly debaucheries would have come as no surprise to the pastor of a Bible Belt Baptist church from Shreveport. He worried about the fifteen recruits from his congregation who were stationed in New Orleans. In a letter to the CTCA, he called the city "the Sodom of the South" and requested that they be relocated to an encampment that would remove them from the occasion of sin.[40]

From her desk at the *Item* where she worked as a reporter, Ethel Hutson complained in a letter to the American Social Hygiene Association that Storyville was "doing a banner business" because of the swarm of uniformed men stationed in New Orleans. "So far as I know," she asserted, "nothing has been done to safeguard these young men from either prostitution or venereal disease."[41] Two months later Jean Gordon again wrote to Baker indicting city politicians for protecting Storyville and even suggesting that they were guilty of felonious behavior in order to keep their hands in the district's till.[42] A representative of the Social Hygiene Association was sent to New Orleans to gauge the VD problem firsthand. He walked Storyville's streets and validated Hutson's report—sailors and soldiers were indeed openly drinking and hanging out in the bordellos and saloons there.

On October 27th, 1917, William Railey alerted Fosdick in a letter, providing him with more data from his volunteers who monitored prostitution and vice in downtown New Orleans.[43] His men confirmed sixty-seven instances

of servicemen drinking or entering "immoral houses" since September 1st—
and they worked only on weekends! Historian Emily Landau reasonably
estimated that perhaps 200 to 470 servicemen were found in and around
Storyville between the first of September and the end of October when
Railey's people were on patrol.[44]

Behrman had done all he could. He had no stomach to contest a government order during the time of war and immediately had a city ordinance
drafted in October. It ended the career of the city's most notorious celebrity,
effective November 12th, 1917. "Our city government has believed that the
situation can best be administered more easily and satisfactorily," proclaimed
the mayor, "by continuing it as a prescribed area. Our experience has taught
us that the reasons for this are unanswerable; but the Navy Department . . .
has decided otherwise." Making sure that he was not depicted as dragging his
feet, Behrman assured the public that his administration would do nothing
"that may be in the remotest degree at variance with the wishes of federal
authorities" during the war. The mayor, not accustomed to losing political
battles during his thirteen years in office, took the high road and delivered
the ordinance to his councilmen in person where it was adopted with little
debate. Brothels were given thirty days to clear out.[45]

The *States* was convinced that "there was no other course open to the
mayor" but condemned the order. In other cities with similar red-light
districts, it instructed, the closings "spread evil" over entire communities
when prostitution was no longer confined. The editorial also wondered what
would happen to the displaced women "who are to be thrown on the mercy
and charity of the community" and hoped that they might find "respectable employment."[46] One citizen displayed less compassion. Writing to the
Picayune, he labeled houses of sin "the agencies of Lucifer" and rejoiced over
the closure. America could now "lift up its manhood from the slough into
which many have sunk."[47]

As the terminal date approached, the city sent out notices to vacate and
ordered firemen to patrol Storyville, anticipating what might be attempts by
unscrupulous building owners to collect on fire insurance by hiring arson-
ists. Many residents had already fled. In their wake "For Rent" signs popped
up—looking more like tombstones to the district's denizens.

In fact, Storyville's commerce had slowly begun to disperse years before
the 1917 death notice. In 1899, City Hall had counted 230 homes of ill repute,
30 assignation houses, and about 2,000 full or part time fallen women in the
restricted district. Eleven years later, the number of brothels had dropped
to 175 with fewer than 700 full-time girls for hire. Now, in November of
1917, only about 100 businesses (16 of which could be termed multi-room

cathouses) were left to close in Storyville, affecting not more than 450 women. Crib prices reflected the district's declining commerce. Landlords in 1904 were getting about $3.50 a night from the working girls. On the eve of the closing, rent had plunged to just 50 cents.[48] New clients from the military temporarily slowed the decline, but the red lights within the district had been fading.

Over four hundred women was still a significant number, or course, and prostitution was not losing its appeal. But fewer women were willing to work the trade in a restricted area, preferring instead to be more prudent about their occupation. Men too were becoming more attentive to community activism against prostitution and were beginning to favor the anonymity of backdoor establishments. Further, the johns were increasingly being held responsible. The war had hastened the rising chorus of voices from women's groups that were particularly vocal about the men, who were held blameless for paid sexual rendezvous with teenage innocents.

Norma Wallace, who operated a brothel in the French Quarter, confirmed Behrman's warnings that Storyville's closure would simply displace the sex trade. "From the river to Rampart, I can't tell you how many whores there were. Between Iberville and St. Louis Streets," she remembered, "and from Bourbon to Rampart, every door had a girl hustling in it."[49] In 1919, Lulu White, the mistress of the opulent Mahogany Hall, alleged that Storyville "is not closed now, never has been closed," and, she maintained, "I can take you to fifty places that are running wide open." She even disclosed names and addresses of places near her property on North Basin Street where women were soliciting men "from the banquette." One of the women, she charged, was living with a city detective.[50] The end of Storyville did little or nothing to end prostitution. In fact, it had metastasized. The musicians knew. One composer made it clear in a parody of a tune called "Hesitation Blues."

> Legislature voted the district down . . .
> Legislature voted the district down . . .
> Damn good way to spread the hookers over town.

Louis Armstrong witnessed the slow collapse, seeing Storyville as a neighborhood rather than a petri dish for vice. Wistful, he related years afterward that he felt sorry for those he had grown to know who lived there. "It sure was a sad scene to watch the law run all those people out of Storyville," he lamented. "They reminded me of refugees. Some of them had spent the best part of their lives there. Others had never known any other life." And when it closed shop, he remarked sarcastically with his signature chuckle, "the people of that section spreaded [sic] out all over the city. . . . So we turned out nice and reformed."[51]

As the clock ticked toward midnight on November 12th, a line of wagons and trucks stacked up on the curbs while men stuffed them with furniture, pool tables, bottles of booze, and trappings from the establishments. A shortage of vehicles resulted in "a stream of women, negro maids, and porters winding their way toward Rampart with furniture and cut glass on their backs and in their hands." Well-groomed men wearing box coats directed the bitter procession. The musicians had already gone, finding new gigs elsewhere in New Orleans and beyond. Here and there unblushing women stood outside to watch the dismantling of their neighborhood, perhaps wondering where they would go next. It looked like a burial at sea, commented the *States*, and the two police captains and fifteen patrolmen who monitored the closing were the morticians. None of them noticed Edna Morris.

Stumbling down the steps of her brothel holding her stomach, Morris had shot herself. Later it was learned that she had tried to escape "the life" by working a while in a canning factory but decided, probably for financial reasons, to return. She was taken to Charity Hospital where she died of her wound.[52] The story of her death hardly attracted notice, occupying a few sentences buried deep inside a newspaper article describing the district's last remaining hours. It has been easy for historians to romanticize the glittery madams, the ostentatious Victorian manors, and the blossoming jazz culture, all of which were part of Storyville's veneer as a whimsical utopia of pleasure. Sadly, the personal lives of struggling women like Edna Morris may never be told.

But that of Nell Kimball was—in her memoirs written in the late 1920s. Kimball was an uneducated refugee from her father's Illinois farm who learned the sex trade as a teenager in St. Louis. She emigrated to New Orleans and became the madam of her own rather spiffy Storyville sporting house, "a fine twenty—dollar luxury house with clean, pretty whores" where she was witness to the last beats of the district.

Midnight I stood under the big hall chandelier, some of its crystals gone, and we all had the last drink of flat champagne, the whores crying, the naked and dressed ones and half-dressed johns coming down from upstairs. It was real sentimental. [53]

As one of Storyville's most self-assured madams, Gertrude Dix did not easily kowtow. A few months after the closing, once the heat had lifted, the feisty entrepreneur covertly reopened for business at her North Basin Street address, with its four luxurious parlors and famous mirrored cherry wood bar. The test did not last long. The predictably nonchalant police winked at her brash defiance, but American Protective League agents spotted the activity and, according to writer Herbert Asbury, arrested her themselves in May of 1918. Four other establishments were also raided in old Storyville. Five women were indicted, including Dix, who was sentenced to five days in the House of Detention.[54]

Lulu White was not as fortunate. She continued to operate in the "closed" district into the summer of 1918, when League members jumped her too for operating a house of ill repute. (Changing the name Mahogany Hall to the White Hotel and Restaurant did not fool many.) White was sentenced in 1919 to a year in jail despite her plea that other brothels were untouched. The "Diamond Queen" of Storyville applied for a pardon while behind bars, and after she had served three months, President Wilson commuted her sentence. The jail term did not dissuade White, however, from continuing her profession. Immediately after she was released, she returned to New Orleans and resumed business until she died in 1931.

Fosdick was almost giddy about the progress he witnessed as he visited the nation's military posts. "Even a city like New Orleans," he exclaimed, "which from a modern social point seemed almost hopeless, so far as moral conditions were concerned, has been cleaned up."[55] The police department concurred, reporting in December that the restricted district "was as quiet as a graveyard" and that the rest of town was swept clean of prostitution. Railey sprung up quickly to dispute that statement in the strongest terms. In a letter to the *Picayune*, he confirmed that his members had spotted twelve brothels still entertaining clients within the shuttered district's boundaries, and there were at least fifty-six more spread throughout the rest of the city. He again supplied the police with their addresses, adding locations of gambling joints as lagniappe. Yet Commissioner Stone continued to insist that his information would not be pursued without the names of those who collected the addresses.[56]

Three months after Storyville's closure, the CTCA, not entirely convinced that the city had reached an appropriate level of virtue, again sent a field officer to New Orleans to measure the state of affairs there. It was not good. The officer guessed that at least twenty-five hundred harlots had returned, never imagining that many of them had never left. "It seems that word had gone out that New Orleans is 'good' and so they are flocking here from far and away."[57] He was right. In June of 1918, for example, nearly two hundred white and seventeen Black working girls were arrested by police in a coordinated raid on ten cabarets and saloons, all in the French Quarter.[58] There

continued to be action within the boundaries of the former restricted district
as well. Eighty-five more men and women were indicted by a federal grand
jury for keeping immoral houses there nine months after it was shuttered.[59]
It was just as Behrman had predicted: "You can make it illegal, but you can't
make it unpopular."

> All, you old-time queens, from New Orleans, who lived in Storyville
> You sang the blues, try to amuse, here's how they pay the bill
> The law step-in and call it sin to have a little fun
> The police car has made a stop and Storyville is done.[60]

THE MORAL PANACEA

Sentiment for prohibition in Louisiana was accelerating with Storyville's
termination. Monroe, parish seat of the last wet parish in the state's northeast, voted to become dry in 1917. It was joining the 2,373 counties (about
80 percent of the US total), which would entirely prohibit alcohol by the
end of the year.[61] Even the *Picayune's* management could not ignore the
pendulum's swing toward the evangelicals. In the wettest city of the entire
South, it stopped running liquor ads in its pages.

Congress was caving to the activists' pressure, so much so that in December of 1917, the Eighteenth Amendment won the necessary two-thirds
vote in both houses and was sent to the states for their approval. Louisiana's
legislature voted yes in August of 1918, and when Nebraska followed suit in
January of 1919, the required thirty-six states was achieved. One year later,
prohibition would be law, a few months ahead of women's suffrage.

Louisiana's support for the controversial amendment was not at all assured. Wet forces, although not nearly as well-organized or as well-funded
as their opponents, insisted that the amendment was an unconstitutional
federal-government overreach. It was the same argument used by some local
women suffragists who opposed a national amendment. Some associated the
Anti-Saloon League prohibitionists with antebellum abolitionists—forcing
their will on the states and placing the country into bondage. The respected
New Orleans Board of Trade reminded everyone that one thousand New
Orleans families were dependent on the brewing industry, seeding the local
economy with a million dollars in yearly wages and salaries. Five thousand
saloon workers, it claimed, would be thrown out of work, and retail grocers,
all of whom sold spirits, would be hard hit as well. Moreover, the city would

have to find revenue to make up for the $700,000 in liquor-license fees and property taxes.[62]

Wets also played the race card. Representative Charles Byrne of New Orleans claimed that if the amendment were to pass, a white person's home, personal property, or business might very well be searched by Black US marshals. And if those assertions failed to convince anyone, opponents pretended that even the US role in the war would be greatly diminished because alcohol, produced by whiskey distillers, was a necessary ingredient in the manufacture of smokeless powder for artillery shells.[63]

In a last-minute move just two days before a showdown vote at the state capitol, a half-page ad appeared in the *Picayune*, paid for and signed by the city's nine local breweries (and four others), meant to convince legislators that there was no need for such an amendment.

It has come to our knowledge that irresponsible individuals, under the cover of night, have surreptitiously furnished to soldiers and sailors intoxication liquors in package form which . . . we denounce and condemn. We denounce any violation of the federal law prohibiting the giving or selling of intoxication liquors to the soldiers and sailors of the Army and Navy.

They, therefore, pledged not to sell packaged intoxication liquor to anyone between the hours of 7 p.m. and 7 a.m. Liquor could only be consumed on the premises.[64] By this time, however, the legislators had likely made up their minds.

A vote to approve the amendment had narrowly failed during the regular session when the state Senate deadlocked in a 20-20 vote. During a special session called in August 1918 to vote once more on the measure, the Senate tally this time was 21-20 in favor, despite an eleventh hour reading of a letter from a wet senator warning that prohibition camouflaged an assault by Washington on the autonomy of the states. It could lead, he wrote, to the lifting of Louisiana's anti-miscegenation law.

The sirens of states' rights and race reappeared, but the fearmongering was not enough to block the inevitable. Soon after the one-vote passage, several senators lumbered in the August heat to one of four saloons near the capitol. Conspicuous among them were a few notable prohibitionists.[65] Shortly thereafter, the Louisiana House, as expected, voted in favor, 69-41, with the delegations from New Orleans and Cajun French parishes voting with the minority. The long fight was over.

Louisiana had finally approved a constitutional amendment to prohibit the manufacture, sale, and transportation of all alcoholic beverages on August 8th, 1918. A report for the *Picayune* captured the special moment, describing supporters shouting out joyously for over a minute once the House vote was revealed. When the din subsided, one representative was recognized by the chair. "Now, Mr. Speaker," he thundered, "I move that the House take a recess in order to give the prohibitionists time in which to 'get tight' and celebrate their victory." This outburst triggered another demonstration, throwing the House floor into tumult.[66] The sarcastic remark also magnified the accusations of hypocrisy leveled at the amendment's proselytizers. Mayor Behrman, an avowed opponent, shared his analysis with some sarcasm. Drys, he was sure, were "strictly local option" supporters. "Their option is to be dry at home and wet when off to a visit." They remain firmly prohibitionists until they visit places like Eunice, Alexandria, or New Orleans so they can "go get wet for a few hours."[67]

The scene on the House floor in Baton Rouge reflected the political polarization that existed in Louisiana over this issue between the mostly Protestant North and the more heavily Roman Catholic, alcohol-friendly South. It was fitting that the Anti-Saloon League's leader in the state was headquartered in Shreveport, embedded within the Bible Belt and supported by likeminded drys. Robert Ewing, for example, published the openly wet *New Orleans States*. But the *Shreveport Times*, his other newspaper, was forced to remain noncommittal on the issue in deference to his readership in that city.[68] Because south Louisiana was the more heavily populated section of the state, the wets had always preferred a public referendum on the issue. This would have practically assured them a victory, but the Constitution stood in their way, requiring a decision by state legislatures.

How did Louisiana succumb to the prohibitionist message? It was surely an aberration. Liquor had always been a companion to Americans since the earliest European settlements of the continent. Even George Washington distilled whiskey at Mount Vernon. And was prohibition not an intrusion into the private lives of citizens? Each of the other previous constitutional amendments, with the exception of the thirteenth, which outlawed slavery, had targeted the behavior of the government, not the people. Historians note the association many rural, mainly Protestant evangelicals were making between immorality and urban life as the population shifted toward the cities at the turn of the century.[69]

Another major contribution came from an alliance with the Progressives, in particular the suffragists, who viewed the temperance movement as a parallel struggle and as a panacea for many of the scourges facing urban society. Even disparate groups like the Ku Klux Klan, which was beginning to explode in memberships, and labor unions, who railed against breweries and other wealthy industries, became allies. And once the income tax amendment was ratified in 1913, the wets no longer could argue that the government could little afford to lose the revenue it depended on from taxes on intoxication beverages.

The outbreak of the First World War played a pivotal role as well, adding to it an emotional element that was missing—patriotism. It was no coincidence that the Eighteenth Amendment was approved by Congress and ratified just after the Armistice. First was the practical matter of protecting servicemen from the temptations of the bottle. But there was also the issue of food conservation, especially grain and corn. American brewers tried educating the public with large ads in major newspapers maintaining that barley was consumed almost exclusively by cattle, not humans. Nevertheless, fears of commodity shortages led Congress to pass a temporary wartime prohibition measure in November of 1918 outlawing the sale of liquor, beer, and even wine effective from June 30, 1919, until demobilization.

Perhaps more persuasive was the linkage people made between the hated German Hun and beer, "the Kaiser's brew." In some corners, drinking beer in itself was seen as an act of disloyalty. As an example, the Anti-Saloon League published a cartoon showing an armed doughboy emerging from his trench to charge the German lines. An oversized arm grabs his ankle, impeding his gallop over the top. Scribbled on the arm is the word "booze."[70] The message was unmistakable—liquor debilitated the military's effectiveness. Moreover, Wilson's idealistic mantra that American participation in the European war was mounted in order to "make the world safe for democracy" blended perfectly with the moral intonations of the Progressives. America will take the lead in making the world a better place. Prohibition was for God and country.

Nine local breweries—the Standard, Dixie, New Orleans, Jackson, American, Columbia, Consumers, National, and Union—halted production once wartime prohibition was enacted, although the announced closures of six of them was a ruse. Two of the breweries planned to convert. The Jackson Brewing Company began installing dehydrating machinery for vegetables, and the New Orleans Brewery hoped to become a vinegar manufacturing plant. Because they remained hopeful that prohibition would be temporary, brewing equipment was stored until good sense and thirsty throats prevailed. Meanwhile, several hundred workers were out of jobs. Saloons also felt a pinch since many depended on these breweries to pay their tax and licenses.[71]

Patriotic gusto was never missing. New Orleans was as solidly behind the war as all other American cities. But prohibition, however well it could be married to the war effort, was still a very tough sell in a city whose genetic code was unconditionally linked to adult beverages. It did not matter to most whether or not their beer was the Kaiser's brew or not—so long as it was cold. Dismembering the city's culture was unacceptable. From the mayor's Mardi Gras day champagne toast to Rex, to the dinner and wine pairings at Antoine's Restaurant, to the grungiest barroom near the river's docks where crewmen gathered regularly for a beer and a smoke, public consumption of alcohol was an indigenous ritual whose origins reached back to the Old World. It was as much a part of life in New Orleans as seafood on Fridays or café au lait and beignets after Sunday mass. Taking this away was like discarding the bass player from a New Orleans jazz ensemble. Many average citizens felt that the entire country had been hijacked by a small but vociferous band of idealistic extremists, renegades from the mainstream, who were able to hoodwink elected officials into their grasp, several of whom were privately against prohibition. Yet they voted for the amendment anyway—worried that a "no" vote would appear to be unpatriotic or irreligious—with little thought given to the impossibility of its enforcement.

A tongue-in-cheek article by "A. Sousc" and entitled "Gloom, Deep Dark and Dismal, Descends as Drought Comes" was printed on page one of the *Picayune* after the amendment's ratification. Most likely representing the majority opinion in a city weaned on wine, it included a poem that the writer called the "Funeral Dirge of the Wets":

The shadows fall—the great dry skeleton
Grips Freedom by the throat. . . .
Our ancient, vaunted Liberty entombed.
Amid a drinking universe we stand alone.
The single land on earth as dry as a bone.
The thirsty millions pray to empty skies;
Oh Bacchus, god of joy and wine, arise;
Bid lightenings strike the Senate, but withhold
Your bolts from Gay and Ransdell, spirits bold,
Who dared to vote to keep the country wet,
And made a hit with all of us, you bet![72]

Chapter 13

SUFFRAGE

"Hearing the Click"

As war waged against wickedness at home, and as Pershing's forces perse-vered against the Germans, another fray that had been fermenting for over half a century was nearing a climax. The quarrel did not inhibit the city's collective reply to their mayor's challenge to support the troops. Yet it did create political fractures and rivaled the war as the most important news story of 1917 and 1918.

In each succeeding year from 1878, an amendment to the Constitution was introduced to Congress that would grant women the right to vote. Called the Susan B. Anthony Amendment, it had slowly but unevenly gained support, reaching a crescendo during the war years, until it was finally approved as the Nineteenth Amendment by the necessary number of states in 1920. The "suffs" had painstakingly chipped away at the patriarchal society that shrouded this natural right. Like Michelangelo's *David*, suffrage had always been trapped within the marble of the Constitution. The suffragists simply carved the marble until it was set free.

Southern women were slow to embrace the crusade for equality at the ballot box. Many had been cultivated in a tradition that discouraged activism, particularly in the realm of politics, a topic strictly confined to men no less so than gambling or sports. Even conversations on the topic were considered unladylike for the demure southern woman, reserved instead for the cigar room after supper, when the ladies were out of sight. Moreover, because many slavery abolitionists had also been strong advocates of the suffrage movement, southerners of both genders often associated the suffragists with the seared memories of the Civil War, Yankee Reconstruction, and what they viewed as federal overreach. According to one suffragist, "the threat of the carpetbaggers to put black heels on white necks throughout the South" was very real.[1]

Anxiety also existed about Washington's views of the South's disfranchisement laws, passed in the late 1800s, which targeted Blacks. Would the government intercede? Any federal interference with state voting qualifications was
too sensitive an issue in the South. As late as 1897, not one southern senator
had supported women's suffrage.

The impresarios of the National American Women's Suffrage Association, the most prominent of the lobbyist groups, created a strategy to make
inroads into the hostile South. One way was to conduct its conventions there.
Atlanta was chosen in 1895, the first southern city to host it. Susan B. Anthony
reluctantly asked her personal friend and supporter, Frederick Douglass, not
to attend for fear of alienating potential southern recruits. Eight years later,
New Orleans was selected for its convention, and Black NAWSA members
were excluded for that same reason. To further defuse southern skeptics,
the organization asserted that it recognized fully a state's right to "arrange
its own affairs in accordance with its own ideas and in harmony with the
customs of its own sections."[2] Southern suffragists were also invited to fill
leadership positions with the national group in order to be more inclusive.
Without these political maneuvers, there was little hope that the states of the
old Confederacy, with the legacy of Reconstruction still simmering, would
ever come into the fold.

Inevitably, the movement gained footing below the Mason-Dixon Line
in the late nineteenth century, and Louisiana women stood near the front
of the queue. They began to "hear the click," as the expression went, the very
moment when a woman realized that her gender was refused political equity.
Caroline Merrick, a pioneer for women's rights in Louisiana, once offered an
example of someone finally hearing the click. A dying woman who was being
cared for by St. Anna's Asylum in New Orleans granted $1,000 to be left to
that institution upon her death. Members of the St. Anna's board witnessed
the signing of her will. They later learned after her passing, however, that the
document was entirely invalid. As women, the board had no legal standing
to witness the signing, and the money went instead to the state. With this
outrage, the suffragists would win new allies.[3]

In New Orleans, the tip of the movement's spear was Kate Gordon. "Miss
Kate," as she was known, was one of five children born of privilege to parents, both teachers, who themselves had been strong advocates of women's
suffrage. Of average build and height, her handsome face displayed one
eyebrow that was elevated slightly higher than the other, each curling over
clear, intelligent eyes that locked onto everyone she met. A determined chin
reinforced her flat and inscrutable mouth. The composite betrayed a woman
with a serious "you'd better believe it" look.

She and her younger sister Jean embraced the activism of the Progressives with a heavy dose of noblesse oblige—demanding sanitation improvements, better care for the disabled, animal cruelty and antivice laws, and exposing political malfeasance. In possession of the most heavily decorated résumés to be found anywhere, they even succeeded in persuading conservative Tulane University to open its medical school for women. The two siblings, the city's most acclaimed change agents in its history, were often referred to as simply "the Gordons," as they generally worked as a team to ignite reforms. Neither one of the powerful duo ever married. Instead, they wedded their lives to what they believed was the common good of their city.

Both sisters' energies were often synchronized in a duet, but Jean's particular touchstone was support for underserved children. She lobbied for legislation toughening enforcement of existing child labor laws and established the city's first institution for the care of "feebleminded" girls, as the mentally challenged were described in the day's parlance. With proper direction, she held, girls with cognitive disabilities in a safe environment could become productive, and the immutable mechanisms of heredity could be softened. At the same time, she preached that sterilization would protect society from the burden of caring for these innocents, or at the very least, the government should prohibit them from marrying.[4]

Sister Kate's hyper-caffeinated vitality and resolve were aligned with her own north star—the fight for an amendment that would span the crevasse that existed between women and the polls—an amendment, that is, to Louisiana's constitution. And it is for this reason that she battled with and split from most other suffragists. Gordon believed adamantly that a federal amendment would ultimately destroy white supremacy in the South, as it would impede state control over elections—code for making sure Blacks did not vote. Taking it even further, she also subscribed to the idea that the ballot box should, ideally, be restricted to informed citizens, society's elite and educated.

In plain terms, Gordon wanted only *white* women to win the right to vote.[5] She maintained that Black disfranchisement was a Progressive reform—Black voters were a wellspring of corruption and a threatened political stability. If southern states passed their own suffrage amendments, they could then continue applying the racial screens that had been inserted into the Louisiana constitution in 1898. Devices like a literacy test and the "understanding" clause (whereby a person would have to interpret the meaning of a passage to the satisfaction of white registrars) effectively disfranchised African American men until the laws were finally outlawed in the 1960s. With a state suffrage amendment, the same laws could then be used to prevent Black women from voting as well. Kate did not deny that these laws were "subterfuges and evasions" of the Fifteenth Amendment to the US Constitution, which awarded suffrage to Black Americans. But they were justified, she affirmed, because the amendment was ratified during Reconstruction, when white males in the South were themselves disfranchised.[6]

With state-managed suffrage, the white vote would presumably be doubled, assuring that Blacks, both male and female, would remain trapped in the dimly lit prison of injustice. A federal amendment, on the other hand, would equalize African American and white women. This was simply unacceptable. "White men," she swore, "would be willing to club Negro men away from the polls" but would balk at doing the same to Black women.[7]

Gordon was not alone in her views. Louisiana's assistant attorney general Harry Gamble, invited by the Press Club to speak on the matter, reiterated the danger of overlooking the racial ramifications of women's suffrage. His speech was framed in states' rights terminology, reminding everyone of the evils of government centralization. "The blighting hand of Washington" was again being forced on the South, and the racial question was in danger of being "thrown into the hands of strangers." Every man should "refuse the poisoned bribe of Washington and demand the vote at home."[8] In the still unreconstructed Bayou State, distrust of Washington had weathered the decades since the last federal occupation troops were withdrawn in 1877. Home rule was quickly restored thereafter, but animosity toward the government diminished only at a glacial pace. Despite Mayor Behrman's plea for his city to "respond to the call" and stand unified in the country's defense, New Orleanians like Gamble and Gordon preferred to continue fighting a political war against the government in order to maintain white supremacy, a war that to them was more crucial—more meaningful.

Miss Kate's first platform, her mouthpiece, was the New Orleans based suffrage organization called the ERA Club, an acronym for Equal Rights for All, formed in 1895.[9] Despite her genteel upbringing, Kate never quite took to waltzing with the issues she cared deeply about. She was more of a square jawed Flamenco dancer, stomping loudly and unrelentingly. When the circumstances required, however, she knew how to present the most gracious model of southern deference and courtesy to the politically powerful—while discreetly poised to strike with a hidden dagger. When the Louisiana state constitutional convention met in New Orleans in 1898, both sisters were there to stare down legislators and petition for full suffrage for women. They got nowhere with this but did win a small but significant victory with an amendment to the Louisiana constitution—if a woman paid taxes, she would at least be allowed to vote on any tax referendum.[10] Here, finally, was a small crack in the wall, which provided suffragists with a critical voting precedent.

The inaugural opportunity to exercise this new freedom arrived in 1899 when a sewerage and drainage bond issue came up for a vote in New Orleans. But many women remained tentative, even panicky, about the simple act of appearing at a precinct to nervously lodge a ballot. These had been places that had always been rooted deep within a man's universe. Voting clashed with cultural norms, which insisted that women could not play on any rough and tumble all-male team, and politics was certainly one of those contact sports. Luckily, proxy voting was then permitted, so Kate, anticipating a woman's apprehension to crash the gender roadblock, went into high gear with a handful of other ERA Club members. After days of painstakingly researching property books and addresses, she and her African American coachman crisscrossed the city to obtain proxies from over three hundred eligible female voters.[11]

Since the law provided that women could not witness legal documents, her driver often stood in as a male witness to the paperwork, hopping out of the car to scratch his name on the document alongside the voters'. This was quite awkward—a barely literate Black man verifying the participation of a white, perhaps highly educated woman during a legal act. Such was the paradox of the day. Armed with the signatures, the two spent the entire election day driving from precinct to precinct casting the proxies, the last one just ten minutes before the polls closed. It was a herculean effort, but it produced the desired result. The New Orleans Progressive Union awarded the thirty-eight-year-old with a medal for her determined, dedicated work, and City Hall recognized her with a public tribute.[12] With this win, her reputation expanded beyond the city's limits.

Gordon's intelligence, bulletproof confidence, and messianic zeal for feminine equality attracted the attention of suffrage icons Carrie Chapman Catt and Susan B. Anthony of the National American Women's Suffrage Association. But its patience with the South's hardcore racism was rapidly thinning, sensitive as it was to negative public opinion.[13] Kate occupied a different frequency from its members. Inflexible as ever, she eventually resigned from her position as the organization's recording secretary. With typical magnification, she testified that she "would rather see my right arm withered in its socket than to raise it in behalf of vitalizing the 15th Amendment and above all destroy the safeguard of our liberty, state sovereignty."[14] Gordon was regurgitating the southern states' rights mantra of the 1850s, the very same chorus that led to secession.

Never did Kate favor universal suffrage. Buying into the radical philosophy of eugenics, she and Jean both envisioned an America polished clean of society's ills by keeping the mentally ill from marriage and procreation—and, indeed, enfranchisement. Only by imposing such laws would the nemesis of crime and the curse of family dislocation be eliminated. Mentally disturbed patients, Jean was sure, had a deleterious effect on city government as well, allowing for political machines and ultimately the "destruction of our civilization" unless the intelligence level of the electorate was elevated.[15]

This blatantly racist position seems so outrageously cruel and irredeemable that one would think that she was a refugee from mainstream society. Not so. In the context of the times, many Americans viewed all people of color as backward and lacking probity—requiring the benevolence of white society. Mainstream groups like the Rockefeller and Carnegie Foundations funded eugenics research. As followers of Social Darwinism, the struggle of the weak to survive, they relied on science as the solution to society's most urgent questions.

However deeply the sisters felt about the dangers of releasing the "feeble minded" onto St. Charles Avenue along with the general population, Kate never disguised her real focus—the continued suppression of African Americans. Her fear was her muse, her motivational tonic. Black men and women would use the franchise, she was convinced, to release themselves from the bondage of Jim Crow segregation. Crime in Black neighborhoods, their music, dress, and the fervor they displayed at their religious services, she offered, were part of a "coon nature." Ugly, ridiculing racial slurs punctuated her speeches, no matter the audience. Terms like "cornfield darkies" and "fool niggers" found their way into the most eloquent and well-constructed of them, italicizing the theme of African American inferiority and the absolute necessity of maintaining the supremacy of the white race—without which, she was convinced, society would be vandalized.[16]

These were not random rages against African Americans. She spoke purposefully. If she could use these demeaning words, then it must be true that whites like herself were indeed superior. There was no airbrushing this. Even in letters to her associates, she seemed never to choose more respectful terms like "Negro" or the more acceptable "colored" when referring to African Americans, in spite of the formal syntax found in the letters of the day—evidence of her inherent bigotry.

Sister Jean was no different in her racial stance. Because of her work with the Milne Home, an asylum for destitute children, she was invited, along with other Progressive civic leaders, to dinner in her honor at the White House with President Roosevelt as the host. She refused the invitation, however, when she learned that Booker T. Washington would join her at the table. According to records, she made no plausible public excuse for not attending. Instead, she took a page from her younger sister and stated exactly what she was thinking, giving as her reason that she would decline to attend any function where she would be placed on equal terms with a Negro. She would apparently never agree to dine with a Black person unless he was filling her water glass—regardless of the host.[17]

Miss Kate was confident in the ultimate success of her crusade, knowing that whites always feared that the Black community might one day assert itself and jolt the pillars of white control. She and her admirers, therefore, had to ensure that white men, the only ones voting, understood the implications of a federal amendment. Southerners would be conceding that the federal government had every right to manage and even supervise state elections, and that would spell the end of white supremacy. In a letter to her associate and confidante in Kentucky, Laura Clay, she wrote of her optimism: "My old point of choice between nigger or woman ... has more truth than poetry to it."[18]

In 1913, not long after resigning from her position in the National American Women's Suffrage Association, she built her own pressure group designed to lobby for state suffrage amendments throughout the entire South. Called the Southern States Woman's Suffrage Conference, it was headquartered in New Orleans at 1800 Prytania Street. She hoped her new group would be the van for suffrage, making other suffrage organizations unnecessary. Its publication, the *New Southern Citizen*, made clear the organization's purpose in its motto: "Make Southern States White."[19]

Despite the hotspur's myopic insistence on a state-sponsored amendment, many suffragists clearly preferred the oft-proposed Anthony Amendment to the US Constitution as a more substantial and permanent solution to their plight. It would enfranchise women, they argued, in one fell swoop rather than having to endure state-by-state political fistfights that might or might not be successful. In Louisiana, these more moderate suffragists were accommodated by the formation in 1913 of the Woman Suffrage Party. Its members desired the ballot however they could get it—whether by state or federal amendment. That more balanced sentiment was unacceptable to the immutable Miss Kate. Always the tallest lightning rod for the cause, she condemned the party because it endangered her self-anointed role as the movement's czar. The schism between these two groups, the Sunnis and Shiites of Louisiana's suffrage contest, would endure in spite of the commonality of their purpose.

The conflict escalated as the captains of each organization attacked each other. The president of the new WSP, New Orleanian Sake Meehan, in a thinly veiled reference to Gordon, announced that her party was committed to be "free of all personalities, jealousies, and antagonisms ... that naturally grow up in a single club dominated ... by a small number of persons."[20] Meehan was even more direct later, insisting that "if Miss Kate could be silenced or eliminated . . . , the cause of suffrage in Louisiana would certainly benefit." In short, Gordon was "a damned nuisance."[21]

Personal attacks would continue, and Kate would cleave to her role as Louisiana's "Wizard of Suffrage" despite damaging the jihad. The feud between the two groups also served to embolden the enemies of suffrage, handing them more ammunition. Here was proof, they hastened to say, that women were too petty and emotional, unable to work together or to compromise to reach a goal. According to this argument, women were just not capable of making judicious decisions and therefore should leave politics to men. This assessment ignored the behavior of thousands of men who for years were herded into polling places and bowed to the wishes of their city's machine boss by way of his stooges, the precinct captains.

Meehan and her apostles also represented the more liberal wing of the Progressive surge, made up of women who not only demanded the vote, but also pushed for social reforms. These women were to become, or at least endure, the flappers of the coming decade, who wore makeup, cut their hair short, and drank in public without male chaperones. Kate, conversely, was a prohibitionist, repelled by the sight of a respectable, refined young woman smoking in public. Never comfortable with women in the fast lane, she was convinced that those who cocktailed with liquor representatives could never be serious voters. Even suffragist allies like Elizabeth Werlein were not immune from Miss Kate's disdain, who watched in controlled horror as Werlein pulled out a cigarette at a table in the dining room of a Baton Rouge hotel, inhaled, and blew smoke through her nose.[22] These personal foibles prevented the "suffs" in Louisiana from fully husbanding their resources. Miss Kate was simply unable to transcend her impulse to judge others, unable to suppress her characteristic hubris, unable to keep her focus.

Loathing for these female modernists who scorned convention was widespread. Gordon was certainly not alone. A letter to the *Picayune* in October, 1918, represented that sentiment:

Take the high heels from your shoes, those silly pointed-toed shoes that make you stalk like a real chicken. Wash the clown-like red and white from your faces, cover up your exposed chests. Wear ankle-length skirts that will not reveal to the world your fatted calves, or spindle shanks, and then, perhaps, with the blessing of God and the respect of man, we may be considered to have brains and common sense enough to have suffrage thrust upon us. Just now, every American woman should think only of helping to win the war.[23]

Another came from a gentleman who too was appalled at the sight of young women using tobacco, surrendering their femininity. "What are we coming to," he barked, "a race of broad-shouldered, frog-breasted, man-dressed women . . . ? I've always worshiped a real woman; she doesn't smoke cigarettes!"[24]

Miss Kate and her followers were yet to embrace the rapid social revolution that was taking place. Evidence of this was everywhere. Jazz, once the bailiwick of African American dance halls and saloons, was shredding through the norms of traditional musical styles. Movies, particularly comedies, ridiculed Victorian customs, the European upper class, and authority of all types. The storyline of the popular cartoon strip "Polly" concerned the difficult time Polly's parents had in controlling her independence. Margaret Sanger had published her controversial 1915 book *Family Limitation*, which promoted birth control. Access to cars was forcing a liberating revolution in courting practices, and job opportunities provided by the war nudged the emancipation process even further. Women were rebelling, frustrated with subjugating rules of "place." This battle over the ballot box was just one more logical step in the creation of a new American woman.

In July of 1918, during some of the heaviest months of combat for Pershing's men, the Gordons and their supporters in the capital finally got through to the governor and enough legislators to present a state suffrage amendment on the floor for a vote. A majority of the legislators were now convinced that with the blessings of the president and both political parties, the nationwide momentum to give women the vote was impending. The tally in each chamber was unambiguous. In the Louisiana House, the count was 80 to 22 while the Senate passed the measure 29 to only 11 against. Victory had finally been achieved. Lydia Holmes, current chair of the state's WSP, was so overcome by the excitement of the roll call that she fainted in the Senate chamber and had to be moved to an adjourning room.[25]

The proposed state amendment would now go before the voters in the November election. Both US senators from Louisiana and all but one of its congressmen were supporters. Governor Pleasant also endorsed the amendment, calling it a citizen's duty to vote for it. Elected in 1916, he reiterated the Gordons' views exactly. Pleasant and his wife Anne joined Kate's scrappy sorority, becoming devotees of what appeared to the couple as a sincere effort to protect Louisiana from the tremors of racial uplift. In one sentence the governor spelled out where he stood: "The South is the stronghold to opposition to the federal amendment because it does not wish to consent to federal control over our local suffrage for fear that it will force the Negro back to the ballot box."[26]

But how would the passage of a state amendment deter a vote for a US constitutional amendment? The strategy was to give southern Congressional representatives leverage in Washington by placing suffrage amendments in their states' constitutions. Then the states' elected leaders on Capitol Hill could argue that there was no longer a need for additional federal action. There was no guarantee that this strategy would work, of course, but it was the only card left to play.

Pleasant, Kate Gordon, and their loyalists had to have recognized that the avalanche of support for a federal amendment was likely impossible to fend off. The National American Women's Suffrage Association was well-organized and well-funded. President Wilson, who was late to support the Anthony Amendment, linked women's suffrage to patriotism and the war effort. And most important of all, public opinion, measured by dozens of newspaper editorials and letters from voters, slanted heavily in their direction. People did not ignore the massive contribution being made by women in every conceivable corner of the war's home front—yet they remained stranded on the periphery of American society. It was time to award them full citizenship.

Still, the skirmish in Louisiana played out. The Woman Suffrage Party sent an olive branch to Gordon while the statewide contest was fought. New Orleans newspapers followed the blood feud and printed Gordon's predictable, succinct reply that she would never grasp hands, even temporarily, with a group that did not stand for states' rights. Letters between Gordon and her soulmate Laura Clay that the two had succumbed to the alarmist belief that the opposition's campaign for the Anthony Amendment was being encouraged in part by "German sympathizers," who hoped that millions of new female voters would enhance pacifist sentiment in the country.[27]

Further inflaming the animosity, Kate's forces had somehow managed to lay claim to the signing ceremony in the governor's office, squeezing out members of the WSP from attending. Gordon and the A-list of the amendment's sponsors, painted with smiles, stood behind the governor and posed for photos as Pleasant signed the proposed amendment with a special gold pen.[28] That did not help matters at all. The image suggested that Gordon, the ERA Club, and her Southern States Women's Suffrage Conference were solely responsible for bringing an amendment to the people for a vote. Lydia Holmes and the WSP were nowhere in sight.

After this rebuff, there could never be a reconciliation. A bipartisan committee of representatives from the rival groups, recognizing the common ground that existed between them, actually forged a provisional cease-fire before the public referendum. They were at odds with each other, but at least the family of suffragists agreed to sit together at dinner.[29] Each faction worked hard through the campaign, but they agreed to keep out of each other's way. The war was always a priority, but their message was clear—women's suffrage and the fight to promote liberty and justice by defeating the Huns were inseparable and compatible goals. But the public bitterness between the two groups was the oxygen which further fueled antisuffrage flames. The inability of them to work smoothly together during the referendum campaign, the antis reiterated, was more evidence that women should focus only on motherhood.

As the November 5th, 1918, election approached, the WSP sent hundreds of mailings to business and community directors, fraternal organizations, and others hunting for converts and attempting to get a bead on the depth of support that existed in the business arena—a kind of primitive public-opinion poll. Ethel Hutson, the party's publicity chair working from a desk in the war room of the Suffrage House, headquarters of the WSP, composed many of those solicitations. Once the chief of the *Item*'s women's bureau, the Baton Rouge native trained in art at Newcomb College and was quickly recognized as one of the most respected painters in New Orleans. But there was much more to this lady. Her passion for the pallet was matched only by her desire to work for women's civil rights.

This referendum represented, she wrote, "a measure of right and justice to the women who pay taxes, obey laws, teach, toil, and serve in every needed capacity needed by men, and who today are supporting the war and all its activities with signal patriotism." Among those returning answers to her inquiries were representatives of the American Federation of Labor, the chairman of the Merchants and Manufacturers Bureau, and the president of the Building Trades Council, as well as lawyers, bankers, and retail managers. They were universally positive, emphasizing the role women played in the war effort.

The responses must have given Hutson and her party a lift. "Women have wonderfully helped to win the war and have done so unselfishly, nobly, and patriotically," one explained. Another remembered that "women have filled the places of men adequately, efficiently, and conscientiously in the industrial world; in private life she has produced and trained the boys who have gone to the front; in political life she has all the finer qualities that men lack." The president of City Bank and Trust wrote that "the liberalizing influence of the progressive age has long since removed the restrictions and prejudices which confirm women to purely domestic relations."[30]

Canal Street was used by the "suffs" in its usual way—as a long, linear platform to get out a message. Yellow banners trimmed in purple and white, the movement's colors, were strung on commercial buildings peppered with pro-vote slogans. Well-dressed volunteers passed out their leaflets to people as they hurried to work or to shop. Between the activists were the "newsies," who cried out the latest German defeat from every busy intersection. As the November 5th vote approached, compelling news of the Kaiser's abdication found itself competing with the suffrage scrimmage.

The volunteers were reinforced by an aggressive teammate. Miss Florence Huberwald, a well-respected local music teacher, was the same impassioned lady who had shared several speaker platforms with the governor and other prominent guests during the Liberty Loan drives. Known for her persuasive, fire-in-the-belly approach, she had been inserting herself on Canal Street's wide sidewalk, spending day after day there for the past months (interrupted only by the influenza epidemic)[31] doing more than just distributing suffrage literature. She attracted small groups of people, both men and women, who huddled around this teacher as she engaged them with the gospel of righteousness, trumpeting the cause.

Huberwald was hardly subtle. "Stop," she would say to a startled businessman as she leaned towards him, hand raised. "I have something to say to you!" Soon they found themselves listening and often laughing at what she had to say. The *Item* described Huberwald's style as "straight from the shoulder" and brief, practiced as she was in the art of proletariat street oratory. "We will remain a territory forever," she exclaimed to several listeners, "and refuse to become a state unless our women . . . can also share our privileges." Despite the hyperbole, she lost no listeners to her prosaic psalm of self-empowerment.

Miss Florence then went on to play the states' rights card, mobilizing her sentences for effect. "In this great cause for equal freedom, will Louisiana be a volunteer or wait to become a conscript through national suffrage?" Another question popped from her: "How long will the United States, the divine trumpeter of freedom, blush at the tardy acknowledgement of justice to her women?" You couldn't take your eyes off of her. And no antidote existed to tame her. Finally, with a rising shout that resonated above the din of the streetcars and newsboys, she swirled to the men who surrounded her, jabbing her finger at them and challenging them eye to eye: "Men of Louisiana—what are you going to do?"[32]

Two unexpected pretenders pulled up seats to the Louisiana game, laying down their chips on the table and preparing to play. One of them was especially controversial—the National Woman's Party led by agitator Alice Paul. The fire-eating suffragist was known for her virulent attacks on President Wilson's early opposition to an amendment. Paul and her militant followers received national publicity for their refusal to comply with the police when

ordered to stop picketing the White House and the Capitol with inflammatory signs. The provocative placards continually referred to the president
as "Kaiser Wilson" and upset the sensibilities of most citizens who looked
upon these women as traitors. The nation was at war, after all, and, to some,
these women seemed less concerned about that fact than their own selfish
agendas. She and over two hundred other women were arrested and jailed in
1917, preferring incarceration to the option of a fine. While imprisoned, Paul,
always the dissident fighter, went on a hunger strike with nineteen others.
Prison officials responded by constraining and torturously force-feeding
them with tubes through their noses three times a day.

Accompanying them behind bars was New Orleanian Mrs. Alice Cosu,
who was sentenced to thirty days in a Virginia "workhouse," as it was called
euphemistically. Her cellmate was a seventy-three-year-old woman from
Florida named Mary Nolan, who recorded her memory of their first night
behind bars. Cosu gave up the only bed to her older inmate and instead
rested on a pad on the cold, concrete floor. As the night fell, Cosu became
progressively ill and suffered some kind of cardiac event. She began vomiting,
but their cries for a doctor went unanswered except for a threat from one
guard to either be silent or be placed with a brace in their mouths.[33]

It is difficult to measure to what extent Paul's smearing offensive against
President Wilson, who was popular throughout the state, had on public
opinion locally. Letters to the editors were angrily averse to their behavior
and seemed to favor the imprisonments. The inclination to suppress anti-
government behavior was practically universal. Any sort of pronouncement
that was even remotely critical of the government was criminalized. Many
were certainly repelled by their extremism. Other suffragists, perhaps, may
have been energized by the attention Paul brought to the plight of women.
Whatever the case, her voice was now in the mix in Louisiana.

Another organization arose in the late summer of 1918, one that would
come bearing another message entirely. Called the Men's Anti-Suffrage
League, its ringleaders were composed of various business and political
operatives throughout the state. They began their campaign late and did
not have nearly the organizational framework of their opponents, but it
was a concern to the suffragists for their vote might be the difference in a
close election.

Louisiana's principal newspapers all endorsed the amendment. Even the
New Orleans States, a longtime opponent of women's suffrage, made public
its change of heart by admitting that state suffrage was much more satisfactory than the federal alternative. According to Lydia Holmes, there was but
one newspaper to her knowledge in the entire state, and a minor one at that,

that was an enemy of the women's vote. When she asked its editor, whom she refused to identify, why he was an enemy of the movement, he simply answered, "Ugh! Don't like women. I'm agin women."[34]

Newspapers were significant allies of the movement to be sure. But there was one politician who would tip the balance and ultimately decide the amendment's fate—Mayor Behrman. It is estimated that he controlled about fourteen thousand votes in New Orleans through his political machine, the Old Regulars. As the master puppeteer, he had the city's seventeen ward leaders connected to a tether through his skillful use of city patronage, and these men had great influence over who manned the precincts as captains in their respective wards. They, in turn, had a knack of persuading their neighbors in the precincts to vote their way, that is, Behrman's way. While he gave lip service in support of the amendment and likely did feel personally that the amendment should pass simply because women deserved it, he was secretly conflicted—and it was not about race. It was about power. If New Orleans women were given the ballot, they would more than likely support political reform efforts. Those most strident about achieving equality were more than comfortable with upsetting the status quo. One of their first targets, he guessed, would be his machine and its tight grip on the city's voters. His order to a caucus of his ward lieutenants to insure the referendum's failure, according to a report in the *Picayune*, was "binding."[35]

Weather had always been an important ingredient in Louisiana's statewide elections. Because of the dreadful condition of its roads, particularly in rural areas where paving was a luxury, rain made it very difficult for voters to reach their precincts, often miles from their homes or farms. Such was the case in the days and weeks before the election as a train of unforgiving rainstorms punished the state. Impassable gravel and mud roads also forced the cancellation of personal appeals and general campaigning for the amendment in hard-to-reach places. Yet another unforeseen complication diminished the vote. Parish after parish throughout the state reported that many of their precincts were closed because of the lingering flu epidemic.[36] But the blow that really staggered and eventually knocked out the amendment was thrown by the mayor.

The Progressive report card was kind to Behrman. His performance during his seventeen years in office marked him as a champion of reform. The checklist was long: targeting the ills of urban society, assaulting particularly the city's most debilitating diseases through science and modern medicine; updating city services like transportation and facilitating advances in sewerage and drainage; paving miles of city streets; improving the natural environment; establishing a public belt railroad; encouraging philanthropy (and being philanthropic himself); spearheading services for society's forgotten; and improving the port.

Despite these impressive accomplishments, he scored poorly on the Progressive litmus test of democratizing politics. His compliant ward kingpins and precinct captains, his "henchmen" as his enemies stigmatized them, produced for the mayor and the Old Regulars the desired vote in Orleans Parish against the hard-fought amendment—5,414 for and an eye opening 14,552 against. Given that New Orleans was ground zero for the suffrage movement in Louisiana, the lopsided vote must have raised eyebrows to outside observers who were unaware of the mayor's curated politics. But this was exactly how big city political machines were supposed to work. Their DNA was expected to be found on the ballots. The statewide referendum lost by a mere 3,525 votes, with only Orleans and six other parishes out of 64 voting the amendment down. It was evident that Orleans Parish issued the verdict, and Behrman was the jury captain.[37]

Lydia Holmes took the results in stride: "The women of Louisiana have done all they can in the state, and we will receive the ballot by federal action."[38] Kate Gordon, zealous as ever, was not as charitable. Shaken by the final results, she moved forward with a very public event that she believed would embarrass the mayor—draping the Liberty Monument, the iconic structure at the foot of Canal Street, in black crepe. Voting down the amendment meant, to her, a capitulation to federal guardianship, disgracing the sixteen martyrs of the so-called White League, who had died near that "holy" site in the 1874 Battle of Liberty Place resisting Louisiana's Reconstruction government.

But Gordon was penetrating into a radioactive sphere. To most New Orleanians, anyone who participated in that rebellion was forever decorated with distinction. Participation in the battle reinforced claims to political leadership, such was the glamor attached to it. A sacred shrine it was—hallowed ground—the city's answer to Griffin's Wharf of Boston Tea Party fame. The monument symbolized resistance against the oppressor, and that is what Miss Kate was likely thinking. But one must be most careful if it was tampered with in any way. Behrman's reaction to her bold threat? "It merely goes to show," he remarked with a shoulder shrug, "how far these women will go.... If they want to drape it, let them go ahead and do it. It rather amuses me."[39]

Meanwhile, Gordon eviscerated the mayor for the defeat, deploying her switchblade-sharp tongue to slash away at this nonbeliever, this mayor who pretended to lead. In a long letter to the *Picayune,* she held back nothing. New Orleanians were by now used to her verbal pyrotechnics, but this seemed even more savage than usual. Nothing pierced like her printed, weaponized words: "It is always a difficult task to fight ignorance," she began. "I extend my hand in sorrow and shame that the dictates of one man can show the farce of what we have believed was free government. . . . The Kaiser who rules the city of New Orleans had ordered out his slaves with the instruction to continue to keep the white women of Louisiana the political inferiors of Negro men."[40]

There was no public response from City Hall to her explosive letter. It would profit no one to trade barbs with her at this point. The seasoned mayor likely placed it aside and dismissed it as an outburst from a frustrated and defeated opponent, experienced as he was in the hard-knuckle politics of his city.

Yet Behrman did not deny her slur that it was his order to ward officers that killed the amendment. Unmoved by Gordon's harangue, he retained his sense of humor about the entire affair. In a gathering at City Hall a week after the provocative letter, Behrman was given a gift—a German infantry helmet by a Salvation Army captain from New Orleans who had confiscated it near the French front. Amused, he winked: "Judging from the battered appearance of the helmet, I wouldn't be surprised if some mayor hadn't worn it over there." Pretending to rub his sore head, he admitted that he was sorry that he did not have its protection during the suffrage struggle when he really could have used it.[41] Behrman then offered what he believed was a major cause of the amendment's defeat—Gordon's behavior aroused public scorn against her crusade.

He was on to something. The Armistice was less than two weeks old. Restrictions were being lifted all over the city, and things were happily returning to normal. Lights were once again brightening the commercial district, food conservation was about to end, and, because the flu epidemic was flickering out in late November, church services were being permitted, schools and theaters were reopening, and public assemblies were allowed. Now the focus was on the return of the boys from France—some thought even by Christmas. It was a time for jubilation! Black crepe? That was a sign of deep mourning. Gordon's scheme was at total variance with the upbeat throb of the city. Draping "looks pretty German to me," commented Mrs. D. A. S. Vaught sardonically, the lady who had lovingly placed flowers at the landmark for the past twenty-seven years as secretary of the monument fund. She had her blood up, angry that such an act would be a sacrilege. "I'm afraid Miss Gordon has upset her own applecart again." She later alluded to the suffragist's infatuation with publicity, adding a remark saturated with contempt: "It's a pity to make a scarecrow of the monument. But I hope they won't get arrested, because nothing would give them so much pleasure and satisfaction."[42]

Hizzoner refused to approve the issuance of a permit for the rally at the monument, but he did instruct the police to be careful not to interfere with any gathering there if Gordon decided to go through with it. Behrman was going on record opposing Gordon's stunt while at the same time allowing her and the rest of her zealots to hang themselves in the public arena.

Gordon must have come to a postmortem realization that her gambit to clothe in black the revered shaft on November 24th was a mistake of impulse. She was thrown off the scent. The rally would go on, but the historic obelisk would remain unclothed. Kate's sudden change of heart was motivated, she explained, because of the possibility that blanketing it might be misinterpreted as dishonoring the men who lost their lives in the defense of liberty in 1874. (Two of the speakers were, however, the sons of White Leaguers, so her explanation was specious.) Instead, she and her vassals quietly dropped the idea and instead brought yellow flowers and wreaths to decorate the granite shrine's pedestal.

Perhaps it was the letters to the *Picayune*, which changed her tactics—like one from "A Mere Man" claiming to be a supporter of women's suffrage: "I voted for women's suffrage," he began, "but never again!" One reason was the abusive denunciation of the mayor. The other was the "impudent proposal" to "desecrate" the Liberty Monument, which, the writer spit out, "is the property of all of our people, and anyone . . . desecrating it should be jailed."[43]

Roughly two hundred members of the ERA Club and Southern States Woman Suffrage Association formed a semicircle around an elevated platform near the monument to hear a half dozen speakers, including a rabbi and two Protestant pastors. Gordon was the last to speak, and she did not disappoint the adoring crowd, which faced her in the chilly forty-degree wind. Bellowing out that the Old Regular ring was "degenerate," her speech angrily castigated Behrman for "disgracing" the spirit of the men who died in the insurrection. Then she played what she thought was her winning hand. As she had done before, Gordon associated the mayor with the dethroned Kaiser Wilhelm. Behrman's gang, she boomed, was nothing more than "a hideous prototype of Prussian autocracy" with white citizens "herded like cattle under a party lash to do the bidding of the political Junkers."[44]

Seven months later, in June of 1919, the Anthony Amendment easily passed both houses of Congress during a special session called by President Wilson. The final step for ratification was now left in the hands of the state legislatures. Three-fourths of them, thirty-six, would be needed. When the Mississippi legislature met in February of 1920, Gordon expanded her pilgrimage to the statehouse in Jackson at the invitation of that city's major antisuffrage newspaper. When the vote on the federal amendment in the Magnolia State failed, she headed back to New Orleans hoping to repeat the victory in her home state. It was North versus South once again. In

Gordon's view, the contest went far beyond Louisiana's borders. There was a commonality of purpose throughout the former Confederacy—Anglo-Saxon superiority—that needed to be re-energized and contoured in a unified vote against the Washington establishment.

Despite this loss in neighboring Mississippi, adamant suffragists throughout Louisiana were invigorated, so close were they to victory. By March, only one more state legislature was left. Thirty-five had approved the Anthony Amendment (including Arkansas and Texas). The walls of the levee were about to break, but Kate Gordon continued sandbagging nonetheless. Holmes and her party attempted to reassure legislators that no federal amendment would ever deny Louisiana control over its own election machinery. The Gordon sisters, on the other hand, refused to bend, soldiering true to their position that the amendment would create massive social disruption. Then, of course, there were also the opponents of woman suffrage, no matter the method.

The balance shifted when the Gordons and their partisans became alien bedfellows with antisuffrage apostates, who professed the very same states' rights argument as the Gordon zealots. "Arrant fools," Kate once called one who refused to recognize the liberties denied to half the population. Yet these groups worked together, sometimes even sharing the same stage, to somehow stave off the long arm of the federal government. All three factions assailed the state's legislators, lobbying them, intercepting them to and from their seats, pleading for their votes.

The unholy alliance worked, for the amendment was defeated by the lawmakers in Baton Rouge in June of 1920. Louisiana lost the opportunity to be acclaimed as the thirty-sixth state to ratify. Two months later, Tennessee instead captured the honor. This was in spite of the efforts of the indefatigable Miss Kate and Mrs. Anne Pleasant, the former First Lady of Louisiana, who traveled with her to Tennessee to assist the antis there once the issue was stillborn in Louisiana.

Over twenty-five million women across America would finally be allowed to vote in the presidential election of November 1920. "My joy," responded Lydia Holmes, "is too great for words." Ethel Hutson was equally concise: "At last we are American citizens." The mayor too claimed to be "delighted," even though he confessed that he "had been" against the amendment. But he regretted that it was Tennessee that consummated the struggle and not Louisiana. Behrman could not resist delivering a final punch to his nemesis: "The women of this city and state know where the blame lies for having cheated them of this high honor which was as sure to come as the day itself." [45]

In the aftermath of the Tennessee vote, it was unusual to see Jean Gordon rather than her outspoken sister issuing a statement to the *Picayune*. Perhaps it was too painful for Kate to reconcile the defeat given her wearying, prolonged effort. Certainly, she felt that the South had betrayed her. Like a woman scorned by her longstanding lover, she found it difficult to talk about it now that the affair was finished. She indicated as much in a 1923 letter to Laura Clay: "It was months before I could allow myself to even think of the whole horrible experience."[46] Jean's bitterness was also evident through her words, recalling the complex emotions that the Gordons were experiencing: "Tennessee has disgraced the South. I can only say that I am glad that it is not Louisiana which has brought ignominy upon us." She continued that she had worked her entire life to legalize the vote for her gender, but "now that it has come about, I do not want it."[47]

Where can the blame be placed for the defeat of the Anthony Amendment in Louisiana? Unquestionably, the shotgun marriage forged between Gordon's forces and the antis was fateful. States' rights activists had slammed the door. Gordon's renowned hubris and jealousies and her antagonistic assaults on the leaders of the Woman Suffrage Party did the movement in Louisiana no good. Two years after the amendment's ratification, Kate remained bitter, even petty. When asked to contribute a chapter in a series of volumes entitled *History of Woman Suffrage*, she began by attributing the movement in Louisiana "largely to the activity of one club"—her ERA Club, intentionally dismissing the significant role played by other suffrage groups.[48] Above all, it was the race issue that complicated the struggle over the amendment and ultimately became its assassin. The drama of the suffrage war in Louisiana must be understood in the context of Jim Crow and fear. The open wounds of Reconstruction healed slowly and painfully.

Once the Nineteenth Amendment had been ratified, the Orleans Parish registrar of voters forecast that many women, despite the constitutional protection they were afforded, would still be cursed with voter anxiety. Others were conflict-averse or found it difficult to liberate themselves from the cultural vice grip they endured in contemporary southern society. To minimize the apprehension he expected from the newly ordained voters, the registrar promised to assign a small squadron of nurse's aides to his office—just in case some may be overcome.[49]

Despite his effort, only 22,299 white women and 1,797 Black women registered in 1920 (just 25 percent of registered voters) as opposed to 56,134 and 802 white and Black men respectively. After a prolonged and laborious struggle, activists hoped for much more participation, but it was not to be. Not until the 1940s did New Orleans women register in numbers that approached half of the electorate. For African American women (and men), percentages remained low for decades.[50] Kate Gordon's alarmist warnings, as it turned out, were misguided. Black disfranchisement remained solidly in place for both Black men and women. The Nineteenth Amendment did little to shake the racial status quo in New Orleans. Perhaps another major wartime push—the crusade against vice—would prove to be more successful.

Chapter 14

WIELDING THE "SWORD OF RIGHTEOUSNESS"

During the months preceding the effective date of the Prohibition Amendment, the Justice Department saw an opportunity to clamp down on the liquor laws already in play and to pay particular attention to military cantonments. The American Protective League would provide the manpower to insulate these installations from the corrosive influences of whiskey and women. APL chief Albert Briggs and his acolytes in Washington were comfortable with the new responsibility since the pursuit of slackers had slowed by mid-1918. The paucity of these cases was creating a morale problem within the organization. This new role would remind American Protective Leaguers that their place in the war remained significant.

Even with Storyville's closing, New Orleans was a priority with its other vice emporiums remaining in full swing. While touring the South's encampments, Briggs typed a letter to partner Charles Frey asking for "all the dope you possibly can regarding the New Orleans situation . . . so I won't have to go back there."[1] Meanwhile, local APL chief Charles Weinberger was appointed to the post of special US commissioner, "commissioned" to target liquor and other vice violations in his hometown. His specific job was to expedite search warrants overnight without waiting for the usual sluggish procedure, collecting a fee of $1,500 for this extra duty. The shift of responsibilities was now official. The emphasis of the APL's detectives was reshaped again—from hunting spies, to identifying slackers, and now to pursuing anyone who strayed from godliness and virtue.[2]

It would not be easy. Eva Wright, a member of the New Orleans Federation of Women's Clubs, revealed to the *Item* a few disquieting matters associated with Camp Nicholls that demanded attention. Brazen, delinquent women, she complained, were picking off innocent (or less so) recruits with relative ease as they moved into and out of the tented encampment where there was a willing customer base for their services.

Many of the young soldiers looked upon commercial sex as a rite of passage during their stint in the army, away from home and family and coaxed on by their buddies. Streetwise women of easy virtue accompanied them to the makeshift brothels that had recently sprouted up on the banks of Bayou St. John near the camp's perimeter. If the soldiers were restricted from coming to them, they would come to the soldiers. It was like hucksters drawn to a carnival. Theirs was a mobile occupation. No need for the men to take a streetcar into town. And all of these potential clients had a few bucks in their pockets with no expenses to worry about, compliments of Uncle Sam, so their entertainment budgets were indulgent. So too would be the girls.

Much more disturbing in Wright's report was the sighting of "large numbers" of young, impressionable teens between fourteen and seventeen years old who remained after dark "visiting" with men in seclusion among City Park's burly live oaks and drapes of Spanish moss. Adult lubricants were no doubt partners in these rendezvous as well. Some of the girls, she presumed, were unmarried and living with their soldier boyfriends, afflicted with a virulent strain of "khaki fever." It was going around. A few were reported missing from their homes by worried parents.[3] Wright's investigation of these conditions was, she said, compiled from interviews, observations, and statements made by "reliable" sources.[4] Drawn to the glamor of associating with a man in uniform, these "charity girls," as they were called (or for some, the less complimentary "patriotutes"), represented what was becoming more evident throughout the country—a class of rebellious youth who eschewed the boundaries of chastity chartered by their parents. Under thirty and eager both to experiment in fashion and to contest the restrictive role of women from the previous generation, they were unwilling to accept the ethic of virginity without question.

The *Item*'s publication of Wright's story created a major stir at Camp Nicholls, and an indignant Colonel Frank Stubbs, the camp's commander, strenuously denied that these activities were factual.[5] Not only was it a slur to the character of the men in uniform, but also to New Orleans's young women. What especially irked the soldiers was confusing visiting female family members with illicit behavior. Outraged by the allegations, several squads of soldiers, unarmed, assembled in front of the *Item*'s headquarters to demonstrate against the paper for publishing the story, demanding to see the owner. Sixty-seven of them were detained by police and returned to Nicholls. On the following day, a reinforced armed guard was ordered to protect the building's entrance on Camp Street.[6]

The *Picayune* watched silently from a neutral corner as the *States* slashed away at its rival, the *Item*, for reporting Wright's claims without corroboration and, with a conspicuous selection of words, for "prostituting the functions of honest journalism." Worse, it blasted its competitor with the ultimate criticism—the *Item* was being "treasonous" and "pro-Kaiser" with its "cowardly attack" on the troops.[7] Smelling blood, the *States* reported that they had located ten enlisted men from Nicholls who were willing to put up $1,000 to anyone who could prove Wright's allegations.[8] Counterpunching, the *Item* wrote unconvincingly that the other dailies were just trying to sell newspapers, accusing the *States* of orchestrating a "raid" on its offices and threatening it with a libel lawsuit.[9] But the *Item*'s publisher, James M. Thomson, finally admitted in a formal, front-page apology to Stubbs, to the men of Camp Nicholls, and to the women who visited the camp that his paper should have verified Wright's "unsupported charges."[10]

Was Wright's report valid? Based on police reports and arrests elsewhere in the city, it is probable that many of her observations about impromptu brothels and sex solicitations did exist, especially when security was lax during the first weeks of the camp's mobilization. It is also likely that teenage girls were making clandestine visits to their boyfriends at Nicholls. The *Item* did indeed run the story without properly acquiring other sources from its own staff of reporters. If it had done so, they would likely have found truth in much of what was alleged and avoided the nasty and very public fistfight with the *States*.

Issues like these raised concern. But maintaining morale was important, and allowing acceptable opportunities for the troops to socialize with young women was a must. Raymond Fosdick's Commission on Training Camp Activities had as its mission to provide tasteful recreational amusements to the young men in uniform during their free time—things like choral groups, libraries, athletics, theaters, education, and "take a soldier home for dinner" programs. The commission also provided diversions for the girls living near the military camps—clubs and socials—to keep their eager minds off of the thousands of young men in uniform suddenly appearing in their communities. It was a tough task. Those uniforms cast a very weighty spell—the glamor of a soldier on a girl's arm, the craving for female companionship. Libidos and sexual curiosity, everyone understood, were at a peak both within a camp's gates and beyond. All of these natural instincts triangulated into an almost impossible force to numb. Magazines, poker, and baseball would do only so much.

The liberal issuance of weekend passes was designed to help. Civic and religious organizations sponsored weekly dances all over the city—each well supervised. Sometimes, however, the affairs were tarnished by the appearance of undesirable women. The problem festered at the Bentley Hotel in Alexandria, Louisiana, near Camp Beauregard, where regular dances were held to entertain Louisiana troops stationed there. Rules were therefore tightened.

First, the dozens of single girls who attended were made to write their names and addresses in the hotel lobby twice—once on a pad under the name of one of the chaperones who became responsible for their conduct and again on a cardboard tag that they pinned on their clothing for easy recognition. Once on the dance floor, couples were closely monitored by female chaperones to ensure that no indecency was on display.

Assisting in the effort was a New Orleans woman named Irene Shields, leader of a local group called the Rescue, Health, and Moral Protective League. Miss Shields intervened if she suspected alcohol, did not recognize an address, or if a girl arrived at the hotel without a parent, a red flag signaling that she was likely searching for more than an innocent dance. In this case the girl would politely be shown the door. It was especially reprehensible to Shields that mothers accompanying their daughters to these affairs would allow them to wear their skirts up to their knees and their hair in curls piled high, dancing with any man who showed interest. An *Item* reporter attended one of the dances and agreed: "Unbelievable as it seems, their mothers sit there . . . and watch them dancing—and smile complacently." Sometimes, the writer added, they even got up to dance too![11]

Area newspapers published this warning, attesting to the concern:

A large number of foolish and vicious women have come to Alexandria from various towns. . . . We wish to warn mothers of the impropriety and danger of permitting young girls to travel alone to a cantonment city. May we emphasize to the parents that even though they have every confidence in their daughters, they should not allow them to be exposed to the pitfalls and temptations with which they are sure to come in contact when visiting Alexandria without a chaperone.

Further, any "suspicious" women would be confined for thirty days in jail. Those without visible means of support would be deemed vagrants and sentenced to jail as well.[12]

Whiskey and women were in the crosshairs of the APL badge flashers. Section 12 and 13 of the Selective Service Act created "moral zones," making it illegal to operate disorderly houses or outlets of any kind that sold alcohol within a prescribed radius of a military facility (five and later ten miles). One APL operative counted eight, fifteen, and sixteen saloons within a half mile of Camp Nicholls, Tulane's Camp Martin, and Jackson Barracks, respectively. All of them were pretending to sell only soft drinks.[13] It was clear that daily compliance with this order would still require monitoring by dozens of League gumshoes. They would be allowed to search cars heading into the encampments, to help law enforcement conduct raids, and to assist in arresting the peddlers of booze and flesh. These methods seemed to work. During its tenure, the New Orleans office handled almost six thousand suspected violations of Sections 12 and 13. (See Appendix A.)

When reports of widespread prostitution and alcohol abuse reached Washington in 1916 during the Pancho Villa affair on the Mexican border, Fosdick was sent to investigate and confirmed the reports of debauchery. Dozens of brothels, accommodating the sexual appetites of the men, materialized from El Paso to San Antonio. In Laredo ten new saloons had opened in just one month to minister to the thirsty. Venereal rates were predictably high as well. In some camps, as many as three hundred soldiers a day were visiting dispensaries for treatment, seriously affecting unit readiness.[14] Fosdick worked tirelessly to ensure that these conditions would not be duplicated.[15]

While the government was occupied policing the brothels, the CTCA and groups with similar missions like the American Social Hygiene Association were taking notes on the girls who were ambushing soldiers at an even faster rate than were the prostitutes. In order to save them from falling entirely into the sex trade, a halfway house was established by the women's division of the CTCA in New Orleans at 1008 Bourbon Street. Designed primarily to guide young women on a straighter path, the Bourbon House, as it was named, provided nineteen rooms for girls no longer tethered to their families.[16]

African Americans too, like members of the Central Congregational Church, contributed to this moral impulse, creating a committee to establish another such home to rescue fallen Black women. Envisioning its race as an affiliate in this initiative, the local branch of the NAACP, in its publication the *Vindicator*, strongly endorsed the movement in partnership with whites. Lamenting that large numbers of women "of both races" were being arrested for prostitution, the organization declared that there "must be a united effort" to "lift our fallen sisters out of the mire." The city must become "a committee of one."[17]

Jean Gordon also sank her teeth into the issue, writing to the secretary of war himself to convince him that federal authorities were needed in New Orleans. It was more than City Hall's cavalier attitude about vice. Her letter was probably triggered in part by the murder of police superintendent James Reynolds in his office, shot by a disgruntled officer over a pay issue. Gordon suspected a conspiracy surrounding the assassination, suggesting in the letter that he was killed because of his insistence on the enforcement of the laws "relative to the open saloons and the conduct in the 'District.'" She had no proof of this allegation, but begged Baker to send a team from Washington to investigate, because "to ask for reports from the city administration or the police force is simply wasting you [sic] time."[18]

Standard procedure dictated that "lost sisters" were first trucked to the Isolation Hospital on North Rampart for examination or treatment before being returned to serve their jail terms. During the war, its doctors conducted 1,981 examinations, a quarter of them infected with a social disease. Crowding was common, as APL agents would send as many as sixty or seventy women there at one time.[19] But the public's attitude toward these women was slowly shifting during the war, and the APL made an enlightened decision to do more than simply help to arrest women of easy virtue. Rehabilitation became the buzzword.

Late in the war, a unique facility in the tradition of Chicago's Hull House opened, repurposed to redeem these women rather than handcuff them to a distressing existence. The resolution to create such a place of salvation was a nod to the Progressive movement, whose devotees preached empathy for those on the edge of society. The APL depended on donations and the sale of the *Spy Glass* for all its activities, but some of the money in New Orleans was budgeted for the creation of this unique facility, where inmate-residents could learn an occupation, take classes in reading, writing, and bookkeeping, maintain a vegetable garden on a six-acre plot, and refine homemaking skills. They were even provided spiritual guidance under the direction of Rabbi Mendel Silber from the Gates of Prayer congregation. The goal was to ween them away from the pit of prostitution and teach them that there were more acceptable opportunities to support themselves than selling their bodies to strangers.

Federal district court Judge Rufus Foster, who originally promoted the concept after he tired of seeing a ceaseless train of these scarlet women escorted before his bench, called the project "a great blessing" and a "very potent factor" in helping to reduce the venereal disease rate.[20] Called the "Amproleague [American Protective League] Farm," it was located in a remote area upriver from the city, three miles west of Kenner, Louisiana, on the former antebellum Frellson sugar plantation. With a $9,000 investment, it was converted into a modern home to accommodate the new tenants. Bedrooms became spaces for sewing machines. Kitchens were installed. Chalkboards were hung for instruction. There were even a piano and a Victrola for entertainment. It was a place of peace—a grove of pecan, oak, and palm trees framed the main building. Residents were not required to wear uniforms and could relax on rocking chairs on the main building's front and rear porches to meditate while viewing the beautiful estate before them.

Attached to it was a fully equipped dormitory built with bedding for fifty women under the care of a sympathetic matron. Two guards limited visitors and insured against runaways.[21]

ATTENDING EVILS

Before the implementation of the Prohibition Amendment in 1920, Weinberger engineered the creation of a liquor bureau within his office, adding some muscle to an agreement made between local breweries and saloons to disallow the sale of beer after 7:00 p.m. throughout the city. League undercover men were assigned to trains cramped with hyperexcited soldiers and sailors on leave looking forward to a night or two of adult diversions in New Orleans, far from the judgmental eyes of their drill sergeants. Their job was preventative—to walk the aisles, badges displayed, to warn the men of the current liquor laws, which prevented retailers from selling them alcohol in uniform, and to make them aware, to their great dismay, that this activity was being watched.

Once the trains came to a halt, the quasi-police of the APL went into action. They weaved their way through the horde of people to stop taxi drivers—the city's vice ambassadors—from intercepting the men stepping off with their luggage before they could share backdoor information with them about easy women and fast booze.[22] Weinberger's men also engaged in coordinated raids of saloons where servicemen were sold forbidden spirits. One tactic was to have pairs of his younger agents, disguised in military uniforms, visit various saloons around town and order beer. If the bartender complied, a raid and arrests would follow.[23]

Even with this kind of auxiliary manpower, enforcement efforts were daunting. Police often closed their eyes to violations. The APL, however, was relentless, enlisting chemists to analyze the contents of several "soft drinks" for sale at stands around town for any trace of alcohol.[24] And when word reached Weinberger's desk in February of 1918 from the local US attorney that the very popular Todo Restaurant on Royal Street was furnishing beer to soldiers (in large cups, straight whiskey in smaller ones), he sent a memo to his entire staff asking, "Will you gentlemen make it a habit to eat at this restaurant, if convenient, during the next three or four days and report quickly on the matter at hand?"[25] If this very established restaurant just steps from busy Canal Street was violating the Selective Service Act prohibiting such sales, it became easier to believe that the practice was widespread and probably unenforceable.

Weinberger and the police leadership planned a coordinated sweep on June 11th, 1918, at 10:30 p.m. APL agents along with squads of police officers descended swiftly and simultaneously on nine cabarets, three of which were tucked in the French Quarter's Tango Belt. Three more were on the grittier river's edge of the French Quarter. Only one, Tom Anderson's "restaurant" on North Basin, was within the old footprint of Storyville. Nearly two hundred white and seventeen Black prostitutes were arrested at these nine establishments, mid-dance in some cases, recognized by the raiders as habitual offenders. A few of the younger girls wailed as they were led away. "Old-timers" laughed it off. As the women were apprehended, their male dance partners stood and watched along with the cabaret managers, escaping arrest.[26] The target area for the closely guarded assault was clear evidence that prostitution had leaned toward the river since Storyville closed eight months prior.

The war was giving vitality to the drive to cleanse the city of its underworld, and, unlike in previous campaigns, it was being fueled by federal government agencies and local religious, civic, and business groups. Weinberger decided to take the vice crusade one step further to capitalize on momentum. Hoping to expand the scope of his local APL office, he sent the League attorney to Washington carrying a petition to Fosdick's Commission in October 1918, asking for support in his plan to stamp out gambling on horse racing in New Orleans. Connecting the effort to the CTCA, Weinberger believed, would establish racing as a detriment to the military. The plan was to use his vice squad to enforce the order while it was not patrolling for streetwalkers day and night. The only way betting on the ponies could be stopped, however, was by handing the entire sport a death sentence.

This was not the first attempt to smother what many believed to be a malignancy nearly as harmful as the wicked enterprise that had operated in Storyville. The press and a coalition of religious leaders of all faiths across the city had been lobbying for the suppression of gambling on horse racing since the turn of the century. New Orleans archbishop James Blenk had been particularly hyperbolic, calling it "a contemplated crime against our children, our homes, and everything else worth living and striving for." The state legislature had outlawed betting at the tracks in 1908, a key vote by one of the city's senators changed at the last hour supposedly after a phone call from the archbishop convinced him to support the ban.[27] But the law was repealed in 1916, and the handicappers and bookies were back in business—legally—at the city's two tracks, the Fair Grounds in Gentilly and the nearby City Park track. Now, with the war in its backstretch, Progressives said it was time to silence the bugle's *Call to Post* once more.

Mayor Behrman was furious, his mind squarely fixed on the positive economic impact horse racing had always had on the city and, most believed, on
the coffers of the Old Regulars. As the machine's boss, he surely had skin in
the game. Once he learned of Weinberger's scheme, he telegraphed the army's
acting chief quartermaster, General R. E. Wood, asking for his intervention.
Wood replied with his own telegram, which Behrman made public, attesting
to the continued need of the army for horses and his hope that the "racing
meets" in New Orleans would continue as they "promote interest in the class
of animal that must be depended upon to produce cavalry mounts."[28] No
mention was made of the associated gambling issue. It seemed like a weak
defense, since it was difficult to believe that because racing "promoted interest" in the animals, the sport should therefore be allowed to continue. But
the mayor played this card anyway, having little else in his hand.

In his post-war summary of the activities of his office, Weinberger listed
his motives for trying to shutter the racing industry for the duration of
the war. It attracted undesirables, caused servicemen to lose their money
while tempting them with liquor, increased the consumption of fuel, diverted
money from "useful channels that could benefit our government," and provided a rendezvous point for arranging assignations with strumpets, who
often prowled the grandstands in between races. Much less convincing was
his stance, a real head-scratcher, that it lowered the military's morale. His
arguments were enough to convince Secretary of War Baker. In an October
1918 communication to Governor Pleasant, the secretary boosted Weinberger's effort by urging Pleasant to "do everything within your power" to
purge the city of "attending evils" at the races, which presented to the men
stationed in New Orleans "crude forms of temptation and danger to their
health."[29] But this all became a moot point. Before any active measures could
be mounted, the war ended.

Just ten days afterward, Judge Foster penned a letter abruptly revoking
Weinberger's position as an ad hoc US commissioner during the APL's hot
pursuit of vice violations. According to Foster, there was no longer a need
for these additional emergency offices once the war ended. The chief was
not happy. When asked by a newspaperman to explain why he thought he
had been scratched so suddenly, Weinberger replied with a hint of bitterness,
as though he had been given an unsatisfactory explanation: "Judge Foster
revoked my commission and I think he should tell why he did it." If he did
not reveal why, Weinberger said, then "I do not think it should be published"
and urged that an "inquiry be made on Judge Foster as to his reason for that
action." In his letter, the judge did briefly thank the chief for his "efficient and
patriotic services." Still, something was amiss.[30]

The answer could very well have been that there existed some suspicion surrounding the misuse of authority in the New Orleans office of the League and, perhaps, the promiscuous issuance of warrants. Foster was a civil libertarian, always emphasizing the citizen's right of privacy and the absolute need for a legally issued warrant before a search could be conducted. Moreover, League director Briggs had again warned APL divisions to tread lightly in their attempts to purge the nation of vice. A column in the November 1918 issue of the *Spy Glass* entitled "Where the Danger Line in League Activities Lies" revealed how worried Briggs and his Washington office had become about having his men diving too deeply into the quagmire of liquor, gambling, and prostitution.

Ten months before, they were girded for the opportunity to sanitize the cities of America. The tone was now very different. Members of the APL "in certain communities" envision themselves as the "public conscience" and the guardian of public morals. "As a result, *through their chiefs* [my emphasis] or otherwise, they inaugurate crusades against gambling and vice," seeking to "discipline, even with force, their local 'bad men;' and in other ways wield the sword of righteousness . . . against the powers of evil." These actions were "destructive," forcing the organization "from the straight path of duty to the Federal Government" and involving each local division "in the disputes of politics, capital, labor, and even religious controversies."[31]

Therein may lie the actual reason for the removal of Weinberger and two other US commissioners. Perhaps the warrants were issued too frivolously during the frenzied last several months of the war, when America's combat role was juiced. Perhaps the commissioners were less than judicious in establishing a strict protocol on how to obtain a warrant. Worse, as the chief of the APL desk in New Orleans, Weinberger likely condoned the actions of his own League agents, who had no legal authority to search or arrest. There is no evidence to confirm that Weinberger or the other special commissioners were guilty of this or any other wrongdoing. In fact, he remained in his position as chief of the League office in New Orleans until it closed in 1919. One can guess, however, that the APL retreated somewhat from its previous willingness to assist in the holy campaign against moral decay for the very same reason it was assailed for the slacker raids—undisciplined overzealousness. And not only in New Orleans. Would the APL continue its bumpy operations if it was allowed to continue into 1919 and beyond? And if so, how much longer would the Justice Department tolerate its repeated indiscretions?

There was another storyline that folded into the mix. The Bureau of Investigation's Bielaski, in a letter to the national directors of the APL a day before the Armistice was signed, vowed that the League would continue indefinitely after the war. "The need for the American Protective League is as great now as it has been in the past, and I am entirely satisfied," he confirmed, "that the need for this organization will continue for some time to come."[32] Attorney General Gregory also gave his assurance that APL activities would be carried out "steadfastly." The League, he warned, "cannot yet be dispensed with. Illegal activities harmful to the public morale . . . must be watched for and reported."[33] Briggs contributed with his own canonization of the APL, which could, he promised, provide assistance to returning doughboys as they reacclimated to civilian life. But then the APL founder went off grid. During a visit to the acclaimed Amproleague Farm just outside New Orleans, he suggested without any authority to reporters gathered around him that the US should cancel all war debts owed them by its allies. His statement was totally in conflict with Wilson's policy position.[34]

That did it. The international embarrassment his remarks caused forced the attorney general to censure Briggs. Gregory had already been under pressure from Treasury Secretary William McAdoo and others to do something about the maverick APL and its leaders. (McAdoo remained miffed at the upstart pretenders ever since it hijacked the label "Secret Service" from its rightful department, the Treasury, and engraved it on its own badges.) Just two short weeks after expressing his hope that League operations would continue, Gregory decided to pull the plug. He invited Victor Elting, as co-chair of the League, to announce that the organization must break camp by February 1st. According to historian Harold Hyman, even the directors were becoming increasingly convinced that peace allowed no room for civilian spy catching.[35] It was time.

Mayor Behrman had to have been relieved upon hearing that Weinberger's operation was officially done. The APL's slow creep from investigating subversives to assaulting New Orleans horse racing, liquor outlets, and vice directly affected the Old Regular machine's source of funds, money that had been used to further entrench Behrman and his deputies in power. Weinberger's organization and companion groups like the Citizen's League had done much during the war to rattle passive tolerance of public malfeasance. Yet the machine would continue to run smoothly after the war, thanks in part to the spread of casino gambling. It would take more than the Progressives to smash City Hall. It would take an unorthodox politician like Huey Long.

EPILOGUE

By mid-September 1918, Germany's collapse was imminent. Every day newspapers reported the Allies swallowing great chunks of enemy real estate. Time-stamped maps for readers substantiated the rapid gains—a deep departure from the stalemate that had been the norm for the past four years on the Western Front. Civil upheaval inside of Germany, prompted by food shortages and unacceptable casualties, were splashed across America's front pages in larger and larger fonts.

The "black day of the German Army," August 8th, 1918, was the beginning of the end. The Kaiser's best infantrymen had been shattered at Armiens, forcing them to limp back to the Hindenberg Line and hope to God they could hang on and survive the carnage awaiting them. Low morale had caused many hundreds to desert. Heavy losses, exhaustion, and a lack of supplies menaced the army all along its tottering front.

September 12th, 1918, marked the beginning of Pershing's greatest offensive, flattening the St. Mihiel salient. The area had been occupied by the Boche since 1914. It was the first and only offensive launched solely by the AEF during the war, and it hinted at the ascendency of American military power. Two weeks later both Austria and Germany sent word to the White House requesting a formal cease-fire. It was now just a matter of agreeing to the syntax.

On the edge of the *Foret de Woevre*, eighteen kilometers east of the Meuse River in northeast France. 8:55 a.m., November 11th, 1918, New Orleanian Sumter Marks, an artillery battery commander with the 21st Field Artillery, scribbled this vivid account to his mother during the last minutes before the Armistice:

> Two hours and five minutes more of war! . . . We have just gotten the message from Army Headquarters. Armistice effective at 11 o'clock. . . . The artillery fire seems to be increasing just at present. I guess a lot of them feel as though they ought to make the most of the short time left. . . .

Now 10:30. Half hour more to go. The heavy firing I spoke of in the beginning of this letter was the damned Huns taking one last pound at our front line infantry. The beasts are spiteful to the last. We are letting the morning pass quietly, but they wouldn't have it. So now we're busy sending 'em back. I'm going to keep it up until about 10 minutes of eleven. I don't want to be guilty of a breach of the armistice. . . . Have permission to use up most of the ammunition on hand and am allowed to choose my own targets. I started on the German front line infantry, shifted to a battery in the rear, and now we're back on the Hun infantry. Guess they're cussing their artillery out for starting anything.

At 10:46 we started our last 40 rounds on the way. I wonder if they'll be the last we fire in the big war! I'm writing this with a telephone receiver up to my ear. From the sound of things around here now you'd think a big offensive was starting. . . .

Three minutes more! Practically everything has stopped. . . . There goes a 75 battery! They must be celebrating. Or perhaps they wanted to fire the last shots of the war. One minute more. There, a gun went just then. Some more going. Time's up according to my watch! Just after time was up the Huns turned loose an awful lot. But one came from our side when they had finished.

It's all over now. Not a gun firing.

It all seems so queer. Almost impossible to believe that the war should come to an end.

11:16 and I'm still safe and sound. . . . So we'll all be together soon and talk it over.

With all the love in the world,

Sumter[1]

When the Armistice was signed at 5:12 a.m. on November 11th, 1918, effective at 11 a.m., in the forest of Compiègne, France, the inconceivable slaughter of more than ten million human lives had mercifully ended. Despite the Great War's epithet as the war to end all wars, it is doubtful that very many survivors affirmed the promise that the 1,564 days of butchery would insure a prolonged peace. As 1918 turned into the new year, post-war sentiments across Europe, once buoyant, turned bleak. A vapor of haunting uncertainty prevailed. Germany, after all, remained unrepentant, its soil unmarred by the boots of allied armies. Bolshevism threatened. Europe's boundaries were redrawn.

In the hours immediately following the joyous news of the cease-fire, British soldier-poet Wilfred Owen's mother received word of her son's death, who had been unable to escape "the shrill, demented choirs of wailing shells" of which he wrote. But for another British family, at least, there was hope. A child was born to them at the very hour of the Armistice. They named him Pax, Latin for peace. But the Great War was soon to be resuscitated, and its scions were Hitler and Stalin. Twenty-one short years later, Pax would be killed in the next war.[2]

At roughly 3:30 a.m. on the Monday morning of the 11th, New Orleans received official word of the Armistice over the Associated Press wire. The riverfront was the first to arouse the city when the dock board signaled orders for all ships to let go their whistles. Railyards were encouraged to do the same, and sleepy engineers chimed in the early morning chorus with their own distinctive blasts, rudely puncturing the night's lunar quiet. By 7:00 a.m. a substantial crowd had already stretched across the city's pivot point, Canal Street, to take part in the revelry—sure to mount as the day advanced.

People spilled into the streets armed with cowbells and makeshift noise-makers like kitchen pots and spoons. Louie Armstrong was tugging coal to Fabacher's Restaurant on St. Charles, "sweating like mad," when he heard a clanging from several cars dragging large cans tied onto their bumpers. "After quite a few cars had passed . . . I asked, 'What's all the fuss about?' 'They're celebratin' 'cause the war is over!'"[3] It appeared as though every musician in town was out with their instruments playing alone or in impromptu bands on open trucks. Newsies thumping tin garbage bins contributed a percussion section. Church bells enriched the symphony. Guns were fired. Cars and trucks glided slowly through the growing throng, their drivers blasting horns and waving flags.

Servicemen, released from duty since noon, were smothered by admirers. When Private T. L. Froix emerged from the quartermaster's office in the Audubon Building, he was wrapped in a large flag and carried down the neutral ground on a stranger's shoulders like a football hero. One vehicle was completely buried in red, white, and blue balloons. Placards were displayed on others delighting in the demise of the Kaiser and extolling President Wilson. "The Kaiser's Funeral," read one on the hood of a truck carrying a small coffin in its bed as it wedged its way through an approving audience. Streetcars plowed through one after another carrying more flag-bearing reinforcements until the thicket of people forced them to halt service. One veteran cop remarked that he had seen crowds about the same size before on Canal, but never before had they remained massed throughout the day.

Businesses closed soon after they received the news, and many of them retreated to the city's restaurants, hotels, and bars to continue the merrymaking indoors. Most establishments ran out of food, but champagne flowed generously and everyone joined in the singing of the usual patriotic songs. APL chief Charles Weinberger dined at La Louisiane with a party of naval officers. Not far away sat former commissioner Harold Newman and his family enjoying the festivity. Elsewhere saloons were handing out free drinks as men, four deep at many bars, were happy to take advantage, quickly taxing inventories. One inebriated fellow staggered out of an establishment, grabbed a six-year-old girl from behind, and reached out to kiss her before realizing that she was African American. An *Item* reporter wrote that he "discovered his error in time" and handed her a dollar bill instead. "A few more such days as Monday," reported the *Picayune*, "and prohibition would not be necessary as far as New Orleans is concerned. There would be no liquor left."[4]

From a camp near the French village of Issoudun near Tours, New Orleanian Pierre Choppin, a pilot with the Second Air Instructional Center, described the celebration in the war zone in a letter to his brother Val, noting with surprise the harsh conditions of the truce: "Why, the terms the beaten Huns accepted do not even leave them with a toothbrush they can call their own." He then went on to portray how the locals were reacting to the news:

> They say that Paris right now is just a big joy factory. Gee, I wish I was there. I know I would be having one hell of a time. They are keeping us pretty tight out here at camp and will not give us a chance to let loose. They know well enough what a bunch of wild birds the fliers are, and if we are given the reins once, they will have a hell of a time checking us all up when they want to call roll again.
>
> There was a pretty wild time last time in the little town near here. The people were going about the streets kissing everybody they met and there are many Yanks who woke to sad reality and found the grizzly beard of a half soused police rubbed across their face as he kissed them with a resounding smack on each cheek.[5]

New Year's Eve 1919 was observed in New Orleans with the usual harbor whistles, factory sirens, and noisemakers. With inviting temperatures in the low 70s, Canal Street, restaurants, and saloons were all jammed in a vortex of self-indulgent natives and visitors alike. It was perhaps the most intemperate greeting to a new year in the city's two-hundred-year history, reminiscent of Carnival. "How many bottles of champagne and other wines, and how many barrels of beer were consumed during the night," one journalist wrote, "is beyond calculation." Horn-blowing cars crept down Canal Street dodging an impromptu parade that formed when a brass troupe tooted its way down the middle of the historic avenue. The ragged procession was followed by a single, intoxicated reveler who listed left and right trying his best to keep up.[6] There was good reason, naturally, for everyone to be in a snappy mood. The Kaiser had fled to neutral Holland, the war was finally over, and the men would soon be returning home. But in the back of everyone's mind that night, another sentiment intruded. In two weeks Nebraska's legislature was expected to ratify the Prohibition Amendment. The necessary three-fourths vote of the states would therefore be reached for it to become law. So while the end of bloodshed was certainly a cause to rejoice, New Orleanians harbored the dread of prohibition and the thought that this would very likely be their last New Year's Eve popping bottles and toasting with bubbly. Celebrate the beginning of 1919 they would. Emotions, though, were mixed.

The scene was repeated the night of June 30th, 1919. At midnight, wartime prohibition commenced, the city's first entrée into an alcohol-restricted landscape until the more rigid Eighteenth Amendment would replace it in January 1920.[7] Hotel clerks reported no vacancies, filled as they were with thirsty visitors from dry territories, who converged on the town hoping to get in on the fun. Several grand hotel bars, like those at the Grunewald and St. Charles, closed as early as mid-afternoon to avoid what they expected to be an uncontrolled bacchanal. Tables were spread over the dance floor at the Cosmopolitan Hotel to accommodate the expected horde of celebrants. Downtown streets were cluttered with the curious and free spirited.

They certainly came, but no one was able to lean and linger at the foot rails to enjoy a cold one. In saloons all over town, thick rows of men pressed toward bars for a drink, trying to elbow their way to the front and scrambling to make eye contact with frazzled bartenders. Many places sold out their stock of booze even before the clock struck 12:00. Outside on the streets, the crowds were surprisingly well behaved. One prankster placed a makeshift tablet at the foot of an unoccupied pedestal in Lafayette Square that read, "In Memory of the Deceased—John Barleycorn. Gone but Not Forgotten, June 30th, 1919."[8]

The expected foolishness fueled by widespread drinking never materialized. Perhaps it was resignation. Or surrender. Time to admit defeat. Already the Anti-Saloon League was planning to open chapters in cities as far away as Singapore and Melbourne and even pressing for prohibition to be included in the Versailles peace treaty. The government's steel heel—the impending Volstead Act, which would strictly enforce the controversial amendment—was ready to fall.

Mayor Behrman was also taken by the almost docile behavior of his imbibing constituents and issued a congratulatory message on the following day. A reporter from the *Item* labeled the evening "a quiet and ladylike affair," depicting the usually edgy Tango Belt as sedate "as an ice cream social." Eighty-five extra police had been deployed to reinforce the federal officers charged with keeping order downtown, with one patrolman for each of the more historic venues of trouble. It was unnecessary. The authorities removed fewer than two hundred people from the streets or saloons for drunkenness or disturbing the peace despite the prolific drinking. The Acme saloon on Royal Street, for instance, had purchased five barrels of whiskey fewer than two weeks before. At midnight, there was still a half barrel left.

But life would go on. Perhaps this sentiment best explains why the last wet day before the "thirsty first," as July 1st was called, was relatively subdued. As glasses clinked for the last time, past stories of camaraderie surfaced at neighborhood saloons. It was a requiem for the mourners, but a requiem with drink and laughter—an Irish wake multiplied dozens of times all over town. Bill Finnin's place on Royal Street was one such spot. For forty-two years it had served cold beer and good conversation. On that last night of cheer, the beloved Irishman placed a sign on the mirror behind his well-worn bar: "On October 12, 1492, we took this country from the Indians. On July 1st, 1919, we give it back."[9]

Five months later, on January 17th, 1920, the Prohibition Amendment officially became the law of the land. It was almost a nonevent, given that alcoholic drinks had already been restricted for the past half year. News coverage of the landmark day was flat and indifferent. People by now were simply weary of it all, tired of the cartoons and metaphors in the papers about the death of John Barleycorn and his final internment. Nor was there much of a fuss inside the remaining saloons given their low inventories and high prices. The feds had made it clear that they would come down hard on any violators.

Yet a few creative New Orleans entrepreneurs and bootleggers were already practiced in sleight-of-hand tricks to ensure that booze was finding its way into dry counties and parishes deprived of their favorite beverages. The law be damned. A year before the Prohibition Amendment, federal inspectors discovered a truck transporting hot-water bottles and gasoline cans from New Orleans on their way to Bessemer, Alabama. The bottles were filled with liquor. Other agents exhumed a suspicious coffin shipped by rail to two undertakers and a physician in Monroe, Louisiana. Just as they guessed, the coffin housed Jack Daniel's rather than Jules Crawford, whose "corpse" was identified on the mortician's certificate.[10] These and other schemes would not end simply because of a new amendment—early signals that enforcement of

the alcohol trade was sure to be a Gordian knot. Mayor Behrman's prostitution maxim that "you can make it illegal, but you can't make it unpopular"
worked just as well for prohibition. Let the games begin. . . .

Neither did the crusade against vice make a dent in the local sex trade. It
became apparent just a few months after the Armistice that the combined efforts of local law enforcement, the Citizen's League, the American Protective
League, and other groups to rid New Orleans of prostitution were failures. A
de facto sex trade continued to prosper into the post-war period at the same
old addresses and beyond. This became a major issue in the 1920 mayor's race
when reformers and an even more vociferous press castigated Behrman for
his "secretive" trip to Washington to save Storyville and for the indifference
of the police to take sustained action against vice.

Nothing much had changed into the new decade. As long as a beat cop's
pockets were nourished periodically, and they surely were, he was happy to
look the other way. Assignation houses were beginning to appear not only
in respectable parts of the business district downtown, but also in residential
areas where they had never before been present. In 1927, a scorching report
from the National Association of Social Hygiene and a parish grand jury
investigation underscored these findings.[11]

Recognizing that the situation was perhaps worse than ever, former Commissioner of Public Safety Harold Newman actually floated the idea in 1922
of reestablishing Storyville as a stopgap measure to quarantine the problem.
Jean Gordon, immediately blasted the proposal: "There is a quiet, irresist-
ible force of reputable men and women in this community who will rise
overnight and show the advocates of that shame of all shames, a restricted
district, that . . . police graft, rent profiteers, and degraded womanhood had
gone forever from our midst, and unless our citizenry has become so over-
whelmingly degenerate, will never be re-established."[12]

Newman's recommendation went nowhere. As long as most residents of
New Orleans remained oblivious to the crib girls seen pandering on their
streets, reacting with eye rolls instead of police alerts, the sex trade would
remain a standard item on the New Orleans bill of fare. It was too easy to
blame local authorities. The city's *c'est la guerre* tolerance of vice and its shal-
low indignation at it were too deeply planted in its old bones.

More successful was the movement to approve a women's suffrage amendment. Yet it would take two more decades for New Orleans women, socially
sequestered as they had been, to capitalize on the hard-fought victory. Conditioned as they were to view politics as a sordid contest unsuitable for
feminine niceties, only a few dared to break out of their orbit and participate

in this gender-bending event. Few women bothered to register to vote in 1920. Four years later the numbers had grown only slightly, and by the end of the 1920s, women were still only 29 percent of the electorate.[13]

Charles Weinberger's force of American Protective League foot soldiers disbanded almost immediately after the war ended, and the hysteria, which had once forced the city's German population underground, slowly disappeared. The Hun was defeated and New Orleanians had short memories. By 1928 a healthy new fraternal organization called the Deutsches Haus had formed to celebrate German customs once more.

Still, a spirit would burn to defend America from anything it deemed a menace to its principles and culture, for other imagined "un-American" enemies beckoned. One especially stood out—the specter of Bolshevism and its wish to unite workers of the world. Much like the APL before it, a vigilante group would reassemble to assist the government and its ardent attorney general, A. Mitchell Palmer, in shielding the nation from the malignancy of Marxism.[14] Leading the new decade's crusade to disinfect the nation would be the Ku Klux Klan. The hysteria continued. Only the targets changed. Many APL men presumably withheld their badges and suspect files into the 1920s, ignoring orders to turn them in and using them for dubious purposes—fingering labor union extremists and suspected Bolsheviks, harassing Blacks, Catholics, immigrants, and Jews, and otherwise "keeping the world safe for democracy." Its fluid, Anglo-Saxon Protestant definition of "American" mirrored the war years.

The Ku Klux Klan, revitalized and eager, hijacked the energy that had been directed at Germans during the war and repurposed it through the early 1920s. This Klan, unlike its Reconstruction-era predecessor, boasted tens of thousands of members from across the US and was applauded by a great many whites as the nation's guardian angel. In 1919 alone, the order made over two hundred appearances in twenty-seven states and added a hundred thousand new members. That same year seventy-six African Americans were lynched. Ten of these were in their WWI uniforms. New Orleans Blacks were spared from these horrific crimes, but they soon learned that wearing Uncle Sam's issue was a risk rather than an insignia of pride. Fear was pervasive, particularly in rural communities where African Americans worked as farm laborers—some fearing that they would be enslaved once again.[15] Moreover, the public promise of some African American leaders that participation in the war and support for the flag would embolden racial uplift never materialized.[16] W. E. B. Dubois wrote eloquently of this familiar pattern. Negro advancement threatened white control. "We return. We return from fighting. We return fighting."[17]

Mardi Gras finally came out of a three-year hibernation and returned in 1920, but it was a much more sober affair than in the prewar years—both literally and figuratively. The city's annual pre-Lenten saturnalia was missing its key additive, compliments of the Prohibition Amendment. It was Thanksgiving without the turkey. This, along with triple canopy rain clouds, wind, and temperatures in the low forties, kept many at home. Contributing to the restrained mood was the loss only two months before of the fabled French Opera House to a devastating fire, a venue dear to the soul of New Orleanians and home to several Carnival balls. The *Picayune* did not finesse the disappointing event. Ash Wednesday's headline read: "N.O. Revels for A Day, but Old Carnival Spirit Fails." One reporter opined that "never had a Carnival met with less enthusiasm." Despite these woes, the krewe of Rex braved the weather to conduct the only parade that day. Drenched krewe members clung to twenty rain-soaked, paper-mache floats behind their masks, trying their best to warm the unanimated crowd below them.

Yet the 1920 celebration was nevertheless memorable because of one special guest of the city—General John J. Pershing. Perched on the grandstand in front of Gallier Hall to witness the spectacle, a Rex officer awarded him a solid gold medallion, knighting him the "Duke of Victory," and anointing him a "peer" of Rex's realm. A limousine then whisked him and his staff to the Boston Club's exclusive seating above Canal Street to view the parade along with the assorted Indians, goblins, and hairy-armed hula "girls" who strolled below. That evening, the former AEF commander attended the Rex ball at the Athenaeum. Entering the auditorium, he was greeted by a loud, standing applause from the formally dressed invitees. As Rex (Mr. John F. Clark) sat at his throne next to his queen (Miss Elinor Bright), Pershing bowed appropriately to the two faux monarchs, who returned the salute with a wave of their scepters.[18] Most unusual was the absence of the mayor, who was too ill to accompany the general during his stay.

Later that year, Martin Behrman would be defeated for reelection, unable to sustain the assaults directed at him from all three dailies. The *Picayune* in particular bludgeoned the mayor with language that might unnerve a sailor, calling him a "crawling, fetid, contaminating monster of the underworld" and a lurking "poisonous adder" because of his association with prostitution, gambling, and machine politics.[19] It also ran a series of stories called "In the Shadow of the Vulture's Wings," which substantiated, through vivid dialogue and solid investigative reporting, the vitality of commercialized sex in the city, with blame placed squarely on Behrman's desk.[20]

Heavier firepower was wheeled into the campaign when newly elected governor John Parker endorsed Andrew McShane, a self-styled reformer who pledged to strike aggressively at corruption and vice. The four-term mayor lost, but the race was close. Fewer than fifteen hundred votes separated him from his fifth consecutive win. Most others would have called it a game once the votes were counted, but after a disappointing four years under McShane, New Orleanians placed the old warhorse back in his Gallier Hall office as mayor once again in 1924. The comeback, however, was short-lived. Fighter that he had always been, Behrman could not lick his degenerative heart disease. He died on January 12th, 1926, less than a year after his final election, in the presence of his wife Julia and their two children, Stanley and Mary, in the simple Algiers home of his youth.

His body lay in state in the grand parlor of City Hall—near his work, exactly as he would have wanted. An estimated twenty thousand came to pay their last respects beginning at 4:00 p.m. and lasting until midnight, the lines often curling around Lafayette Square's leafy perimeter. The next morning's funeral procession was an impressive display of respect and sorrow. Amid the slow, mourning toll of church bells and half-mast flags, his bronze coffin was carried to St. Louis Cathedral on a caisson led by six horses and eight rigid soldiers. Immediately following were two units of mounted cavalry, then family members, police, firemen, and even crew members of a visiting French warship. Next came city officials and employees, fraternal groups, and finally the common citizens of his city. When the head of the cortege reached Jackson Square, they were swallowed by a throng of people hoping to get a last glimpse. With the help of police, the solemn crowd stepped back, and the pallbearers carefully walked the flag-draped casket into the historic church.

Once the requiem mass was celebrated, the procession formed again for Metairie Cemetery four miles away. There, after closing prayers were said under a white tent, the mayor was given a final gun salute fired by soldiers of the Washington Artillery as a lone bugler played "Taps." Behrman's body was buried amongst seven Louisiana governors, two renowned Civil War generals, illustrious city benefactors, and Josie Arlington, one of the most well-known—and most well-off—Storyville madams.

On the one-year anniversary of the Armistice, the people of New Orleans erected the first permanent World War I memorial in the United States. Dr. E. S. Kelly, a prominent physician, and lawyer St. Clair Adams, organized a committee that raised almost $8,000 for the construction of a commemorative arch in McCarty Square in the city's Ninth Ward neighborhood. Over a period of several months, volunteers canvassed that neighborhood for donations and held fundraisers to pay for the solid granite monument that measured over twenty-eight feet high. Ironically, the arch was carved by a German-born New Orleanian named Albert Weiblen.

Four cast bronze plaques adorned the monument inscribed with the 1,231 names of all those in the proud Ninth Ward who served, headed by the ten white men who were killed in action or died from disease. Along with those ten were other tablets honoring white and African American surviving war veterans and the five Ninth Ward "colored men" who died in service from disease or accident. Today, the memorial is known much less as a tribute to those who gave their lives for their country as it is proof of how Black participation in the war did little to soften racial attitudes—their names, even in death, segregated in bronze. The structure, much like the abortive peace treaty, is perhaps a metaphor for the Great War's muddled legacy in New Orleans—a spoiled opportunity to move toward a just and more tolerant society.

APPENDIXES

APPENDIX A

Cases Handled (approximate) by the American Protective League, New Orleans Division From "A Summary of the Activities of the APL," January, 1919

Alien enemy activities: 292
Citizen disloyalty and sedition: 1,626
Sabotage, bombs, dynamite, defective manufacture: 24
Anti-military activity, interference with the draft: 34
Propaganda, word of mouth and printed: 1,326
Bribery, graft, theft, and embezzlement: 82
Naturalization, impersonation, etc.: 827
Radical organizations—I.W.W., etc.:43
Counter espionage for military intelligence: 2
Selective Service regulations under boards: 2,194
In slacker raids, estimated: 20,000
Of local and district board members: 4
Work or fight order: 254
Character and loyalty—civilian applicants: 103
Applicants for commissions: 57
Training Camp Activities, Section 12: 2,909
Training Camp Activities, Section 13: 2,843
Camp desertions and AWOL: 140
Collection of foreign maps, etc., estimated: 3,500
Counter espionage for naval intelligence: 206
Collection of binoculars, etc.: 8
Food Administration—hoarding, destruction, etc.: 453
Fuel Administration—hoarding, destruction, etc.: 964
Department of State—miscellaneous: 7
Treasury Department-War Risk Insurance, etc.: 625

U.S. Shipping Board: 15
Alien Property Custodian—miscellaneous: 7
Red Cross loyalty investigations: 409

APPENDIX B

American Protective League Expenditures
(in dollars, financed through private subscriptions)
From "A Summary of the Activities of the APL," January, 1919

Furniture and fixtures: 5,200
Uniforms and pistols: 116
Salaries (office force): 8,700
Automobile hire: 21
Postage: 623
Liquor violations: 2,500
Rent: 1,100
Telephone and telegraph: 678
Office expense: 995
Electric light: 205
Stationery and printing: 2,100
Miscellaneous expenses: 2,084
Vice violations: 1,400
Insurance: 161
Amproleague Farm investment: 9,000

TOTAL: 34,883

APPENDIX C

Resignation letter, Charlton R. Beattie, 2-4-18
To the Administrators of the Tulane Educational Fund
503-505 Tulane-Newcomb Building
New Orleans, La.

Sirs:
Your communication notifying me of certain resolutions adopted by your
Board on January 23rd, 1918, has been received.

I find the following to be one of the resolutions:

"That in order to remove every suspicion of disloyalty, each person connected with the university be required to sign at once the following statement:

"I am a citizen of_____."

"I will loyally uphold the Government of the United States in the prosecution of the war against Germany and her Allies."

I decline to sign this statement, and cannot but consider the resolutions requiring same, impertinent, if not insulting. Your requirement of signatures to the statement is useless and vain. No disloyal person would hesitate to sign, or would be deterred from signing from acts of disloyalty.

It is noted that, in accordance with the resolutions, my refusal to sign will be construed, by your Board, as an act of disloyalty of an American citizen, or the act of an enemy alien.

I cannot allow myself to be driven to sign this statement, by the threat of being considered disloyal.

I am an American citizen, and am of the sixth generation of my family, born on American soil.

Some of my ancestors have served in every war in which this country has ever been engaged. They fought and died on the battlefields of the American Revolution that made this country free and independent.

I trust that the sentiment running through the resolutions adopted by your Board will not become part and parcel of the ethics, to be held and taught by the great institution over which you at present preside.

Every citizen's loyalty to his country is, and must be presumed.

That it is not, by your Board, places me, so far as your Board is concerned, in the category of the disloyal, and as no one you place under this ban should be allowed by you to instruct the students at Tulane, my resignation, as professor, in your College of Law, is hereby tendered to you.

Respectfully,
Charlton R. Beattie

APPENDIX D

Record of the New Orleans War Finance Activities (subscribed monies) From "Putting Over the Fourth Liberty Loan in New Orleans, 1919", Williams Research Center, HNOC; Louisiana in the War, 33

1st Liberty Loan Drive $9,227,650
2nd Liberty Loan Drive $15,248,900
3rd Liberty Loan Drive $15,667,500
4th Liberty Loan Drive $30,800,000
War Savings Stamps $8,365,000
War Camp Recreational Fund $33,000
1st & 2nd Red Cross War Funds $1,952,239
Red Cross Christmas Membership Drives 1917 and 1918 . . . . $124,000
YWCA & YMCA Funds $275,000
Boy Scout Drives 1918 and 1919 . . . . $34,158
Jewish Relief Fund $250,424
United War Work Fund $697,863

Total . . . . **$103,203,184**[*]

*A fifth Liberty Loan drive coming after the Armistice netted another $20.5 million

NOTES

INTRODUCTION

1. Despite the crisis of war, a French speaking delegation from New Orleans was invited to the Sorbonne in Paris in 1917 to celebrate the city's bicentennial. Such was the affiliation between France and its former colony. An account of that visit, delivered in a speech by Paul Villere, member of the delegation, can be found in Tulane University's Louisiana Collections, M459.

2. Second Report of the Provost Marshal General to the Secretary of War, 526.

CHAPTER 1

1. *Times-Picayune* (*TP*), May 8, 1915, 1; May 9, 1915, 10; *New Orleans Item*, May 8, 1915, 1.

2. *TP*, May 9, 1915, 8.

3. https://uselections.org.

4. *TP*, December 23, 1914, 1.

5. The *Daily Picayune*, February 9, 1876, 1. The *Boston Post* reported the same story under a headline that read, "The Duello Still Flourishes in the South," but provided more details. According to the article, friends of the two fought a proxy duel with swords soon after the original encounter. Both duelists were cut but not seriously. Then the two principles themselves, once released from jail, met "on the field of honor" for a rifle duel at forty paces. Neither one was struck, whereupon their seconds "succeeded in adjusting" the matter. *Boston Post*, February 18, 1876, p. 4.

6. *DP*, June 26, 1879, 2; October 23, 1879, 1.

7. *Los Angeles Herald*, May 28, 1887, 1; *Ft. Worth Daily Gazette*, April 13, 1991, 8.

8. *The European War*, vol 10, 857.

9. *The St Tammany Farmer* (*STF*), December 10, 1921, 1.

10. Asher, 80–81.

11. *Item*, March 4, 1915, 1.

12. *TP*, May 19, 1931, 1–2; *New Orleans States*, May 19, 1931, 1.

13. *Ogden Standard-Examiner*, July 5, 1931, 21; *Brooklyn Daily Eagle*, May 21, 1931, 3.

CHAPTER 2

1. Department of Health and Sanitary Survey, 22.

2. The term refers to a unique stratum of African Americans of mixed race who composed a separate tier of society in New Orleans. They were middle class leaders of the Black community—professionals or engaged in such enterprises as funeral home operators, insurance agents, or property owners. Most were educated, Catholic, and had ancestral connections to white Creoles and Free People of Color in antebellum New Orleans. See Virginia Domingues, *White By Definition: Social Classifications in Creole Louisiana*, LSU Press, 1986; Sybil Klein, *The History and Legacy of Louisiana's Free People of Color*, LSU Press, 2000; Kimberly Hanger, *Bounded Lives, Bounded Places: Free Black Society in Colonial New Orleans*, Duke University Press, 1997; Arnold Hirsch and Joseph Logsdon, eds., *Creole New Orleans: Race and Americanization*, LSU Press, 1992; Connie Eble, "Creole in Louisiana," *South Atlantic Review* 73, no. 2 (2008), 39–53; Nikki Dugar, "I Am What I Say I Am: Racial and Cultural Identity among Creoles of Color in New Orleans," University of New Orleans master's thesis, 2009.

3. *DP*, July 2, 1911, 14.

4. *Item*, August 8, 1912, 9; Carter, *The Past as Prelude*, 242.

5. Stoddard, 45.

6. Hersch, 31; Hair, 77.

7. LaFarge, 118.

8. Anderson and Kelly, 95.

9. Levitt, 169.

10. Percy, 14–15.

11. Carter, *Southern Legacy*, 106.

12. Barker, 5.

13. Campanella, "Remembering the Old French Opera House," 17.

14. Thirteenth Census, 1910, 827; Fourteenth Census, 1920, 402.

15. LaFarge, 118.

16. Barker, 102.

17. *States*, January 1, 1918, 1.

18. *TP*, January 1, 1918, 13.

19. Costa interview, January 30, 1985.

20. *Leslie's Illustrated News*, 562.

21. *TP*, May 16, 1919, 6.

22. For a sympathetic overview of Behrman's administrations and his responsibility for the city's economic and civic improvements, consult "Martin Behrman and New Orleans Civic Development, 1904–1920" in *Louisiana History* by Robert W. Williams Jr. The author writes that Behrman is "perhaps the most neglected among the city political bosses of the late nineteenth and early twentieth centuries." See also *Machine Politics in New Orleans, 1897–1926* by George Reynolds. Chapter 1 provides a glimpse at the city's economic condition during the Behrman years.

23. *TP*, January 2, 1917, 11; May 22, 1917, 1; *Item*, April 29, 1917, 1, 12; Arnesen, 211.

24. *Item*, June 24, 1917, 27.

25. *STF*, April 27, 1917, 1; January 1, 1917, 8; *States*, October 27, 1918, 9; Piston, 169.

26. *Item*, April 29, 1917, 1, 12; *TP*, September 1, 1918, A34.

27. *TP*, January 2, 1917, 11; August 12, 1917, 14B.

28. *TP*, January 2, 1918, 1; *Item*, July 8, 1917, section 2, 1.

29. *Item*, October 22, 1918, 2.

30. *TP*, February 25, 1917, A12; *Item*, April 29, 1917, 1, 12.

CHAPTER 3

1. Krist, 145.

2. Rose, 31, 96. Al Rose's *Storyville, New Orleans: Being an Authentic, Illustrated Account of the Notorious Red Light District* provides interviews with several of Storyville's madams. These women are unabashed in relating some of the lurid details of their enterprise. The book suffers, however, from the author's failure to provide documentation.

3. Warren Ogden interview, July 18, 1978, in Vyhnanek, 133.

4. Widmer, 33; Armstrong, 105.

5. Lomax, Library of Congress interview.

6. Armstrong, 110–11.

7. Lomax, Mister Jelly Roll, 437.

8. Levy, 61.

9. Rose. 98; *Item*, December 20, 1909, 1.

10. *Item*, February 23, 1910, 1; March 22, 1910, 1.

11. Elder Papers, "Rules for Student Residence," NA-029, box 7. 1918, Newcomb Archives.

12. Rose, 136, 138, 139; Arceneaux, 129.

13. Arceneaux, 50.

14. William Russell Jazz Files, MSS 536 f.25, District folder, HNOC; Rose, 31.

15. Police investigations of illegal drug sales was tepid, at best, See *Item*, August 29, 1907, 1, 4, 6.

16. Asbury, 440, 443, 446–7; Levy, 66.

17. *Collier's* February 29, 1908, in Asbury, 434.

18. Armstrong, 8, 94.

19. Arceneaux, 31.

20. Consult Emily Clark's *The Strange History of the American Quadroon* for background on pre-WWI women of color and plaçage in antebellum New Orleans. *Brothels, Depravity, and Abandoned Women* by Judith Schafer describes the legislative and judicial evolution of the interracial sex scene in New Orleans, also primarily prior to WWI.

21. Ord. 4118, NOPL; Rose, Appendix E; Krist, 236.

22. *TP*, March 18, 1917, A15.

23. *TP*, September 6, 17, 6.

24. Krist, 115.

25. Rose, 52; Maren-Hogan, 1.

26. W. Piazza v. City of N.O. (1917), Civ Dist Court of N.O., Docket #119538; City of N.O. v. W. Piazza (1917), Sup Crt of LA, Docket #22624; Maren-Hogan, 26–29.

27. N.O. Commission Council Series. Ordinance 4485.

28. Long, Babylon, 94.

29. Rose, 178.

30. Saxon, 1, 2.

31. Ory unpublished autobiography, in McCusker, 59; Hersch, 52; Ward and Burns, 38, 40.

CHAPTER 4

1. Kemp, *Behrman of NOLA*, 59.

2. Allan Lacombe, author interview, December 2, 1998.

3. *Item*, August 6, 1912, 1; August 18, 1912, 1; October 14, 1911, 1; Levy, 117.

4. *Item*, July 5, 1917, 6.

5. There are few if any extant records of the Behrman administrations, particularly those of his early terms in office. The few that are in existence are housed in the Louisiana Collection of the N.O. Public Library, although they contain mostly innocuous letters that shed little light on what was one of the city's most important mayors. There are no records whatsoever covering the war years.

6. Barker, 20.

7. *TP*, September 2, 1917, B12.

8. *TP*, June 20, 1918, 4.

9. *Item*, September 14, 1917, 4.

10. Atkins, 145.

11. Hersch, 5.

12. *Item*, November 19, 1918, 8.

13. Hersch, 161.

14. Marquis, 18.

15. Charters, 130; Stoddard, 32.

16. Souchon, 5.

17. *TP*, July 13, 2015, 16.

18. *TP*, August 2, 2015, 5.

19. H. J. Boisseau interview in Charters, 74.

20. For a more complete history of Spanish Fort, see Richard Campanella's article in the *Times-Picayune*, September 8, 1919, p. 12A.

21. *DP*, December 9, 1896, 12.

CHAPTER 5

1. See "Inventory of the Records of World War Emergency Activities in Louisiana, 1916–1920" at the Louisiana Division, N.O. Public Library, for locations of depositories throughout Louisiana housing records of local councils of defense and other agencies. The state council published a weekly journal, "The Louisiana War Bulletin," which may be of interest to researchers.

2. *Item*, February 21, 17, 6.

3. *Item*, March 12, 17, 9.

4. Rose, 178, 181. A more complete investigation of the Baby Dolls can be found in *Walking Raddy: The Baby Dolls of New Orleans* edited by Kim Vaz-Deville. See also Deville's earlier work, *The Baby Dolls: Breaking the Race and Gender Barriers of the New Orleans Mardi Gras Tradition.*

5. *TP*, February 20, 1917, 5.

6. *TP*, February 20, 1917, 7.

7. Rose, 180.

8. *TP*, February 19, 1917, 1.

9. *TP*, February 21, 1917, 4.

10. Gill, 138; Rose, 22, 64; Atkins, 154–5.

11. *Herald*, January 3, 1918, 1; *TP*, February 13, 1918, 5.

12. *TP*, April 2, 1917, 4.

13. *TP*, February 8, 1917, 4.

14. *TP*, February 7, 1917, 1.

15. Fortier, 42.

16. *TP*, March 2, 1917, 8.

17. *TP*, March 9, 1917, 13.

18. *TP*, March 16, 1917, 8.

19. *TP*, March 11, 1917, 8A.

20. *TP*, March 15, 1917, 8.

21. *Item*, March 30, 1917, 12.

22. *States*, March 28, 1917, 1, 7.

23. *TP*, March 25, 1917, A15.

24. *Item*, March 23, 1917, 1.

25. *Item*, March 25, 1917, section 2, 1.

26. *Weekly Clarion-Ledger*, July 30, 1903, 3.

27. *TP*, March 25, 1917, 1, 14.

28. *TP*, April 6, 1917, 10.

29. *TP*, April 3, 1917, 9.

30. *TP*, April 5, 1917, 11.

31. *TP*, April 5, 1917, 8.

32. *TP*, April 13, 1917, 8.

33. *TP*, April 5, 1917, 1

34. *TP*, March 31, 1917, 8.

35. Fleming, 13.

36. *TP*, April 6, 1917, 1.

37. *TP*, April 7, 1917, 4.

38. Hutson Family Papers, April 12, 1917.

CHAPTER 6

1. *Item*, April 24, 1917, 6
2. See David Kennedy's thoughtful *Over Here: The First World War in American Society*, pp 144–158 for more on the issues surrounding conscription.
3. *Item*, April 21, 1917, 1; *TP*, April 24, 1917, 2.
4. Congressional Record, 6061. Jeanette Keith's study of southern resistance to the draft among both Blacks and whites, *Rich Man's War, Poor Man's Fight: Race, Class, and Power during the First World War*, is an important source for anyone searching for answers to this antimilitaristic phenomenon during a time of patriotic exuberance. Vardaman is liberally referenced. See also *To Raise an Army: The Draft Comes to Modern America* by John Chambers and *The White Chief: James Kimble Vardaman* by William F. Holmes.
5. *The Crisis* 14, no. 1 (May 1917), 23.
6. Dyer, 182, 184.
7. *Jambalaya*, 138.
8. *TP*, January 17, 1919, 1.
9. Minutes, UCV 27th annual reunion, October 4–5, 1917
10. *TP*, Trench and Camp section, December 10, 1917, 4.
11. *TP*, February 17, 1918, A10.
12. Report, Provost Marshal, 1917, 113–14. For data on the Selective Service Act, e.g., claims for exemptions, physical disqualifications, and details on dependencies, aliens, age limits, mobilization, etc., see all three wartime reports of the provost marshal general and *Selective Service Regulations*, both digitized on the Hathi Trust.
13. McClellan, 16.
14. *Washington Post*, July 21, 1917, 1.
15. *TP*, June 5, 1917, 1.
16. LA State Archives, Vital Records Index.
17. *Second Report of the Provost Marshal General*, 121.
18. *TP*, December 15, 1917, 13.
19. See chapter 4 of Greta de Jong's *A Different Day: African American Struggles for Justice in Rural Louisiana, 1900–1970* for parish data and details of the Great Migration in Louisiana. New Orleans Creole and civil rights leader A. P. Tureaud (University of New Orleans Special Collections, MS 164) provides a unique personal perspective of his experiences in Chicago in 1917, saying that in Chicago, racial discrimination was "even more hostile" than in his hometown. Correspondence from migrants can be found in Emmett J. Scott's "Letters of Negro Migrants of 1916–1918," *Journal of Negro History* IV, no. 3 (July 1918); and "More Letters of Negro Migrants of 1916–1918," *Journal of Negro History* IV, no. 4 (October 1919).

See also James Grossman's *Land of Hope: Chicago, Black Southerners, and the Great Migration* and Peter Gottlieb's *Making Their Own Way: Southern Blacks' Migration to Pittsburgh, 1916–30* for excellent and highly detailed studies of the episode in two representative cities.

20. The complete act can be found at *Acts Passed by the General Assembly of the State of Louisiana at the Regular Session*, Act No. 139, July 9, 1918, 137–8.

21. See New Orleans Commission Council Series Ordinance No. 5268, October 29, 1918.

22. *TP*, April 21, 1918, B7.

23. *States*, October 28, 1918, 1.

24. *TP*, August 15, 1918, 1.

25. "The Immigrant Army: Immigrant Service Members in World War I," n.p.

26. Mary Connoly, interviewed by Joe Maselli, American-Italian Archives, Jefferson Parish Public Libra.

27. WWL Staff, "How the Son of Sicilian Immigrants Became One of New Orleans' Greatest Athletes," https://tinyurl.com/sqmhkzr.

28. *TP*, November 22, 1917, 8.

29. *TP*, November 24, 17, 8.

30. Gisclair, "Pete Herman," knowlouisiana.org., *Encyclopedia of Louisiana*; Wiltz, *The Last Madam*, 21.

31. *Report of the Provost Marshal*, 1917, 86, 113–14; *TP*, June 9, 1917, 5.

32. David Kennedy's *Over Here*, 158–163, includes an objective overview of the administration's difficulties in incorporating Black men into the service. Segregation would continue to be the policy, but there were several other problems to confront. The Selective Service's discriminatory policies concerning Black exemptions are also explained.

33. "The City School Reduced in Grace," *Southwestern Christian Advocate*, July 5, 1900; Stern, 70, 73, 74.

34. 13th Census, 1910, Volume 1, 1238.

35. African Americans could choose between the four private secondary schools in New Orleans that were founded during Reconstruction: Leland College—an institution endowed by the Baptist Church, closed after the 1915 hurricane, Xavier Normal School (later University) for Catholics, the Methodist Episcopal New Orleans University, or the Congregationalist sponsored Straight College. (The latter two merged in 1935 to form Dillard University.) Each of these private institutions, however, was tuition-based and therefore opened to only a select few.

36. Yerkes, 282–85.

37. https://www.archives.gov/atlanta/wwi-draft/armstrong.html.

38. *TP*, June 7, 1917, 2.

39. Archdiocese of N.O. Archives, WWI correspondence, box 1, folder "Misc. Catholic Activity," undated.

40. *Louisiana in the War*, 23. This valuable resource was published by the *Times-Picayune* to provide readers with an account of both the material and human contributions made by Louisiana during the war. Written in independent "chapters" by different authors, it covers such items as the military presence in the state, decorated servicemen, war fund raising, the press, education, medical mobilization, the economic boom, conscription, and various civilian organizations that assisted in the war effort. The publication also lists hundreds of names of those connected to these activities and profiles the most eminent (Jackson Barracks archives in New Orleans).

41. *TP*, October 18, 1917, 1, 7.

42. *States*, September 19, 1917, 1.

43. *TP*, September 20, 1917, 1; *States*, September 19, 1917, 1.

44. *TP*, September 23, 1917, 4.

45. *The NY Times Current History: The European War*, vol. 12, 7–8.

46. *TP*, June 15, 1917, 3.

47. Mayer, *To the Border and Back by the First Louisiana Infantry*.

48. *TP*, February 26, 1918, 12.

49. Pettijohn February 3, 1918, Washington Artillery Collection, 2000.024.

50. Kimball, 279.

51. Powell, 128.

52. *LA in the War*, 11.

53. *Le Meschacébé*, May 10, 1919, 1, LSU Special Collections.

54. McConnell papers TU LA Collection #156, box 4, folders 7, 8.

55. Loving, Confidential Memo to Gen. Marlborough Churchill, Director of Military Intelligence, November 18, 1918, NARA, RG 165, file 10218–256, Fold 3, Military Intelligence file; Mjagkij, 181–2.

56. Lefferts, 39.

57. Russell interviews, October 12, 1958, and August 22, 1958, identifier items 43 and 27.

58. LA Council of Defense records, TU Collection # 847, box 1, folder 3, May 2, 1918.

59. Hannefin, Daughters of Charity Provincial Archives, RG7-5-3, https://dcarchives .files.wordpress.com/2013/12/stlouis-world-war-one.docx

60. *LA in the War*, 13–14.

61. *Item*, June 20, 1918, 7; *LA in the War*, 85–87.

CHAPTER 7

1. For a comprehensive investigation of US war financing, see Julia Ott's *When Wall Street Met Main Street: The Quest for an Investor's Democracy*, Harvard University Press, 2011.

2. *Item*, October 7, 1918, 10.

3. *TP*, June 16, 1917, 14.

4. *TP*, October 21, 1917, 1.

5. "Putting Over the Fourth Liberty Loan in New Orleans, 1919," 79-031-RL, Williams Reach Center; *TP*, September 7, 1917, 3.

6. *TP*, October 24, 1917, 5.

7. *TP*, June 4, 1917, 1; *TP*, April 8, 1918, 16.

8. *TP*, April 7, 1918, 1A.

9. *TP*, May 4, 1918, 8.

10. *TP*, April 24, 1918, 1, 7.

11. The so-called Spanish influenza would commit over 54,000 New Orleanians to bed between October 1918 and April 1919. Worldwide, the disease dispatched between 50 and 100 million people in a mere 15 months, including as many as 670,000 Americans, far exceeding its WWI combat deaths. A shocking 3,489 New Orleanians would die during the epidemic—a mortality rate of 6.5 percent. Only Pittsburgh and Philadelphia had higher rates. October 1918 would become the deadliest month in city history. See John Barry's *The*

Great Influenza: The Story of the Greatest Pandemic in History for a comprehensive narrative. For details of the crisis in New Orleans, consult "The American Influenza Epidemic,
1917–18" at https://www.influenzaarchive.org/

12. *TP*, September 29, 1918, B13; *Item*, September 29, 1918, 1.

13. "Putting Over the Fourth Liberty Loan in New Orleans," 1919, 79-013-RL, HNOC,
Williams Research Center. *States*, October 5, 1918, 1; *TP*, October 6, 1918, 1, B10.

14. "Putting Over the Fourth Liberty Loan in New Orleans."

15. *Herald*, June 20, 1918, 5.

16. *TP*, October 24, 1917, 5.

17. *Herald*, June 20, 1918, 1.

18. *States*, June 30, 1918, 12.

19. *Item*, November 5, 1918, 5; *TP*, November 5, 1918, 1.

20. Lyons letter to the *Mixer and Server: Journal of the Hotel and Restaurant Employees
International and Bartender's League of America*, October 26, 1918, 22.

21. *LA in the War*, 32.

CHAPTER 8

1. *TP*, March 7, 1918, 7.

2. K. W. Watson Appointment Rules, 231.3, Telephone Operators, Office of the Chief
Signal Corps Correspondence, RG 111, NARA, in Frahm, the *Journal of the Gilded Age and
Progressive Era* 3, no. 3 (2004), 286, http://www.jstor.org/stable/25144374; Frahm, "Women
Telephone Operators in World War I France." Center for Cryptologic History. 2016, 5–6.
https://tinyurl.com/r22dymr; Dr. Elizabeth Cobbs, Texas A&M University, personal papers.

3. *TP*, January 26, 1918, 11.

4. *Item*, June 17, 1917, section 2, 1.

5. *TP*, April 22, 1917, A15.

6. *TP*, October 13, 1918, B2.

7. *TP*, September 8, 1918, B9.

8. *TP*, December 24, 1918, 8.

9. *States*, October 17, 1918, 11.

10. *Item*, November 4, 1932, 10.

11. *Item*, October 7, 1917, Section 1, 8.

12. *TP*, November 7, 1917, 7.

13. *TP*, August 11, 1918, 9.

14. *Item*, December 8, 1918, section 2, 7.

15. Gavin, *American Women in WWI: They Also Served*, University of Colorado, Boulder,
1997, in Fortier, "Behind the Banner of Patriotism," 5.

16. *TP*, December 20, 1918, 18.

17. *Newcomb Arcade* XI, no. 1 (November 1918), 39; and *Newcomb Arcade* IX, no. 3 (April
1917), 218–19.

18. Dixon, 182.

19. American Red Cross, *Department of Chapters –Auxiliaries, 1*, in Fortier, "Behind the
Barriers," 10.

20. An account of these three women, their impact on racial uplift, and the contribution the auxiliaries made to the war effort can be found in Chapter 6 of Paula Fortier's "Behind the Banner of Patriotism: The New Orleans Chapter of the American Red Cross and Auxiliary Branches 6 and 11 (1914–1917)." See also "Red Cross in Louisiana" and "The Red Cross in New Orleans" in the manuscript "Louisiana in the War," n.p., for details of the organization's work during the war and the flu epidemic. Included is a list of the chapters' officers in the various parishes.

21. *Herald*, May 23, 1918; June 6, 1918, 1.

22. *TP*, October 28, 1917, A5.

CHAPTER 9

1. *TP*, September 4, 1917, 6.

2. Mjagkij, 82.

3. *TP*, October 8, 1917, 1; *States*, October 8, 1917, 2.

4. Elliott Rudwick's *Race Riot at East St. Louis, July 2, 1917*, University of Illinois Press, 1982, is perhaps the most rigorously researched narrative of this violent clash.

5. See "The Houston Mutiny and Riot of 1917" by Robert V. Haynes in the *Southwestern Historical Quarterly* 76, no. 4 (April 1973), 418–439.

6. *TP*, October 13, 1917, 8.

7. *States*, October 28, 1917, 1; *TP*, A6.

8. Project HAL Data Collection Project, database, https://tinyurl.com/yd2qpcuh.

9. *TP*, April 25, 1918, 17.

10. *TP*, September 5, 1917, 1.

11. Barbeau and Henri, 164–66.

12. *TP*, April 5, 1917, 2.

13. Ellis, *Race, War, and Surveillance*, 10.

14. WWI, Military Intelligence, Negro Subversion, Fold 3; Ellis, *Race, War, and Surveillance*, 228.

15. Williams, *Sidelights on Negro Soldiers*, 70–71.

16. *Spy Glass*, June 4, 1918, 3.

17. Ellis, *Race, War, and Surveillance*, 73.

18. *TP*, April 24, 1917, 8.

19. *TP*, April 15, 1917, B6.

20. For more about cooperation between New Orleans Creoles of Color and white leaders, see Kevin Gaines, *Uplifting the Race: Black Leadership, Politics, and Culture in the Twentieth Century*, University of North Carolina Press, 1996; in *Attacking Jim Crow: Black Activism in New Orleans*, 1925–41, LSU dissertation, 2009, pp 87–88, Sharlene DeCuir claims that among Black leaders, there existed an "unwillingness to pose a threat" to the local white power structure, "petitioning, not picketing." This was because they saw no hope that change was imminent, appealing to their moral consciousness and waiting for concessions within the Jim Crow system. New Orleans Civil Rights leader A. P. Tureaud (in Hirsch and Logsdon's *Creole New Orleans, Race and Americanization*, pp 264–5, 268) further explains

that Black leaders used personal contacts with whites in authority to air grievances, which led to moderate yet visible successes. Louisiana's NAACP field director Harvey H. Britton also maintained that "there was always an underlying feeling in Louisiana of some kind of comradeship between blacks and whites" (1987 taped interview by Adam Fairclough, Amistad Research Center, Tulane University). One impatient local NAACP member, however, complained: "Our population . . . is so thoroughly mixed that approximately seventy-five percent have . . . a 'white complex.' Although they associate with those of darker hue, they are not willing to assist in righting wrongs" (Dr. Ernest Cherrie to William L. Andrews, July 6, 1931, part I, series G, NAACP Papers, Library of Congress).

21. *The Vindicator*, September 3, 1918, Selected Branch Files, 1913–39, Part 12, Series A, Reel 14, NAACP Papers, Cambridge University Library, in Downs and Floyd, 8.

22. Negro Civic League of Louisiana, pamphlet, APL report, March 3, 1918, BI File OG 83017, RG 65, NARA, in Ellis, *Race, War, and Surveillance*, 65.

23. *Piron and Williams*, www.loc.gov/item/2014562599/

24. Nickerson, www.loc.gov/item/2013568816/.

25. *States*, October 6, 1918, 11.

26. *TP*, April 16, 1917, 5; April 9, 1917, 9.

27. *TP*, April 11, 1917, 8.

28. *TP*, April 4, 1917, 8.

29. *TP*, April 6, 1917, 8.

30. "Trench and Camp Section," *TP*, April 8, 1917, A16.

31. *STF*, June 15, 1918, 2.

32. *Vicksburg Weekly Herald*, May 16, 1919, in Barbeau and Henri, 175.

33. Robert Moton's autobiography, *Finding a Way Out*, offers a firsthand account of Washington's concerns about racial issues within the ranks of the troops and the sensitivity with which those concerns were addressed. See also Charles P. Procee's 2019 thesis "The Line That Belts the World: Transnationality, the Colour Line, and Race during the Great War," Concordia University, for his interesting comparison between what he calls America's "brutal racism" and France's "benevolent racism."

34. Moton, 263.

35. Keene, 88, 90.

36. "Secret Information Concerning Black American Troops," reprinted in *The Crisis*, vol. 18, no. 1 (May 1919), 16–18.

37. *TP*, May 30, 1917, 3.

38. *TP*, July 15, 1918, 3.

39. *Southwestern Christian Advocate*, January 3, 1918, 2.

40. *The Crisis* 16, no. 3, July 1918, 111.

41. *Item*, November 24, 1918, 10.

CHAPTER 10

1. *TP*, June 3, 1917, section 2, 1.

2. *TP*, May 10, 1917, 7.

3. Munro, et al, 9, 13.

4. The local Austrian population numbered just over eight hundred, but they received little attention, even after the US war declaration against Austria-Hungary in December of 1917.

5. *Bureau of the Census, Supplement—1910*, Statistics for Louisiana, 1913, 586.

6. "Atrocity Stories," box 1; "Correspondence 1914–1918," box 2, Archdiocese of N.O. Archives.

7. *Neue Deutsche Zeitung*, May 16, 1915, 4; *TP*, April 2, 1915, 4.

8. *States*, February 12, 1916, 12; *TP*, February 10, 1915, 2.

9. Deutsches Haus Collection, MSS 609, items 9, 35 (microfilm), HNOC, in Kuss, 195.

10. Gerard, 173; *States*, June 3, 1918, 5.

11. *TP*, April 5, 1917, 8.

12. *Item*, April 8, 1917, 22; *States*, April 7, 1917, 8.

13. Kolb, 22.

14. *Neue Deutsche Zeitung*, April 15, 1917, 8.

15. N.O. City Directory, 1917–19 in Berchtold, 29.

16. Berchtold, 30.

17. Louisiana Acts, 1918, no. 138.

18. *STF*, May 25, 1918, 1.

19. *The Salem Echo*, 5–18, 5, in Berchtold, 30. The trend to remove "German" from the names of some New Orleans churches had begun a decade or more before the war to reflect demographic shifts in their congregations, not necessarily in reaction to the war

20. Weyer, WWL-TV, recorded interview, German-American Cultural Center, c. 1975

21. *TP*, April 20, 1918, 5.

22. Gorman, WWL-TV, recorded interview, German-American Cultural Center, c. 1975.

23. *TP*, April 27, 1918, 1.

24. *States*, October 6, 1918, 1.

25. *TP*, April 8, 1918, 12.

26. *States*, April 4, 1918, 8.

27. Augusto Miceli Papers, #924, box 7, "Pickwick Club Manuscript," Part II, Tulane Special Collections.

28. *TP*, May 10, 1917, 7.

29. *TP*, July 16, 1917, 8.

30. *TP*, May 1, 1917, 7.

31. *TP*, November 10, 1918, C6; March 28, 1917, 3.

32. *Item*, April 17, 1917, 4.

33. *TP*, April 5, 1917, 8.

34. *Item*, July 21, 1917, 1.

35. *TP*, December 9, 1917, 15.

36. *TP*, February 8, 1918, 6.

37. *TP*, January 21, 1918, 4.

38. *STF*, June 8, 1918, 2.

39. Bear, Interviewed by Dorothy Schlesinger. June 5, 1975.

40. *TP*, February 17, 1918, 14.

41. *TP*, January 18, 1918, 4.

42. *STF*, May 11, 1918, 5.

43. *TP*, August 17, 1918, 6

44. Louisiana Acts, 1918, no. 114.

45. OPSB Minutes, February 22, 1918, May 10, 1918; Merrill, 235.

46. *TP*, July 6, 1918, 4.

47. *TP*, October 3, 1917, 8.

48. See Jean M. Palmer's "The Impact of World War I on Louisiana's Schools and Community Life," in *Louisiana History* 7, no. 4, (Autumn 1966), 323–32.

49. Louisiana Acts, 1918, no. 177.

50. McCord, 151–3, 158.

51. *TP*, December 1, 1917, 9.

52. *TP*, April 12, 1918, 8.

53. *TP*, September 22, 1918, 14B.

54. *TP*, March 29, 1918, 16; OPSB minutes, March 8, 1918, 291, and May 10, 1918, 324, UNO Special Collections.

55. Minutes, OPSB, April 8, 1918, 291, 301.

56. *TP*, April 12, 1917, 11.

57. Board Resolutions, 1917–27, 190–1, NAC-008, box 1, folder 2, Newcomb Archives.

58. Board of Administrators, Tulane Educational Fund, Minutes, vol. 13, 198.

59. *TP*, February 18, 1918, 9.

60. Board of Administrators, Tulane Educational Fund, Minutes, vol. 13, 199.

61. *TP*, February 16, 1918, 7.

62. Dyer, 185; Board of Administrators, Tulane Educational Fund, vol. 13, 1916–1918, 283–4.

63. FBI Case Files, Old German Files, Case #8000–79302, 84, 95, Fold 3; APL, LaRC-487, box 1, folder 1, Tulane Louisiana Research Collection.

64. *TP*, April 16, 1915, 8; April 29, 1915, 10; May 3, 1915, 5; *Report of the President of the German Society of N.O., La., Annual Reports for the 69th Fiscal Year*, Series II, Deutsches Haus Collection, HNOC.

65. *Report of the President of the German Society of N.O. for the 68th Fiscal Year.*

66. *TP*, December 18, 1916, 4.

67. *Report of the President of the German Society of N.O., 71st Fiscal Year.*

68. *TP*, March 12, 1918, 7; *Item*, March 12, 1918, 2; November 12, 1918, 10; and March 9, 1918, 1; FBI Case Files, Old German Files, Case #8000–6976, Fold 3.

69. *Report of the President of the German Society of N.O., La., Annual Report for the 71st Fiscal Year.*

70. Deutsches Haus Collection, MSS 609, item 9, HNOC.

CHAPTER 11

1. *TP*, March 28, 1917, 9.

2. Gregory to J. W. Byrns, May 9, 1917, RG 60, NARA in Hyman, 271–2.

3. Bielaski to All Special Agents and Local Officers, March 22, 1917, Frey Papers, Collection 743, box 6, UCLA Special Collections.

4. Mills, 23, 105.

5. Membership roles were inaccurate. Local chapters were reluctant to report their numbers, perhaps in an effort to maintain the anonymity of their agents. Whatever the case, Harold Hyman set the final number at 350,000. See his *To Try Men's Souls: Loyalty Tests in American History*, 273.

6. McAdoo to Gregory. June 2, 1917. The Papers of Woodrow Wilson Digital Edition 42, https://tinyurl.com/y7aqmn9s.

7. Weinberger, 7.

8. Blum, 14.

9. Jensen, 48.

10. Jensen, 49; Mills, 187.

11. Jensen, 133, 136.

12. Hyman, 274.

13. One Louisiana state senator was prosecuted for violating the Sedition Act. See Tammie A. McDaniel's "The Politics of Sedition: The Trial of Winnfield's Senator S.J. Harper" *Louisiana History* 53 (2012): 51–67.

14. *Spy Glass*, vol. 1, no. 1, June 4, 1918, 1.

15. *Annual Report of the Attorney General*, 1918, 104; Kornweibel, 174.

16. *TP*, April 27, 1918, 1.

17. *TP*, April 28, 1918, B8.

18. *TP*, April 29, 1918, 2.

19. *States*, April 29, 1918, 1, 3.

20. *TP*, May 4, 1918, 7.

21. *TP*, April 29, 1918, 1; April 30, 1918, 1; *States*, April 29, 1918, 1.

22. *States*, October 3, 1918, 7.

23. FBI Case Files, December 12, 1917, Military Intelligence Division, Negro Subversion, 3, Fold 3.

24. FBI Case Files, Old German Files, Case # 8000–79302, 95, 84, Fold 3.

25. American Protective League, Manuscript Collection 487, folders 2 and 3, Tulane Special Collections.

26. *TP*, August 25, 1918, B9.

27. *Spy Glass*, vol. 1, no. 1, June 4, 1918, 2.

28. O'Brian, "Civil Liberties in War Time," *Proceedings of the 42nd Annual Meeting, New York Bar Association*, 304, in Swisher, *Political Science Quarterly* 55, no. 3 (9–40), 328.

29. FBI Case Files, Old German Files, Cases 19940, 1; 217789, 4, Fold 3.

30. FBI Case Files, Old German Files, Case 10069, 1, 4; Case 17151, 7, Fold 3.

31. *Spy Glass*, August 24, 1918, 1.

32. Gregory to T. U. Taylor, April 15, 1918, Gregory Papers, box 1, Manuscript Division, Library of Congress, in Ross, 272.

33. Hough, 326.

34. WWI Case Files, Negro Subversion, Cases 10218–108; 10218–191, Fold 3.

35. LA Council of Defense bulletins 46 & 50, July 2, 1918 and July 27, 1918, Tulane LA Research Collection, # 847, box 1, folder 4.

36. Hutson Papers, Collection #14, box 2, folder 10, February 24, 1917, TU Special Collections; WWI Correspondence, box 2, "War, Various" folder, Archdiocese of New Orleans archives.

37. Old German Files, Mil Intel Division, Negro Subversion, Case 10218-273, Fold 3.

38. Old German Files, Mil Intel Division—Negro Subversion, cases 10218-170, 1; 10218-186, 2; 10218-188, 1; 10218-317, 2, Fold 3.

39. Hyman, 278.

40. *Spy Glass*, vol. 1 no. 9, October 5, 1918, 3.

41. AG annual report, 1918, 44; Kornweibel, 23; Hough, 327; *TP*, December 15, 1918, C1.

42. *Spy Glass*, vol. 1, no. 8, September 21, 1919, 1.

43. *TP*, March 22, 1918, 1, 9.

44. *TP*, April 30, 1918, 5.

45. Old German Files, FBI Case Files, Case 282939, 89, Fold 3.

46. *TP*, September 12, 1918, 8.

47. *States*, October 6, 1918, Features Financial Section, 1.

CHAPTER 12

1. By the time the Eighteenth Amendment went into effect in 1920, thirty parishes representing 52.9 percent of Louisiana's population were already dry. Joy Jackson, "Prohibition in N.O.", 263.

2. Louisiana Legislative Act 176, 1908.

3. Leathem, 226.

4. *TP*, November 25, 1917, B10.

5. *DP*, January 7, 1909, 4.

6. *Item*, January 7, 1914, 3.

7. *Item*, February 15, 1910, 1.

8. *DP*, April 1, 1910, 7.

9. *TP*, January 26, 1917, 4.

10. *TP*, February 9, 1917, 8; January 30, 1917, 8; February 5, 1917, 6.

11. Krist, 236.

12. Levy, 148.

13. *TP*, February 19, 1917, 8.

14. *TP*, January 24, 1917, 1.

15. *Item*, February 6, 1914, 4.

16. *TP*, February 5, 1917, 5.

17. *TP*, February 6, 1917, 4.

18. *TP*, February 22, 1917, 8.

19. *Item*, June 20, 1917, 5.

20. *TP*, March 10, 1917, 4.

21. TP, March 13, 1917, 14.

22. *States*, July 7, 1917, 1; *TP*, July 8, 1917, 9.

23. *TP*, June 20, 1917, 1. Given that neighborhood groceries also sold alcoholic beverages, that number was probably too small. Another report estimated that there was one liquor outlet for every eighty New Orleanians compared to one in every five hundred people in New York City. If these numbers were accurate, there were over four thousand places to inspect. *TP*, March 5, 1917, 12.

24. *Item*, June 19, 1917, 1.

25. *TP*, April 22, 1917, B10.

26. *Item*, January 27, 1917, 1, 3.

27. *TP*, January 29, 1917, 1.

28. *TP*, July 29, 1917, A10.

29. Brandt, 75.

30. FBI Case Files, Old German Files, Fold 3, Case 79302, 72.

31. *TP*, February 21, 1918, 7.

32. Report on N.O., LA, Supplemental Report No. 1, September 25, 1917, box 8, entry 395, NARA RG 65, in Bristow, 105.

33. *TP*, November 18, 1917, B9; Kemp, *Behrman of NOLA*, 308.

34. Kemp, *Behrman of NOLA*, 319.

35. *States*, November 12, 1917, 11. Behrman wrote in his memoir that neither of the Gordon sisters ever gave up a fight. In a backhanded compliment to his lethal adversary Kate, he wrote, "If Miss Gordon had been in the Confederate Army, she would still be carrying a gun and debating constitutional points about secession." Kemp, *Behrman of NOLA*, p. 306.

36. Gordon to Baker, September 14, 1917, NARA RG 165, box 582, in Brandt, 74.

37. *TP*, November 18, 1917, B9; Fosdick to Daniels, September 11, 1917, Daniels MMS, box 458 in Brandt, 75.

38. Kimball, 278.

39. *Item*, July 1, 1917, section 2, 5; Asher, "Last Days of Storyville," New Orleans Magazine, October 2017, 83.

40. War Department Records, War College and War Plans Division, Subordinate Offices—Education and Recreation Branch, CTCA, Entry 395, 1917, NARA, RG 165, box 8, in Long, *Babylon*, 226.

41. War Department Records, NARA, in Landau, 185.

42. Gordon to Baker, August 22, 1917, War Department Records, File 4659, NARA in Landau, 185–6.

43. Railey worked hand in hand with Fosdick on their vice crusade, as evidenced by their letters. See "The Sexual Economy of War: Regulation of Sexuality and the U.S. Army, 1898–1940" by J. A. Byers, a 2012 Duke University dissertation, 245–50, for more on their partnership.

44. FBI Case Files, Old German Files, Fold 3, Case 79302, 18, 19; Landau, 186.

45. Kemp, *Behrman of N.O.*, 308–11; *TP*, October 3, 1917, 5.

46. *States*, October 3, 1917, 6.

47. *TP*, October 13, 1917, 8.

48. Rose, 169; Asbury, 455.

49. Wiltz, 17–18.

50. *TP*, March 2, 1919, B14.

51. Armstrong, 96–7; Teachout, 45.

52. *States*, November 13, 1917, 3.

53. Kimball, 282.

54. Asbury, 453.

55. Fosdick, "The Commission on Training Camp Activities," 2–18, 169–70, https://ti nyurl.com/tqnwvmr.

56. *TP*, December 30, 1917, 11.

57. Cpt. J. B. Collins, February 11, 1919, quoted in letter of William Zinsser, Social Hygiene Div., to F.P. Keppel, February 24, 1919, doc. 46661, box entry 393, RG 165, NARA, in Bristow, 105.

58. *TP*, June 12, 1918, 1.

59. *TP*, August 25, 1918, B8.

60. From "Farewell to Storyville," Clarence and Spencer Williams, 1926, recorded by Armstrong and Billie Holiday

61. *TP*, February 17, 1918, 10.

62. *Item*, May 14, 1917, 1; *TP*, July 12, 1917, 5.

63. *TP*, January 6, 1918, A10.

64. *TP*, August 4, 1918, A11.

65. *TP*, August 7, 1918, 4.

66. *TP*, August 9, 1918, 1.

67. Kemp, *Behrman of NOLA*, 279–80.

68. Jackson, 262.

69. For a scholarly analysis of the prohibition vote, see Michael Lewis, "Access to Saloons, Wet Voter Turnout, and Statewide Prohibition Referenda, 1907–1919," *Social Science History* 32, no. 3 (Fall 2008), 373–404.

70. Cherrington, 182–83.

71. *TP*, December 1, 1918, B10.

72. *TP*, October 29, 1919, 1.

CHAPTER 13

1. Green, *Southern Strategies*, 128.

2. Graham, 24.

3. Merrick, 125.

4. Carrasco, 311–12.

5. See Marjorie Wheeler's *New Women of the New South: The Leaders of the Woman Suffrage Movement in the Southern States*, Oxford University Press, 1993, 120–25 for details on how Gordon leveraged the "Negro problem."

6. *TP*, May 5, 1918, A9.

7. ERA Club Papers, newspaper clipping, "Federal Law Called Useless by the ERA Club," NOPL, n.d.

8. *TP*, March 12, 1918, 4.

9. The ERA "Equal Rights for All" Club was born of its 1892 predecessor, the much tamer Portia Club, Louisiana's first women's suffrage organization. The ERA Club was misnamed, for under Gordon's direction, it was emphatic in its opposition to suffrage for Black women. According to the Portia Club founder Caroline Merrick, however, the division of the two was amicable. They would later merge. For a first-person account of the origins of these groups, see Merrick's *Old Times in Dixie Land: A Southern Matron's Memoirs*, Grafton Press, 1901, chapter XIX. The most important primary source on the topic is *History of Woman Suffrage*, Fowler and Webb, 1922, conceived by suffragists Elizabeth Cady Stanton, Susan B. Anthony, and Matilda Joslyn Gage. In vol. VI, chapter XVII, 1900–1920, both Kate Gordon and Ethel Hutson of the State Woman Suffrage Association describe the fight over ratification of the suffrage amendment in Louisiana.

10. Gilley, 291–3.

11. Gilley, 293.

12. Lindig, 116–17.

13. Green, *Southern Strategies*, note 12, 237.

14. Kate to Ida Boyer, September 16, 1918, Clay Papers, Special Collections, University of Kentucky Libraries, in A. Smith, "The History of the Women's Suffrage Movement," *Louisiana Law Review* 62, no. 2, (Winter 2002), 551

15. Milne Papers, Annual Report, 1922, in K. Kemp, "Jean and Kate Gordon, New Orleans Social Reformers, 1898–1933," *Louisiana History* 24, no. 4 (Autumn 1983), 397.

16. A. Smith, 548.

17. Milne Papers, Annual Report, 1908 in K. Kemp, "Jean and Kate Gordon, New Orleans Social Reformers, 1898–1933," *Louisiana History* 24, no. 4 (Autumn 1983), 393.

18. Gordon to Clay, December 5, 1907, Clay Papers, Special Collections, University of Kentucky Libraries.

19. Kate Gordon, ed, 1914–17, Louisiana Research Collection, Tulane University.

20. Meehan to Agnes Ryan, May 24, 1913, Women Suffragettes Papers, LaRC-700, Tulane Special Collections.

21. Meehan to Grace Chamberlain, August 2, 1913, Grace Chamberlain Papers, LA Historical Center, LA State Museum, box 2, folder 188.

22. Stanonius, "A Woman of Boundless Energy," 12.

23. *TP*, October 11, 1918, 8.

24. *TP*, June 1, 1917, 8.

25. *States*, June 21, 1918, 6.

26. *TP*, October 27, 1918, A3.

27. Gordon to Clay, March 14, 1918, Clay to Gordon, July 6, 1918, Laura Clay Papers, Special Collections, University of Kentucky Libraries.

28. *States*, June 21, 1918, 6.

29. *TP*, September 8, 1918, B8.

30. Ethel Hutson Papers, Tulane Manuscript Collection #14, box 1, folder 1.

31. The disease placed over 54,000 New Orleanians on their backs between October, 1918 and April of the following year. A shocking 3,489 of those victims died—a mortality rate of 6.5 percent. Only Pittsburg and Philadelphia had higher death rates. See David Morens et al., "The 1918 Influenza Pandemic: Lessons for 2009 and the Future." *Critical Care*

Medicine 38.4 Suppl (2010): e10–e20. John Barry's *The Great Influenza*. Penguin, 2005. For specific information about the epidemic in New Orleans, see "The Influenza Encyclopedia, the American Influenza Epidemic of 1917–1918," New Orleans, University of Michigan Center for the History of Medicine. Web.

32. *Item*, October 27, 1918, section 2, 4.

33. Stevens, 197–8.

34. *Item*, November 29, 1918, 6.

35. *TP*, October 31, 1918, 4.

36. Harper, 224.

37. Report of the Secretary of State to His Excellency the Governor of Louisiana, January 1, 1919, 275.

38. *TP*, November 6, 1918, 1.

39. *TP*, November 21, 1918, 5.

40. *TP*, November 7, 1918, 1, 8.

41. *Item*, November 19, 1918, 9.

42. *TP*, November 21, 1918, 5.

43. *TP*, November 22, 1918, 8.

44. Era Club Papers, Minute Book, MS 25, NOPL; *Item*, October 25, 1918, 6.

45. *TP*, August 19, 1920, 2.

46. Gordon to Clay, March 22, 1923, Clay Papers, in Green, "The Rest of . . ." 188.

47. *TP*, August 19, 1920, 2.

48. Harper, 219.

49. *Item*, September 5, 1920, Section 2, 1.

50. Report of the Sec of State to His Excellency the Governor of LA, 1921, 337.

CHAPTER 14

1. Briggs to Frey, January 8, 1918, Frey Papers, Collection 743, box 2, UCLA Special Collections.

2. Weinberger, 13.

3. The local Traveler's Aid Society was understaffed at train terminals, attempting to intercept runaways (both Black and white) attracted to the abundance of servicemen in town. (C. W. Hutson Papers, Tulane Special Collections #140, box 35, folder 6, February 2, 1918.) Mrs. George Denegre, its leader, was distraught. In June of 1918, she wrote, "This month was positively lurid. Girls were running away after the soldiers with a spirit of wildness with which it was almost impossible to cope." (T.A.S. report, 3–19, Tulane Special Collections #365, box 1, folder 31).

4. *Item*, July 1, 1917, section 2, 5.

5. *TP*, July 3, 1917, 9.

6. *TP*, July 5, 1917, 1.

7. *States*, July 5, 1917, 6.

8. *States*, July 3, 1917, 4.

9. *Item*, July 7, 1917, 4; *States*, July 5, 1917, 6.

10. *Item*, July 6, 1917, 1.

11. *Item*, October 13, 1918, section 2, 9.

12. *STF*, June 8, 1918, 1.

13. FBI Case Files, Old German Files, Case 8000–79302, 68, Fold 3.

14. Fosdick to Baker, August 10, 1916, Fosdick Papers, Series 1, Correspondence, Princeton University Special Collections.

15. US forces lost 6,804,818 days of active duty due to venereal disease during the war, and hospitals treated an astounding 100,000 more men for venereal disease than for the total number of US casualties. One out of every ten servicemen contracted syphilis or gonorrhea, called "big and little casino" by the men (Ireland, 263, 271). French prime minister Georges Clemenceau invited Pershing's men to avail themselves of his state-managed brothels or *maisons tolérées*, where the girls were licensed. Pershing politely refused. When Secretary Baker heard of the offer, he reportedly exclaimed, "For God's sake, Raymond, don't show this to the President or he'll stop the war" (Fosdick, *Chronicle of a Generation*, 171). Report of the Surgeon-General of the Army," Annual Report of the War Department, vol. I, Washington, DC: War Department, 1919, 955.

16. *TP*, September 1, 1918, Magazine Sect, 4.

17. *The Vindicator*, August 20, 1918, Selected Branch Files, 1913–39, Part 12, Series A, Reel 14, NAACP, in Downs and Floyd, 173.

18. Jean Gordon to Baker, August 22, 1917, NARA File doc 4659, War Department Records, in Landau, 186.

19. *LA in the War*, 73.

20. For a comprehensive study of the VD problem during WWI, see Allan Brandt, *No Magic Bullet: A Social History of Venereal Disease in the United States since 1880.*

21. *TP*, November 10, 1918, C7; Weinberger, 11; *Item*, November 7, 1918, 14.

22. Hough, 329.

23. *TP*, March 7, 1918, 14.

24. Hough, 327.

25. American Protective League archive, Tulane Special Collections, Collection # 487, box 1, folder 1.

26. *TP*, June 12, 1918, 1.

27. *Tensas Gazette*, June 10, 1910, in Perreault, 87, 109; *Item*, November 22, 1918, 5.

28. *States*, October 22, 1918, 1.

29. Weinberger, 11–13.

30. *TP*, November 23, 1918, 1; Weinberger, 13–14.

31. *Spy Glass*, vol. 1, no. 11, November 4, 1918, 2.

32. *Spy Glass*, vol. 1, no. 11, November 4, 1918, 1.

33. *States*, November 22, 1918, 16.

34. *TP*, November 10, 1918, A14.

35. Hyman, 293; Gregory to Briggs, November 21, 1918, MSS 24109, box 1, RG 60, Library of Congress.

EPILOGUE

1. Cpt. Sumter D. Marks Jr., 21st Field Artillery, private collection of Berthe Marks Amoss.

2. *Nottingham Journal*, May 4, 1940, 1 in Cuthbertson, 242.

3. Armstrong, 144.

4. *TP*, November 12, 1918, 10; *States*, November 11, 1918, 1; *Item*, November 11, 1918, 12.

5. Choppin papers, MSS 757, Williams Research Center, HNOC, folder 7.

6. *TP*, January 1, 1919, 1.

7. Drinks with less than 2.75 percent alcoholic content were permitted under the act but not under the amendment.

8. *TP*, July 1, 1919, 15.

9. *Item*, July 1, 1919, 1, 10; *States*, July 1, 1919, 1, 13.

10. *TP*, January 6, 1919, 2; January 8, 1919, 16.

11. *Item*, January 26, 1921, 1, 2; *TP*, March 8, 1927, 1; July 15, 1927, 22. Louisiana law enforcement officers made roughly 2,700 arrests for prostitution in 1924, according to a report by Dr. L.C. Scott of the Louisiana Board of Health. L. C. Scott, "The Prostitution and Venereal Disease Problem in Louisiana," *National Municipal Review* 13 (1924): 200–202.

12. *TP*, July 22, 1922, 1.

13. Report of the Secretary of State to His Excellency the Governor, 1929, 328.

14. For a contemporary look at the causes of right-wing vigilantism, see Madeline Albright, *Fascism: A Warning*, Harper Collins, 2018. She argues that when fear grips the public, it wants quick action on the part of the government and welcomes strong, unquestioned direction from its leaders. This, in turn, often leads to exploitation of nationalistic symbols—the flag, for example—and the public's prejudices against those who are identified as threats to American values.

15. *TP*, November 20, 1918, 5.

16. Capozzola, 1379; Franklin and Moss, 346–52.

17. *The Crisis*, May 1919, 14.

18. *TP*, February 18, 1920, 1; *States*, February 17, 1920, 1.

19. *TP*, January 15, 1920, 1.

20. *TP*, September 7, 1920, 1, et al.

BIBLIOGRAPHY

ARCHIVAL MATERIALS, GOVERNMENT DOCUMENTS, BULLETINS, REPORTS, AND OTHER PRIMARY SOURCES

Abstract of the Fourteenth Census of the United States. US Census Bureau. Washington: Government Printing Office, 1923. https://tinyurl.com/s7thv2c.

American Protective League records. LaRC-487. Box 1. Folders 1–3. Tulane Louisiana Research Collection.

Annual Report of the Attorney General of the United States for the Year 1918. Washington: Government Printing Office, 1918.

Bear, Renee Samuel. June 5, 1975. Friends of the Cabildo Oral History Project. Interviewed by Dorothy Schlesinger. New Orleans Public Library (NOPL).

Behrman, Martin. "New Orleans: A History of Three Great Public Utilities, Sewerage, Water, and Drainage and Their Influence upon the Health and Progress of a Big City." Paper read by Behrman to the League of American Municipalities, September 29, 1914.

Biannual Report of the Board of Health for the Parish of Orleans and the City of New Orleans, 1918–1919. New Orleans: Brandao Printing Co., 1919.

"Board Resolutions, 1917–27." NAC-008. Box 1. Folder 2. Newcomb College Archives.

Board of Administrators. Tulane Educational Fund, 1916–1918. Minutes 13. University Archives, Tulane Special Collections.

Correspondence 1914–1918. "Atrocity Stories." Box 1. Archdiocese of N.O. Archives.

Correspondence 1914–1918. "War, Various." Box 2. Archdiocese of N.O. Archives

Chamberlain, Grace, and O.W. Papers. RG 14. Box 2. Folder 188. Louisiana State Museum Historical Center.

Choppin, Pierre, Papers. MSS 757. Folder 7. Williams Research Center, Historic New Orleans Collection (HNOC).

Christian, Marcus Collection. "A Black History of Louisiana." MSS 011. The Dillard Project. Works Progress Administration. University of New Orleans archives, 1942.

City of N.O. v. Willie Piazza. Supreme Court of Louisiana. Docket #22624 (1917). 142 *Louisiana Reports,* 167.

Clay, Laura, Papers. University of Kentucky Special Collections Research Center.

Cobbs, Elizabeth. Texas A & M University, personal papers.

Compilation of War Laws of the Various States and Insular Possessions. Washington: Government Printing Office, 1919.

Connoly, Mary. 1971. Interviewed by Joseph Maselli. Jefferson Parish American-Italian Archives.

Costa, Mildred. Friends of the Cabildo Oral History Project. Interviewed by Dorothy Schlesinger. January 5, 1985. NOPL.

Davenport, Charles, Papers. MSS.B.D27. Box 83. American Philosophical Society Library. https://tinyurl.com/yae95sp2.

Department of Commerce and Labor, Bureau of the Census, Supplement–1910 Statistics for Louisiana. Washington: Government Printing Office, 1913

Department of Health Sanitary Survey of the City of New Orleans, 1918–1919. New Orleans: Brandao Printing, 1919. Louisiana Collection. NOPL.

Durand, Maurice. August 22, 1958. Hogan Jazz Archives, Oral History Collections. Item 27. Interviewed by William Russell. Tulane Special Collections.

Elder, Katherine Lucinda Wilson, Papers. "Rules for Student Residence." House Regulations. NA-029. Box 7. 1918. Newcomb College archives.

ERA Club Papers. 1914–1925. MS-25. Newspaper clipping. "Federal Law Called Useless by the ERA Club." Louisiana Collections, NOPL

Era Club Records. Minute Book. MS 25. Resolution of November 24, 1918. NOPL.

Fosdick, Raymond, Papers. Raymond Fosdick to Newton Baker. August 10, 1916. Box 1. Princeton University Archives.

Frey, Charles Papers (1917–1919). Collection 743. "Memo to All Special Agents and Local Officers." March 22, 1917. Box 6. UCLA Special Collections.

Historic New Orleans Collection. MSS 536, f.25. District folder.

Historic Record of Camp Nicholls, New Orleans, New Orleans: Robert True Co., 1917, Louisiana Digital Library.

Hutson, Family Papers. April 12, 1917. Manuscript Collection 140. Box 35. Folder 9. Tulane Special Collections.

Hutson, Ethel, Papers. Manuscript Collection 14. Box 1. Folder 10. Tulane Special Collections.

Ireland, M. W. *The Medical Department of the United States Army in the World War IX.* Washington: US Government Printing Office, 1928.

Jambalaya. Tulane University 1919 yearbook. Tulane Archives.

Johnson, Bascom. Report on New Orleans, LA. Supplemental Report No. 1. September 25, 1917. RG 65. Box 8. Entry 395. Quoted in Nancy Bristow. *Making Men Moral: Social Engineering during the Great War.* NYU Press, 1996, 105.

Johnson, G. R. G.R. Johnson to Cpt. Louis M. Evans. Office of the Chief, Signal Corps correspondence. 1917–1940. Base Operations and Planning. 231.3. Telephone Operator. RG 111. Folder 1. National Archives and Record Administration (NARA). February 23, 1928.

Keller, Anatole, Family Papers, Mss 2910. Box 1. Folder 9. LSU Special Collections.

Lacombe, Allen. December 2, 1998. Interviewed by the author. Author's collection.

Link, Arthur S., ed. William McAdoo to Thomas Watt Gregory. June 2, 1917. The Papers of Woodrow Wilson Digital Edition 42. University of Virginia Press. https://tinyurl.com/y7aqmn9s

Louisiana Acts Passed by the General Assembly of the State of Louisiana at the Regular Session. Baton Rouge: Ramirez-Jones Printing Co., 1918.

Louisiana Council of Defense Records. #847. Box 1. Folder 3. Bulletins 46 & 50. July 2, 1918, and July 26, 1918. Tulane Special Collections.

Loving, Walter H. Walter Loving to Gen. Marlborough Churchill, Director of Military Intelligence. Folder 3. RG 165, file 10218–256. Military Intelligence file. NARA. November 18, 1918.

Mayer, Herbert. *To the Border and Back by the First Louisiana Infantry: Mexican Border Service from* Alexandria *to San Benito, Rio Hondo and Home.* Object #2013.005.058, New Orleans: Town Talk Print, 1916. Louisiana National Guard Archives, Jackson Barracks.

Marks, Sumter. Sumter Marks to Berthe Marks Amoss. Personal collection of Berthe Marks Amoss. November 11, 1918.

McAdoo, W. G. W. G. McAdoo to Thomas W. Gregory. World War I Letters. June 2, 1917. WWP21462. Wilson Presidential Library. http://presidentwilson.org/collections/show/8.

McClellan, Edwin. *The United States Marine Corps in the World War.* Washington: Government Printing Office, 1920.

McConnell Family Papers. LaRC156. Box 4. Folders 7, 8. Tulane Special Collections.

Miceli, Augusto Papers. #924. Box 7. "Pickwick Club Manuscript, Part II." Tulane Special Collections.

Minutes, New Orleans Bureau of Health October 9, 1918. FF 300. NOPL.

Minutes, Orleans Parish School Board. January 11, 1918; January 25, 1918; March 8, 1918; April 8, 1918; May 10, 1918. Louisiana Collection, University of New Orleans.

Munro, Dana, George Sellery, and August Krey, eds. *German War Practices.* Part 1. Treatment of Civilians. Washington: Committee on Public Information, 1918.

Minutes, New Orleans Board of Health. October 9, 1918. FF 300. Louisiana Collection. NOPL.

New Orleans Thirty-Second Semi-Annual Report of the Sewage & Water Board, New Orleans. New Orleans: American Printing Co, 1916.

O'Brian, John L. "Civil Liberties in War Time." *Proceedings of the 42nd Annual Meeting, New York Bar Association* 42 (1919): 304. In *Political Science Quarterly* 55. no. 3 (9–40), 328.

Old German Files. Suspected German Activities. Cases #22806, 9940, 217605, 217789, 10069, 187170, 243269, 17151, 126596, 282939. Fold 3. RG 65. NARA.

Old German Files. FBI Case Files. Mil Intel Division—Negro Subversion. Cases #74, 8000–79302, 108, 191 170, 186, 188, 317. Fold 3. RG 65. NARA.

Old German Files. FBI Case Files. Mil Intel Division—Negro Subversion. Report of Cpt. R.G. Heard, Assistant Intelligence Officer to Military Intelligence Division Chief, 17th Division. Case #273. Fold 3. RG 65. NARA.

Ordinance 4118. Commission Council Series. 2–17; Ordinance 4485. CCS. 7–17. New Orleans City Archives. NOPL.

Pettijohn, Wayne Sheldon. "Journal of WWI Travels." February 3, 1918. Collection 2000 024. Washington Artillery Archives.

Piazza, Willie, v. City of N.O. Civil District Court of N.O. Docket #119538 (1917). NOPL.

"Putting Over the Fourth Liberty Loan in New Orleans, 1919." 79-031-RL. New Orleans: The Chamber's Agency, Inc. c.1919. Williams Research Center. HNOC.

Report, New Orleans Traveler's Aid Society. 3–19. LaRC 365. Box 1. Folder 31. Tulane Special
Collections.

Report of the Board of Administrators of the Charity Hospital to the General Assembly of
the State of Louisiana, 1918.

Report of the Provost Marshal General to the Secretary of War on the Operations of the
Selective Service System, 1917. Washington: Government Printing Office, 1918.

Reports of the President of the German Society of N.O., La. Annual Reports for the 68th,
69th, and 71st Fiscal Years, 1915, 1916, 1918. Series II. Deutsches Haus Archives. HNOC.

Reports of the Secretary of State to His Excellency, the Governor of Louisiana. Baton
Rouge: Ramires-James Printing Co., 1919, 1921, 1929.

Robinson, Jim. October 12, 1958. Hogan Jazz Archives Oral History Collections. Item 43.
Interviewed by William Russell. Tulane Special Collections.

Second Report of the Provost Marshal General to the Secretary of War, on the First Draft
of the Selective Service System to Dec. 20th, 1918. Washington: Government Printing
Office, 1919.

*Selective Service Regulations: Prescribed by the President under the Authority Vested in
Him by the Terms of the Selective Service Law (Act of Congress Approved May 18th, 1917,
with Supplementary and Amendatory Acts and Resolutions).* Washington: Government
Printing Office, 1918.

State of Louisiana. *Official Journal of the House of Representatives, 1st Extra Session, 1917*
Baton Rouge: Ramirez-Jones Printing Co., 1917.

Stier, Emile. American National Red Cross, New Orleans, Louisiana Chapter. Excerpt from
"Report of the New Orleans Chapter of the American Red Cross." Digital Public Library
of America. https://dp.la/item/909dce97401a7518b730b0a61a809346.

State of Louisiana. *Official Journal of the House of Representatives.* 1st Extra Session, 1917.
2nd Regular Session, 1918. Baton Rouge: Ramirez-Jones Publishing Co. 1917, 1918.

The Register: Bulletin of the Tulane University of Louisiana, 1917–1918. Series 19, no. 13. New
Orleans: Tulane University, October 1, 1918.

Thirteenth Census of the United States Taken in the Year 1910 1. Department of Commerce
and Labor, Bureau of the Census. Chapter VII, XIII. Washington: Government Printing
Office, 1913. https://tinyurl.com/v9a0s3l

United Confederate Veterans of Louisiana minutes. 27th annual reunion.

US Bureau of Labor Statistics. *Monthly Review.* Washington: Government Printing Office,
2–1918.

US Department of Labor, Office of the Secretary, Division of Negro Economics. *Negro
Migration in 1916–17.* Washington: Government Printing Office, 1919.

US Food Administration: Report of the Administrative Division, Part I. 1917–1919.
Washington: Government Printing Office, 1921.

Vardaman, James K. "Recent Disturbances in East St. Louis." *Congressional Record* 55
(August 6, 1917): 6061–6067.

Voelkel, Stephen J. Papers. Box 2. Folder 10. Louisiana National Guard Archives, Jackson
Barracks.

War Department Records. War College and War Plans Division, Subordinate Offices—
Education and Recreation Branch, Commission on Training Camp Activities. Box 8.
File 4659. Entry 395. RG 165. NARA.

Weinberger, Charles. *A Summary of the Activities of the New Orleans Division of the American Protective League.* 1919. Atlanta: Emory University.

Weyer, Harry and Doris Ann Gorman, c. 1975. Recorded interview. German-American Cultural Center.

Women Suffragettes Papers, LaRC-700, Tulane Special Collections.

THESES, DISSERTATIONS AND UNPUBLISHED MANUSCRIPTS

Berchtold, Raimund. "The Decline of German Ethnicity in New Orleans, 1880–1930." Master's thesis, University of New Orleans University (UNO), 1984.

Byers, John A. "The Sexual Economy of War: Regulation of Sexuality and the U.S. Army, 1898–1940." PhD dissertation, Duke University, 2012.

Dossie, Porsha. "Animal-Like and Depraved: Racist Stereotypes, Commercial Sex, and Black Women's Identity in New Orleans, 1825–1917." Honors thesis, University of Central Florida, 2014.

Dupont, Robert L. "Progressive Civic Development and Political Conflict: Regular Democrats and Reformers in New Orleans, 1896–1912." PhD dissertation, Louisiana State University, 1999.

Fortier, Paula A. "Crescent City Nightingales: Gender, Race, Class, and the Professionalism of Nursing for Women in New Orleans, Louisiana, 1881–1950." PhD dissertation, Paper 1168. UNO, 2014.

Fortier, Paula A. "Behind the Barrier of Patriotism: The N.O. Chapter of the Am Red Cross and Auxiliary Branches 6 and 11, 1914–1917." PhD dissertation, UNO, 2010.

Leathem, Karen. "'A Carnival According to Their Own Desires': Gender and Mardi Gras in New Orleans, 1870–1941." PhD dissertation, University of North Carolina, 1994.

Levy, Russell. "Of Bards and Bawds: New Orleans Before and During the Storyville Era, 1897–1913." Master's thesis, Tulane University, 1967.

Maren-Hogan, Masha. "The Appalling Appeal of the Octoroon: The Shifting Status Mixed Race Prostitutes in Early Twentieth Century New Orleans," Senior thesis, University of North Carolina at Ashville, 2012.

McCord, Stanley J. "A Historical and Linguistic Study of the German Settlement at Roberts Cove, Louisiana." PhD dissertation, LSU, 1969.

Perreault, Matthew Saul. "Jockeying for Position: Horse Racing in New Orleans, 1865–1920." Master's thesis, LSU, 2016.

Smallwood, Betty. "Milneburg, New Orleans: An Anthropological History of a Troubled Neighborhood." Master's thesis, UNO, 2011.

Sutherland, Robert, "An Analysis of Negro Churches in Chicago." PhD dissertation, University of Chicago, 1930.

PERIODICALS

Asher, Sally. "The Last Days of Storyville." *New Orleans Magazine* 50, no. 12 (October 2017): 78–83.

Barry, John, "Journal of the Plague Year." *Smithsonian* 48, no. 7 (November 2017): 34–44. https://tinyurl.com/ubrdre4

Cain, Timothy. "Silence and Cowardice at the University of Michigan: World War I and the Pursuit of Un-American Faculty." *History of Education Quarterly* 51, no 3 (August 2011): 296–329. https://tinyurl.com/ujhd2wd

Campanella, Richard. "The Ursuline Nuns' Lost Landmark on the Mississippi River, 1827–1912." *Preservation in Print* (December 2015): 14–15. https://tinyurl.com/t8bcewk

Campanella, Richard. "Remembering the Old French Opera House." *Preservation in Print* 40, no 1 (February, 2013): 16–18. https://tinyurl.com/u3vj353

Capozzola, Christopher. "The Only Badge Needed Is Your Patriotic Fervor: Vigilance, Coercion, and the Law in World War I America." *The Journal of American History* 88, no. 4 (March 2002): 1354–1382. https://www.jstor.org/stable/2700601?seq=1

Carrasco, Rebecca S. "The Gift House: Jean M. Gordon and the Making of the Milne Home, 1904-0150 1931." *Louisiana History* 34, no. 3 (Summer 1993): 309–325. https://tinyurl.com/u29jj2d

Donald, Henderson H. "The Negro Migration of 1916–1918." *Journal of Negro History* 6, no. 4 (October 1921): 90. https://www.jstor.org/stable/i327539

Du Bois, W. E. B. "Close Ranks." *The Crisis* 16, no. 3 (July 1918): 111. https://tinyurl.com/rw8bfyw.

"The Looking Glass." *The Crisis* 14, no. 1 (May 1917): 23.

"The Looking Glass: Secret Information Concerning Black American Troops." *The Crisis* 18, no. 1 (May 1919): 16–18. https://tinyurl.com/wz4skrt.

"The Looking Glass: Returning Soldiers." *The Crisis* 18 (May 1919): 13–14. https://tinyurl.com/wz4skrt

Fosdick, Raymond. "The Commission on Training Camp Activities." *Proceedings of the Academy of Political Science in the City of New York* 7, no. 4 (February 1918): 163–170. https://tinyurl.com/tqnwvmr

Foster, Craig. "Tarnished Angels: Prostitution in Storyville, New Orleans, 1900–1920." *Louisiana History* 31, no. 4 (Winter 1990): 387–397. https://www.jstor.org/stable/4232839?seq=1

Frahm, Jill. "The Hello Girls: Women Telephone Operators with the American Expeditionary Forces during World War I." *The Journal of the Gilded Age and Progressive Era* 3, no. 3 (July 2004): 271–93. https://www.jstor.org/stable/25144374?seq=1

Gilley, B. H. "Kate Gordon and Louisiana Woman Suffrage." *Louisiana History* 24, no. 3 (Summer 1983): 289–306. https://tinyurl.com/yd6ry7ta.

Green, Elna. "The Rest of the Story: Kate Gordon and the Opposition to the Nineteenth Amendment in the South," *Louisiana History* 33, no. 2 (Spring 1992): 171–189. https://www.jstor.org/stable/4232938?seq=1

Grossman, James R. "Blowing the Trumpet: The 'Chicago Defender' and Black Migration during World War I. *Illinois Historical Journal* 78, no. 2 (Summer, 1985): 85–96. https://www.jstor.org/stable/40191833?seq=1

Haydel, Jennifer. "The Wood Screw Pump: A Study of the Drainage Development of New Orleans." *The Student Historical Journal* 27 (1995–96): 14–23. https://tinyurl.com/ts9u8pt

Jackson, Joy. "Prohibition in New Orleans: The Unlikeliest Crusade." *Louisiana History* 19, no. 3 (Summer 1978): 261–284. https://www.jstor.org/stable/4231785?seq=1.

Johnson, Bascom. "Eliminating Vice from Camp Cities." *Annals of the American Academy of Political and Social Science* 78 (1918): 60–64.

Johnson, Jerah. "Jim Crow Laws of the 1890s and the Origins of New Orleans Jazz: Correction of an Error." *Popular Music* 19, no. 2 (April 2000): 243–251. https://www.jstor.org/stable/853671?seq=1

Johnson, Kenneth R. "Kate Gordon and the Woman-Suffrage Movement in the South." *The Journal of Southern History* 38, no. 3 (August 1972): 365–392. https://www.jstor.org/stable/2206099

Kemp, Katherine. "Jean and Kate Gordon: New Orleans Social Reformers, 1898–1933." *Louisiana History* 24, no. 4 (Autumn 1983): 389–401. https://www.jstor.org/stable/4232307?seq=1

Kmen, Henry. "The Joys of Milneburg." *New Orleans Magazine* (May 1969): 16–19.

Kuss, Mark. "Hey Man! Watch Your Language: Treatment of Germans and German Americans in New Orleans During World War I." *Louisiana History* 56, no. 2 (Spring 2015): 178–198. https://www.jstor.org/stable/24396453?seq=1

Landphair, Juliette. "Sewerage, Sidewalks, and Schools: The New Orleans Ninth Ward and Public School Desegregation." *Louisiana History* 40, no. 1 (Winter 1999): 35–62. https://www.jstor.org/stable/4233555

"My Country 'Tis of Thee." *Life Magazine* 67, no. 1767 (February 10, 1916): cover. https://tinyurl.com/y7ps8kar.

Lyons, Robert. *Mixer and Server: Journal of the Hotel and Restaurant Employees International and Bartender's League of America* 27 (October 1918): 22. https://tinyurl.com/tdfmct6

May, Zachary. "The Government's Moral Crusade: America's Campaign against Venereal Disease during World War I." *Bound Away: The Liberty Journal of History* 1, no. 1 (2015): 1–12. https://digitalcommons.liberty.edu/ljh/vol1/iss1/6

Mixer and Server: The Journal of the Hotel and Restaurant Employee's International Alliance and Bartender's League of America 26, no. 1 (January 15, 1917): 48. https://tinyurl.com/tldmn7b

Parker, Walter. "Facilities of the Port of New Orleans." *Annals of the American Academy of Political Science and Social Science* 86 (November 1919): 188–198. https://tinyurl.com/utgtpfl.

Piston, William. "Maritime Shipbuilding and Related Activities in Louisiana, 1542–1986." *Louisiana History* 29, no. 2 (Spring 1988): 163–175. https://tinyurl.com/r6fgkes.

Smith, Armantine. "The History of the Women's Suffrage Movement in Louisiana." *Louisiana Law Review* 62, no. 2 (Winter 2002): 509–560.

Souchon, Edward. "The Town is Ended ... but the Melody Lives on." *Record Changer* 12, no. 2 (1953): 3–5.

Stanonis, Anthony. "A Woman of Boundless Energy: Elizabeth Werlein and Her Times." *Louisiana History* 46, no. 1 (Winter 2005): https://www.jstor.org/stable/i390488.

Watson, K. W. Appointment Rules 231.3. Telephone Operators, Office of the Chief Signal Corps Correspondence. College Park, MD: NARA. Quoted in Jill Frahm, "The Hello Girls: Women Telephone Operators with the American Expeditionary Forces during

World War I." *Journal of the Gilded Age and Progressive Era* 3, no. 3 (2004): 271–291. https://www.jstor.org/stable/i25144370.

Williams, Robert W. Jr. "Martin Behrman & N.O. Civic Development, 1904–1920. *Louisiana History* 3 (fall 1961): 141–153. https://www.jstor.org/stable/4232262?seq=1.

WEBSITES AND TV BROADCASTS

"1920 Census: Abstract of the Fourteenth Census of the United States." US Census Bureau. 1923. https://tinyurl.com/s7thv2c.

"At Home and at War: 1917–1919." Historic New Orleans Collection. December 9, 2015. https://tinyurl.com/tpjwa74.

Brister, Nancy. "Old New Orleans." Accessed April 22, 2018. http://old-new-orleans.com/ NO_Cotton_Exchange.html.

Derby, Gisclair S. "Pete Herman." David Johnson, ed. *Encyclopedia of Louisiana*. Louisiana Endowment for the Humanities. January 24, 2014. www.knowlouisiana.com.

Frahm, Jill, "Women Telephone Operators in World War I France." Center for Cryptologic History. 2016. https://tinyurl.com/r22dymr.

Gisclair, S. Derby. "Pete Herman." KnowLA: *Encyclopedia of Louisiana*. David Johnson, ed. Louisiana Endowment for the Humanities. January 24, 2014. www.knowlouisiana.org.

Hannefin, Daniel D. C. Sr. "Records of Daughters of Charity Service in World War I." National Archives and Record Administration (NARA). 1989. https://dcarchives.files. wordpress.com/2013/12/stlouis-world-war-one.docx

Helgason, Gudmundur. Accessed July 12, 1916. https://uboat.net.

"How the Son of Sicilian Immigrants Became One of New Orleans' Greatest Athletes." WWLTV broadcast. January 9, 1917. https://tinyurl.com/sqmhkzr.

"Home of Heroes." Medal of Honor and Military History. 2019. Accessed November 29, 2017. www.homeofheroes.com.

"Library of Congress Narrative: Jelly Roll Martin and Alan Lomax." Monrovia Sound Studio. 1999. http://www.doctorjazz.co.uk/locspeech1.html.

"Louisiana Secretary of State, Vital Records Index, Orleans Parish Marriage Records." Accessed May 2, 1917. https://tinyurl.com/ubl8wqu.

Nickerson, W. J. "The Colored Soldier Boys of Uncle Sam We're Coming." L. Grunewald Co. Inc. New Orleans: 1918. Notated Music. https://www.loc.gov/item/2013568816/.

"Online Public Vital Records Index." Orleans Parish Marriage Records. Accessed February 21, 2017. https://tinyurl.com/ubl8wqu.

Piron, Armand J, Samuel J Perrault, and Clarence Williams. "America They Are Both for You." Monographic. 1911. Notated Music. https://www.loc.gov/item/2014562599/.

"Records of Rights," US Labor Department, Letter Regarding Labor Agents, July 14th, 1917, Web, 16, Mar, 2018 www.recordsofrights.org/records/98/letter-regarding-labor-agents.

Reonas, Matthew. "'World War I.' KnowLA: *Encyclopedia of Louisiana*. Louisiana Endowment for the Humanities. David Johnson, ed. December 16, 2011. http://www .knowla.org/entry/823/.

Schumm, Laura. "Food Rationing in Wartime America." A&E Television Networks, LLC. December 18, 2015. http://www.history.com/news/hungry-history/food-rationing-in -wartime-america.

"The Immigrant Army: Immigrant Service Members in World War I." US Citizenship and Immigration Services. https://tinyurl.com/v97c8rw.

Tyler, Pamela "Woman Suffrage." David Johnson, ed. *Encyclopedia of Louisiana*. Louisiana Endowment for the Humanities. 2018. https://64parishes.org/entry/woman-suffrage.

Watkins, John. "Records of Rights." Letter Regarding Labor Agents, July 14, 1917, National Archives, General Records, Department of Labor, www.recordsofrights.org/records/98/ letter-regarding-labor-agents

Williams, Spenser. "Farewell to Storyville." Accessed January 13, 1917. http://www.metrolyr ics.com/farewell-to-storyville-lyrics-billie-holiday.html,

"World War I Draft Cards: Louis Armstrong." NARA. Accessed March 7, 18. https://www .archives.gov/atlanta/wwi-draft/armstrong.html.

BOOKS

Allured, Janet and Michael Martin, eds. *Louisiana Legacies: Readings in the History of the Pelican State*. Hoboken, NJ: Wiley-Blackwell, 2013.

Anderson, Elizabeth, and Gerald Kelly. *Miss Elizabeth: A Memoir*. Boston: Little Brown and Co., 1969.

Armstrong, Louis. *Satchmo: My Life in New Orleans*. New York: Prentiss-Hall, 1954.

Arnesen, Eric. *Waterfront Workers of New Orleans: Race, Class, and Politics, 1863–1923*. Oxford: Oxford University Press, 1991.

Arceneaux, Pamela D. *Guidebooks to Sin: The Bluebooks of Storyville, New Orleans*. New Orleans: The Historic New Orleans Collection, 2017.

Asbury, Herbert. *The French Quarter: An Informal History of the New Orleans Underworld*. New York: Alfred Knopf, 2003.

Atkins, Jennifer. *New Orleans Carnival Balls: The Secret Side of Mardi Gras, 1870–1920*. Baton Rouge: LSU Press, 2017.

Barbeau, Arthur, and Henri Florette. *The Unknown Soldiers: Black American Troops in World War*. Philadelphia: Temple University Press, 1974.

Barker, Danny. *Buddy Bolden and the Last Days of Storyville*. Alyn Shipton, ed. New York: Cassell Press, 1998.

Barker, Danny. *A Life in Jazz*. Alyn Shipton, ed. Oxford: Oxford University Press, 1986.

Barnes, Harper. *Never Been a Time: The 1917 Race Riot That Sparked the Civil Rights Movement*. New York: Walker and Co., 2008.

Bauerlein, George. *The Book of New Orleans and the Industrial South*. New Orleans: Searcy & Pfaff, 1919.

Behrman, Martin. *The Story of Mayor Behrman's National Campaign to Advertise New Orleans and its Advantages to the Entire United States*. New Orleans: Ferry-Hanly Advertising Co., 1918.

Bennett, James. *Religion and the Rise of Jim Crow in New Orleans*. Princeton: Princeton University Press, 2005.

Blanke, David. *The 1910s*. Westport, CT: Greenwood Press, 2002.

Blum, Richard, ed. *Surveillance and Espionage in a Free Society: A Report by the Planning Group on Intelligence and Security to the Policy Council of the Democratic National Committee*, Westport, CT: Praeger Publishers, 1972.

Brandt, Allan. *No Magic Bullet: A Social History of Venereal Disease in the United States since 1880*. Oxford: Oxford University Press, 1987.

Bristow, Nancy. *Making Men Moral: Social Engineering during the Great War*. New York: NYU Press, 1996.

Brothers, Thomas, ed. *Louis Armstrong in His Own Words*. Oxford: Oxford University Press, 1999.

Cable, Mary. *Lost New Orleans*. Boston: Houghton Mifflin Harcourt, 1980.

Cajun, Andre. *Basin Street*. New Orleans: Pelican Publishing Co., 2013.

Campanella, Richard. *Bourbon Street: A History*. Baton Rouge: LSU Press, 2014.

Campanella, Richard. *Lost New Orleans*. London: Pavilion Books, 2015.

Carney, Court. *Cutting Up: How Early Jazz Got America's Ear*. Lawrence: University Press of Kansas, 2009.

Carter, Hodding, ed. *The Past as Prelude: New Orleans, 1718–1968*. New Orleans: Tulane University, 1968.

Carter, Hodding. *Southern Legacy*. Baton Rouge: LSU Press, 1950.

Casey, Powell A. *Try Us: The Story of the Washington Artillery in World War II*. Baton Rouge: Claitor's Publishing, 1971.

Casso, Evans J. *Louisiana Legacy: A History of the State National Guard*. New Orleans: Pelican Press, 1926.

Charters, Samuel. *A Trumpet around the Corner: The Story of New Orleans Jazz*. Jackson: University Press of Mississippi, 2008.

Cherrington, Ernest Hurst. *Standard Encyclopedia of the Alcohol Problem*, Vol. I. Westerville, OH: American Issue Publishing Co., 1925.

Cobbs, Elizabeth. *The Hello Girls: America's First Women Soldiers*. Boston: Harvard University Press, 2017.

Coyle, Katy, and Nadiene Van Dyke. "Sex, Smashing, and Storyville." In John Howard, ed., *Carryin' On in the Lesbian and Gay South*. New York: NYU Press, 1997.

Cuthbertson, Guy. *Peace at Last: A Portrait of Armistice Day, 11 November, 1918*. New Haven, CT: Yale University Press, 1918.

Devore, Donald, and Joseph Logsdon. *Crescent City Schools: Public Education in Louisiana, 1841–1991*. Lafayette: Center for Louisiana Studies, 1991.

Dixon, Brandt V. B. *A Brief History of H. Sophie Newcomb Memorial College, 1887–1919: A Personal Reminiscence*. New Orleans: Friends of Newcomb College, 1995.

Downs, Matthew, and M. Ryan Floyd. *The American South and the Great War, 1914–1924*. Baton Rouge: LSU Press, 2018.

Dyer, John P. *Tulane: The Biography of a University*. New York: Harper and Row, 1966.

Early, Gerald, ed. *Ain't But a Place: An Anthology of African-American Writings about St. Louis*. St. Louis: Missouri Historical Society Press, 1998.

Ellis, Mark. *Race, War, and Surveillance: African-Americans and the U.S. Government during World War I*. Bloomington: Indiana University Press, 2001.

Ellis, Scott S. *Madame Vieux Carré: The French Quarter in the Twentieth Century*. Oxford: University of Mississippi Press, 2009.

Englund, Peter. *The Beauty and the Sorrow: An Intimate History of the First World War*. New York: Random House, 2012.

Farwell, Byron. *Over There: The United States in the Great War, 1917–1918*. New York: W. W. Norton & Co., 1999.

Fleming, Thomas. *The Illusion of Victory: America in World War I*. New York: Basic Books, 2003.

Flynn, J.Q. *Flynn's Digest of the City Ordinances: of the City Ordinances, Together with the Constitutional Provisions, Acts of the General Assembly, and Decisions of the Courts Relative to the Government of the City of New Orleans*. New Orleans: L. Graham and Son, 1896.

Fosdick, Raymond. *Chronicles of a Generation*. New York: Harper and Brothers, 1958.

Franklin, John Hope, and Alfred Moss Jr. *From Slavery to Freedom: A History of African Americans*. New York: McGraw-Hill Publishers, 1994.

Fuller, Paul E. *Laura Clay and the Woman's Rights Movement*. Lexington: University Press of Kentucky, 1975.

Fussell, Paul. *The Great War and Modern Memory*. Oxford: Oxford University Press, 1995.

Gerard, James W. *My Four Years in Germany*. New York: Grosset and Dunlap, 1917.

Gill, James. *Lords of Misrule: Mardi Gras and the Politics of Race in New Orleans*. Oxford: University of Mississippi Press, 1997.

Graham, Susan Hunter. *Woman Suffrage and the New Democracy*. New Haven, CT: Yale University Press, 1996.

Grant, Joanne, ed. *Black Protest: History, Documents, and Analysis, 1619 to the Present*. Robbinsdale, MN: Fawcett Books, 1968.

Green, Elna C. *Southern Strategies: Southern Women and the Woman Suffrage Question*. Chapel Hill: University of North Carolina Press, 1997.

Gratton, Brian, and Myron Gutmann. *Historical Statistics of the US*. Cambridge: Cambridge University Press, 2006.

Harper, Ida, ed. *History of Woman Suffrage. Vol VI, 1900–1920*. New York: Fowler and Webb, 1922.

Harvey, Chance. *The Life and Selected Letters of Lyle Saxon*. Gretna, LA: Pelican Press, 2013.

Hersch, Charles. *Subversive Sounds: Race and the Birth of Jazz in New Orleans*. Chicago: University of Chicago Press, 2007.

Higham, John. *Strangers in the Land: Patterns of Nativism, 1860–1925*. New Brunswick, NJ: Rutgers University, 1955.

Hirsch, Arnold and Joseph Logsdon, eds. *Creole New Orleans: Race and Americanization*. Baton Rouge: LSU Press, 1992.

Hough, Emerson. *The Web: A Revelation of Patriotism*. National Directors of the APL Chicago: Reilly & Lee, 1919.

Hughes, M., and Matthew Seligmann, eds. "James Watson Gerard: American Diplomat as Domestic Propagandist," in *Leadership in Conflict 1914–1918*. Barnsley, UK: Pen & Sword, 2000.

Hyman, Harold M. *To Try Men's Souls: Loyalty Tests in American History.* Berkeley: University of California Press, 1959.

Jackson, Joy J. *New Orleans in the Gilded Age: Politics and Urban Progress, 1880–1896.* 2nd ed. Baton Rouge: Louisiana Historical Association in cooperation with the Center for Louisiana Studies of the University of Southwestern Louisiana, 1997.

Jensen, Joan M. *The Price of Vigilance.* New York: Rand McNally Company, 1968.

Jones, Max. *Talking Jazz.* New York: W. W. Norton and Co., 1988.

Kane, Harnett T. *Queen New Orleans: City by the River.* New York: Bonanza Books, 1949.

Keene, Jennifer. *Doughboys, the Great War, and the Remaking of America.* Baltimore: Johns Hopkins Press, 2001.

Kendall, John. *History of New Orleans.* Chicago and New York: Lewis Publishing Co., 1922.

Keire, Mara. *For Business and Pleasure: Red-Light Districts and the Regulation of Vice in the United States, 1890–1933.* Baltimore: Johns Hopkins Press, 2010.

Keith, Jeanette. *Rich Man's War, Poor Man's Fight: Race, Class, and Power in the Rural South during the First World War.* Chapel Hill: University of North Carolina Press, 2004.

Kemp, John. *Martin Behrman of New Orleans: Memoirs of a City Boss.* Baton Rouge: LSU Press, 1997.

Kemp, John. *New Orleans: An Illustrated History.* Brightwaters, NY: Windsor Publishers, 1981.

Kennedy, Al. *Chief of Chiefs: Nathaniel Lee and the Mardi Gras Indians of New Orleans, 1915–2001.* Gretna, LA: Pelican Press, 2018.

Kennedy, David. *Over Here: The First World War and American Society.* Oxford: Oxford University Press, 1980.

Kimball, Nell. *Nell Kimball: Her Life as an American Madame.* Stephen Longstreet, ed. New York: Macmillan, 1970.

Kolb, Carolyn. *New Orleans Memories: One Writer's City.* Oxford: University of Mississippi Press, 2013.

Kornweibel, Theodore, Jr. *Investigate Everything: Federal Efforts to Compel Black Loyalty During World War I.* Bloomington: Indiana University Press, 2002.

Krist, Gary. *Empire of Sin: A Story of Sex, Jazz, Murder, and the Battle for Modern New Orleans.* New York: Crown Publishers, 2014.

LaFarge, Oscar. *Raw Material: An Autobiographical Examination of an Artist's Journey into Maturity.* London: Victor Gollancz, 1946.

Landau, Emily. *Spectacular Wickedness: Sex, Race, and Memory in Storyville, New Orleans.* Baton Rouge: LSU Press, 2013.

Lee, Everett S., "State of Birth," 1870–1950." Vol 3. Philadelphia: University of Pennsylvania Studies of Population, Redistribution & Economic Growth 1953.

Lefferts, Peter. *Black US Army Bands and Their Bandmasters in World War I.* Lincoln: University of Nebraska-Lincoln, 2012.

Levitt, Mel. *A Short History of New Orleans.* San Francisco: Lexikos, 1982.

Lindig, Carmen. *The Path from the Parlor: Louisiana Women, 1879–1920.* Lafayette: University of Louisiana at Lafayette Press, 1986.

Lomax, Alan. *Mister Jelly Roll: The Fortunes of Jelly Roll Morton, New Orleans Creole and "Inventor of Jazz."* Berkeley: Duell Sloan & Pierce, 1950.

Long, Alecia. *The Great Southern Babylon: Sex, Race, and Respectability in New Orleans, 1865–1920*. Baton Rouge: LSU Press, 2004.

Long, Alecia. "A Notorious Attraction: Sex and Tourism in New Orleans, 1897–1917," In *Southern Journeys: Tourism, History, and Culture in the Modern South*. Edited by Richard Starnes. Tuscaloosa: University of Alabama Press, 2003.

Margavio, A. V. and Jerome Salomone. *Bread and Respect: The Italians of Louisiana*. Gretna, LA: Pelican Publishing, 2002.

Marquis, Donald. *In Search of Buddy Bolden*. Baton Rouge: LSU Press, 1978.

Medley, Keith. *Black Life in Old New Orleans*. Gretna, LA: Pelican Press, 2014.

Melden, Charles M. *From Citizen to Slave*. New York: Methodist Book Concern, 1921.

Merrick, Caroline. *Old Times in Dixieland: A Southern Matron's Memories*. New York: Grafton Press, 1901.

Michaeli, Ethan. *The Defender: How the Legendary Newspaper Changed America*. New York: Houghton Mifflin, 2016.

Mills, Bill. *The League: The True Story of Average Americans on the Hunt for WWI Spies*. New York: Skyhorse Publishing, 2013.

Mjagkij, Nina. *Loyalty in Time of Trial: The African-American Experience during World War I*. Lanham, MD: Rowman and Littlefield, 2011.

Moton, Robert. *Finding a Way Out*. New York: Doubleday, 1920.

Neiberg, Michael. *The Path to War: How the First World War Created Modern America*. Oxford: Oxford Press, 2016.

Soards' New Orleans City Directory for 1917. Soards Directory Co., Ltd., New Orleans, 1917. Louisiana Collections, New Orleans Public Library.

New Orleans: What to See and What to Visit, A Standard Guide to the City of New Orleans. New Orleans Progressive Union Press of Louisiana, 1909.

Persico, Joseph. *Eleventh Month, Eleventh Day, Eleventh Hour: Armistice Day, 1918 World War I and Its Violent Climax*. New York: Random House, 2005.

Pietrusza, David. *1932: The Rise of Hitler and FDR-Two Tales of Politics, Betrayal, and Unlikely Destiny*. Lanham, MD: Rowman and Littlefield, 2016.

Reed, John S. *Dixie Bohemia: A French Quarter Circle in the 1920s*. Baton Rouge: LSU Press, 2014.

Reynolds, George. *Machine Politics in New Orleans, 1987–1926*. New York: Columbia University Press, 1936.

Richey, Emma, and Evelina Kean. *The New Orleans Book*. New Orleans: Searcy & Pfaff, 1919.

Richey, Emma, and Evelina Kean. *The New Orleans Book*. New Orleans: The L. Graham Co., Ltd., Printers, 1915.

Rose, Al. *Storyville, New Orleans: Being an Authentic, Illustrated Account of the Notorious Red Light District*. Tuscaloosa: University of Alabama Press, 1976.

Ross, William B. *World War I and the American Constitution*. Cambridge: Cambridge University Press, 2017.

Saxon, Lyle. *Gumbo Ya Ya: Folk Tales of Louisiana*. Gretna, LA: Pelican Press, 1998.

Schneider, Dorothy and Carl. *Into the Breech: American Women Overseas in World War I*. New York: Viking, 1991.

Seiferth, Herman, ed. *Louisiana in the War*. New Orleans, n.d.

25

Smith, Normand R. *Footprints of Black Louisiana*. Bloomington, IL: Xlibris Corp., 2010.

Stanonis, Anthony. *Creating the Big Easy: New Orleans and the Emergence of Modern Tourism, 1918–1945*. Athens: University of Georgia Press, 2006.

Stern, Walter C. *Race and Education in New Orleans: Creating the Segregated City, 1764–1960*. Baton Rouge: LSU Press, 2018.

Stevens, Doris. *Jailed for Freedom*. New York: Boni and *Liveright*, 1920.

Stoddard, Tom. *The Autobiography of Pops Foster, New Orleans Jazzman*. Berkeley: University of California Press, 1971.

Symanski, Richard. *The Immoral Landscape: Female Prostitution in Western Societies*. Toronto: Butterworth and Co., 1981.

Tallant, Robert. *The Romantic New Orleans*. New York: E. P. Dutton, 1950.

Taylor, Troy. *Wicked New Orleans: The Dark Side of the Big Easy*. Cheltenham, UK: History Press, 2010.

Teachout, Terry. *Pops: A Life of Louis Armstrong*. New York: Houghton Mifflin Harcourt, 2009.

The European War. New York Times Current History. 20 vols. New York: New York Times Co, 1917.

Tydings, Millard. *Before and After Prohibition*. New York: McMillan, 1930.

Tyler, Pamela. *Silk Stockings and Ballot Boxes: Women and Politics in New Orleans, 1920–1963*. Athens: University of Georgia Press, 2009.

Vaz, Kim Marie. *The Baby Dolls: Breaking the Race and Gender Barriers of the Mardi Gras Traditions*. Baton Rouge: LSU Press, 2013.

Voss, Louis. *History of the German Society of New Orleans*. New Orleans: Sendker Printing Service, 1927.

Vyhnanvk, Louis. *Unorganized Crime: New Orleans in the 1920s*. Lafayette: University of Southwest Louisiana, 1998.

Widmer, Mary Lou. *New Orleans, 1900–1920*. Gretna, LA: Pelican Publishing Co., 2007.

Wilkerson, Isabel. *The Warmth of Other Suns. The Epic Story of America's Great Migration*. New York: Vintage Books, 2010.

Wiltz, Christine. *The Last Madam: A Life in the New Orleans Underworld*. Boston: Da Capo Press, 2000.

Williams, Charles. *Sidelights on Negro Soldiers*. Boston: B. J. Brimmer, 1923.

Yerkes, Robert, ed. "Psychological Examining in the U.S. Army." *Memoirs of the National Academy of Sciences* 15 (1921): 1–875. https://tinyurl.com/unzv6a8

NEWSPAPERS

Le Meschacébé (Lucy, LA)
Leslie's Illustrated News
Neue Deutsche Zeitung (New Orleans)
The Boston Post
The Brooklyn Daily Eagle
The Chicago Defender

The Crisis
The Daily Picayune
The Ft. Worth Daily Gazette
The Herald (Algiers, LA)
The Los Angeles Herald
The Ogden Standard-Examiner
The Times-Picayune
The Negro Advocate
The Newcomb Arcade
The New Orleans. Daily Democrat
The New Orleans Item
The New Orleans States
The St. Tammany Farmer
The Southwestern Christian Advocate
The Spy Glass (June to Dec, 1918) www.ancestry.com
The Tensas Gazette
The Vindicator (New Orleans)
The Washington Post
The Weekly Clarion-Ledger (Jackson, MS)

FURTHER READING

Annual Report of the Surgeon General, U. S. Army, 1919. Washington: General Printing Office, (1920) 1:125–141.

Baiamonte, John V. *Spirit of Vengence: Nativism and Louisiana Justice, 1921–1924.* Baton Rouge: LSU Press, 1986.

Behrman, Martin. "A History of Three Great Public Utilities—Sewage, Water, and Drainage—and Their Influence Upon the Health and Progress of a Big City." Paper delivered at the convention of the League of American Municipalities, Milwaukee, WI, September 29, 1914.

Boulard, Garry, "Blacks, Italians, and the Making of New Orleans Jazz." *Journal of Ethnic Studies* 16, no.1 (Spring 1988): 53–66.

Campanella, Richard. *Bienville's Dilemma: A Historical Geography of New Orleans.* Lafayette: Center for Louisiana Studies, 2008.

Collins, Philip R. "The Old Regular Democratic Organization in New Orleans," Master's thesis, Georgetown University, 1948.

Connelly, Mark T. *The Response to Prostitution in the Progressive Era.* Chapel Hill: UNC Press, 1980.

Craig, Anne O. and Maia Harris, "Storyville," *Louisiana Cultural Vistas* (Spring 1997): 44–51.

Davis, Miriam. *The Axeman of New Orleans: The True Story.* Chicago: Chicago Review Press, 2017.

Deacon, William. *Martin Behrman Administration Biography, 1904–1916.* New Orleans: John Weihing Printing Co., 1917.

Dominguez, Virginia R. *White by Definition: Social Classification in Creole Louisiana*. New Brunswick, NJ: Rutgers University Press, 1986.

Fairclough, Adam. *Race and Democracy: The Civil Rights Struggle in Louisiana, 1915–1972*. Athens: University of Georgia Press, 1995.

Gambino, Richard. *Vendetta: The True Story of the Largest Lynching in United States History*. Toronto: Guernica Press, 1998.

Gavin, Lettie. *American Women in World War I: They Also Served*. Boulder: University Press of Colorado, 1997.

Genthe, Arnold. *Impressions of Old New Orleans: A Book of Pictures*. New York: George H. Doran, 1926.

Gisclair, S. Derby. *Baseball in New Orleans*. Charleston, SC: Arcadia Publishing, 2004.

Gordon, Kate M., ed. *New Southern Citizen*. 3 vols. 1914–17. Tulane University. Louisiana Research Collection.

Grossman, James R. *Land of Hope: Chicago, Black Southerners, and the Great Migration*. Chicago: University of Chicago Press, 1989.

Hair, William Ivy. *Carnival of Fury: Robert Charles and the New Orleans Race Riot of 1900*. Baton Rouge: LSU Press, 1976.

Hennick, Louis and E. Harper Charlton. *The Streetcars of New Orleans, Vol II*. Gretna, LA: Pelican Press, 1965.

Higham, John. *Strangers in the Land: Patterns of Nativism, 1860–1925*. New Brunswick, NJ: University, 1955.

Jackson, Joy J. "Bosses and Businessmen in Gilded Age New Orleans Politics." *Louisiana History* 5, no. 4 (Autumn, 1964): 387–400.

Katz, Hélena. *Cold Cases: Famous Unsolved Mysteries, Crimes, and Disappearances in America*. Santa Barbara, CA: Greenwood Printing, 2010.

Kaufman, Burton. "New Orleans and the Panama Canal, 1900–1914." *Louisiana History* 14, no. 4 (Autumn, 1973): 333–346. https://www.jstor.org/stable/4231348?seq=1

Larson, Edward J. *Sex, Race, and Science: Eugenics in the Deep South*. Baltimore: Johns Hopkins University Press, 1994.

Leavell, R. H., T. R. Snavely, et al. "Negro Migration in 1916–1917." Reports of the US Department of Labor, Division of Negro Economics. Washington: Government Printing Office, 1919.

Long, Alecia, "Willie Piazza: A Storyville Madam Who Challenged Racial Segregation," *Louisiana Cultural Vistas* (Summer 2000): 8–10.

Mackey, Thomas C. *Red Lights Out: A Legal History of Prostitution, Disorderly Houses, and Vice Districts, 1870–1917*. New York: Garland Publishing, 1987.

Marquis, Donald M. "Lincoln Park, Johnson Park, and Buddy Bolden." *Second Line* (fall 1976): 27–28.

McCafferty, Kerri. *St. Joseph Alters*. Gretna, LA: Pelican Press, 2002.

McCain, William. "The Papers of the Food Administration for Louisiana, 1917–1918." *Louisiana Historical Quarterly* 21 (July 1938).

Merrill, Ellen. *Germans of Louisiana*. Gretna, LA: Pelican, 2005.

Michaeli, Ethan. *The Defender: How the Legendary Black Newspaper Changed America*. New York: Houghton Mifflin Harcourt, 2016.

Mir, Jasmine, *Marketplace of Desire: Storyville and the Making of a Tourist City in New Orleans, 1890–1920*. PhD dissertation, New York University, 2005.

Mullen, Bill. *Popular Fronts: Chicago and African-American Cultural Politics, 1935–46.* Champagne, IL: University of Illinois, 1999.

Mullendore, William C. and Ralph Lutz. *History of the United States Food Administration, 1917–1918.* Palo Alto, CA: Stanford University Press, 1941.

Nation, Carry. *The Use and Need of the Life of Carry A. Nation.* Topeka, KA: F. M. Steves and Sons, 1908.

O'Hara, Joseph A. "Feeble-Minded." *New Orleans Medical and Surgical Journal* 70 (1917): 350–351. https://tinyurl.com/tlln4az

Paddock, Grace B. "I was a "Hello Girl." *The World Wars Remembered*, ed by Timothy Clark, Dublin, New Hampshire: Yankee, Inc. 1979.

Percy, Walker. *The Moviegoer.* New York: Alfred Knopf, 1961.

P'Pool, Elbert E. "Commercialized Amusements in New Orleans." Master's thesis. Tulane University, 1930.

Reed, Germaine A. "Race Legislation in Louisiana, 1864–1920." *Louisiana History* 6, no. 4 (Autumn 1965): 379–92.

Reich, Steven A., ed., "Primary Documents," *Encyclopedia of the Great Black Migration.* Santa Barbara, CA: Greenwood Press, 2006.

Schott, Matthew J. "The New Orleans Machine and Progressivism." *Louisiana History* 24, no. 2 (Spring 1983): 141–53.

Smith, Clarence B., Jr. "Closing the New Orleans District." *National Municipal Review* 11 (1922): 266–68.

Shepherd, Samuel C., Jr. "In Pursuit of Louisiana Progressives." *Louisiana History* 46, no. 4 (Autumn 2005): 389–406.

Soileau, Lydia. "The Germans of Roberts Cove, Louisiana: German Rice Cultivation and the Making of a German Community in Acadia Parish, 1881–1917." Master's thesis, University of New Orleans, 2010.

The Behrman Administration: Work Accomplished during the Eight Years of the Honorable Martin Behrman as Mayor of the City of New Orleans Compiled and Condensed from the Records and Official Reports in the Various Departments of the City Government. City of New Orleans, 1912.

Warburton, Clark. *The Economic Results of Prohibition.* New York: Columbia University Press, 1932.

Williams, T. Harry. *Huey Long.* New York: Alfred Knopf, 1969.

Zink, Harold. *City Bosses in the United States: A Study of Twenty Municipal Bosses.* New York: AMS Press, 1968.

INDEX

Reims Cathedral, 117
Rescue, Health, and Moral Protective
    League, 197
Reuther, Joseph, 119
Rex, Krewe of, 52, 53, 213
Reynolds, James, 198
Richardson Aeroplane Corporation, 26
Ricks, Adolph, 119
Robinson, Jim, 82
Roh, Paul, 119–20, 132
Roosevelt, Teddy, 12, 49, 135
Rosen, Charles, 129–30
Ross, Louise, 102
Rotary Clubs, 123
Runkel, Herman, 10
Ruth, Babe, 29

Saint Nazaire Stevedore Band, 82
Salem Evangelical Church, 122
Salvation Army, 90, 94, 97
Schaffer, Gypsy, 33
Schlitz, Theo, 123
Schroeder, John, 126
Schwartz, S. J., 56
Scott, Natalie, 101
Sedition Act, 140, 143–44, 146, 147
segregation, 5, 8, 34–38, 46–47, 48, 73–74, 82,
    102, 106, 108, 114, 152, 226n32
Selective Draft Law, 65
Selective Service Act, 68
Shields, Irene, 197
Signal Corps, 98
Silber, Mendel, 199
Simpson, Grace, 33
slacker raids, 149
slackers, 69–71, 148–51
Society for the Uplift of the Negro Race, 34
Sommers, George, 13
Southern District of the Lutheran Synod,
    122
Southern Railways Terminal Station, 31, 78,
    141, 154
Southern Shipbuilding, 26
Southern States Woman's Suffrage
    Conference, 180–81, 183–84, 190

Southwestern Christian Advocate, 111, 115–16
SS Sidney, 45
State Negro Civic League of Louisiana, 111
Story, Sidney, 29
Storyville, 6–7, 8, 27–28, 29–38, 40, 51–52,
    154–56, 162–69, 201; Behrman support,
    162–65; Black Storyville, 34–38, 51; Blue
    Book, 31, 32–33; City Ordinance 4118,
    34–35; closing, 162–69; crime, 37–38;
    economic impact, 29, 155–56, 165–66;
    interracial sex, 30, 33, 34–38, 154–55;
    octoroon women, 35; opposition, 32,
    34, 162–69; owners, 31, 33, 35–36, 222n2;
    segregation, 34–38; soldiers, 162–65;
    tourism, 29
Stubbs, Frank, 79, 195, 196
Student Army Training Corps (SATC), 66
Sullivan, Dan, 85–86
Sullivan, John L., 29
Sunday Law, 157–58, 161
Sunday Sun, The, 33

Thomas, Daniel, 11
Thompson, James M., 196
Times-Picayune, The, 12, 50–51, 62, 65, 117,
    124, 125–26, 170, 195, 213, 226n40
To Hell with the Kaiser (Irving), 127
Todo Restaurant, 200
Trench and Camp, 115
Tulane University, 66, 85, 129, 130, 176

United Confederate Veterans, 67
United Daughters of the Confederacy, 97
United Spanish War Veterans, 57
United States Department of Justice, 5, 136,
    137, 150, 194, 203–4
United States Department of Labor, 101
US Mint, 55
USS Maine, 53

Vance, J. Madison, 104
Vardaman, James, 59, 65, 113
Vaught, Mrs. D. A. S., 189
venereal disease, 6–7, 162, 164, 198, 199,
    239n15

ABOUT THE AUTHOR

Photo by Helen Reed

Brian Altobello received his undergraduate and master's degrees in US history from LSU. He concluded his career as a high school teacher to work for the Louisiana Department of Education and was named a Distinguished Educator. Altobello is the author of *Into the Shadows Furious: The Brutal Battle for New Georgia* and is an educational consultant in New Orleans, where he lives with his wife, Denise.

Printed in the United States
by Baker & Taylor Publisher Services